The
Accidental
Taxonomist

Heather Hedden

Information Today, Inc.
Medford, New Jersey

First Printing, 2010

The Accidental Taxonomist

Copyright © 2010 by Heather Hedden

Library of Congress Cataloging-in-Publication Data

Hedden, Heather.
  The accidental taxonomist / Heather Hedden.
    p. cm.
  Includes bibliographical references and index.
  ISBN 978-1-57387-397-0
  1. Information organization. 2. Classification. 3. Indexing. 4. Subject headings. 5. Cross references (Information retrieval). 6. Thesauri. I. Title.
  Z666.5.H43 2010
  025--dc22

                                     2010008320

Printed and bound in the United States of America

President and CEO: Thomas H. Hogan, Sr.
Editor-in-Chief and Publisher: John B. Bryans
Managing Editor: Amy M. Reeve
VP Graphics and Production: M. Heide Dengler
Book Designer: Kara Mia Jalkowski
Cover Designer: Ashlee Caruolo

www.infotoday.com

Contents

Figures and Tables

Foreword

In one sense, taxonomy work, as the practice of naming and organizing things, is an ancient art. In another sense, it is a thoroughly modern one, taking on new and more challenging characteristics as organizations and human societies have become more information intensive.

With the arrival of affordable computing in the 1980s, simple economics pushed information into digital formats. The economic opportunities for distributing information on much larger scales also required the development of new tools and more specialized skills for organizing and retrieving digital content collections. This activity was still fairly localized within the holders of large content collections: libraries, publishers, and content aggregators such as online databases.

We can trace the first generation of modern taxonomists to this new activity in the digital domain in the 1980s.

The blossoming of the internet in the 1990s began a much more universal information availability cascade, and this made problems of information navigation and retrieval both more widespread and more acute.

This problem has largely been addressed on the internet through increasingly sophisticated search. Search can satisfy this need on the internet because it can exploit two unique features of the internet:

- Super availability of information means that useful content can be found for almost any purpose.

- Social clues about useful content such as links and references can lift content that has been recognized as useful to the top of search results.

So the internet in itself had little direct impact on the nature or importance of taxonomy work and taxonomy professionals, except to illustrate that there are other mechanisms than the use of taxonomies and taxonomists to support navigation and retrieval.

The internet has had an indirect impact and a much more far reaching one for taxonomists than that first affair with digital information in the 1980s. The public world of the internet and the technology it represents has put incredible pressure on enterprises and governments to become faster, better, and cheaper at what they do—and the ability to manipulate data and information has become a key competitive driver.

Organizational information, whether exposed to the world through ecommerce websites or databases, or whether transferred and accessed within firewalls, cannot easily leverage the two features of the internet, super-abundance of information and social clues:

- They have abundance (which drives the need to organize and navigate) but not super-abundance.

- they are typically organized into functional or market silos, and so social clues about value are not readily available, because there is little linking activity across silos to leverage.

Taxonomists and taxonomies have therefore become major instruments for analyzing content, purposes, and needs, and designing taxonomies to help people find content whatever their need. Technology-driven tools have not yet demonstrated that they can reliably substitute for the skills of taxonomists for helping information systems meet the diverse and specialized purposes and needs of knowledge workers within enterprises.

The past decade has therefore seen a much larger demand for taxonomy work and a greater variety of types of taxonomy work. An ancient art has become a thoroughly modern practice, with quite new and quite challenging characteristics. One of those is that taxonomy work is now very diverse. It no longer has the clearly defined boundaries it used to have.

Taxonomy professionals need to know about the technology environments they are designing for; they need to be able to analyze the business needs of their clients; they need to understand the information and knowledge requirements of their users, the characteristics of the content they are covering; they need consulting, project management, and communication skills; they need to know about the use of standards and the current developments and trends in both technology and standards, because they are constantly changing. This is all over and above the traditional theory and specialized skills that go into the creation and application of effective taxonomies.

There are no taxonomy schools out there to supply this need, as Heather Hedden points out in this book. The need for information organization has drawn practitioners from several loosely related disciplines: librarianship, publishing, information architecture, indexing, data, and information and knowledge management, among others. So we have a loose coalition of taxonomy professionals of varying levels of experience, many of them teleported into taxonomy work from elsewhere (or "accidental" taxonomists, as Hedden puts it), many of them combining taxonomy responsibilities with other duties, and bringing different backgrounds, skills, and approaches to their work.

The field desperately needs a practical literature to bring together the key elements of taxonomy work for this diverse range of practitioners, particularly for those who have found themselves with taxonomy responsibilities without much prior theoretical or technical preparation.

This is slowly starting to change. When I published my book *Organising Knowledge* (2007), there was no other comparable book in the field of taxonomy work. Bowker and Star's *Sorting Things Out* (1999) provided a brilliant theoretical underpinning for modern taxonomy work, but there was little guidance on how to bring this theory to meet the problems of organizational information and knowledge management. If we use an aerial metaphor, Bowker and Star provided a perspective at 30,000 feet.

My goal in *Organising Knowledge* was to give a perspective closer to the ground, but because it focuses on the value of taxonomy work as a strategic intervention, it still works at a fairly high level—let's say 1,000 feet. Darin Stewart's book, *Building Enterprise Taxonomies* (2008), functions as a useful primer for approaching taxonomy work, but it is also still at a fairly high level. David Weinberger's book *Everything Is Miscellaneous* (2007) gives an engaging account of the history of taxonomy work but fails to deliver any actionable insights for the practitioner.

Hedden's book, *The Accidental Taxonomist*, provides that critical link at the 100 feet "how do I do this?" level, and rather than focusing on the enterprise as Stewart and I have done, she has focused on what a taxonomy *practitioner*—especially the "accidental" taxonomist—needs to know, in all its nitty gritty, technical glory. She has done this in an accessible, systematic, clear and organized way, covering the pathways into taxonomy work, what it means to build and manage taxonomies, how to work with taxonomy software, how to make a living as a taxonomist, where to network and build knowledge and skills, and how to plan and run taxonomy projects.

The best use of this book, I am sure, will be as a practical field guide to taxonomy work. Every taxonomist, accidental or not, should have a copy close by. This is a formidable piece of work, whose success will be measured by the well-grounded confidence it inspires, and the consistency and quality of the taxonomy work that it enables.

—Patrick Lambe

References

Bowker, Geoffrey and Star, Susan Leigh. 1999. *Sorting Things Out: Classification and its Consequences.* Cambridge, MA: MIT Press.

Lambe, Patrick. 2007. *Organising Knowledge: Taxonomies, Knowledge and Organisational Effectiveness.* Oxford, U.K.: Chandos

Stewart, Darin L. 2008. *Building Enterprise Taxonomies.* Portland, OR: Mokita Press

Weinberger, David. 2007. *Everything Is Miscellaneous: The Power of the New Digital Disorder.* New York: Times Books.

Patrick Lambe is the author of *Organising Knowledge* (Chandos, 2007), which was the first book to place taxonomy work firmly in the mainstream of knowledge and information management issues. He is the founder of Straits Knowledge, a Singapore-based consulting and research firm focused on knowledge management and taxonomy work, two-term former President of the Information and Knowledge Management Society (www.ikms.org), and an Adjunct Professor at the Hong Kong Polytechnic University. He speaks regularly at international conferences, and his weblog is at www.greenchameleon.com.

Acknowledgments

The field of taxonomies is broad and multidisciplined, and thus no single taxonomist-author could comprehensively cover the subject without getting input and insights from others with different experiences. I am very grateful to the colleagues of mine who have contributed to this book. I especially want to acknowledge the very thorough review of my book by two expert reviewers, Lynda Moulton and Alice Redmond-Neal, who voluntarily took time out of their busy schedules to meticulously go through every chapter. In addition to providing suggestions for better wordings and corrections to any inaccurate generalizations and assumptions, they each contributed some additional bits of information and insights from their own experience that I incorporated. Additional expert review on certain sections and chapters came from Margot Diltz and Tom Reamy. I want to give a big thank you to my friend and indexing colleague Jean Jesensky for giving my book its initial read-through for clarity. Thanks also go to the taxonomy consultants I interviewed and the other taxonomists who completed my online surveys.

In addition to those who helped directly with this book, I wish to acknowledge all those who contributed indirectly, such as by teaching or mentoring me or by giving me opportunities. My primary mentors in the area of controlled vocabularies and taxonomies were my manager at what was then Information Access Company (now Cengage Learning), Margot Diltz, and consultant Jessica Milstead. Through Gale's partnership with Synaptica, I also got feedback on my vocabulary work from Trish Yancey. Even the students I taught in my online courses helped me indirectly by asking questions, which I realized needed to be addressed. So I also thank Kris Liberman for giving me the opportunity to teach numerous sessions of my taxonomies workshop through the continuing education program of Simmons GSLIS. Finally, thanks go to my husband, Tom, also a freelancer, who has had to work more this past year to help financially support us while I was writing this book.

About the Website

www.accidental-taxonomist.com

The Accidental Taxonomist mentions a number of websites throughout. These include examples of online taxonomies, software vendor sites, and useful reference sites. These websites are all collected in Appendix D. To facilitate quick access to these resources, a website with links to all these related sites can be found at www.accidental-taxonomist.com. Furthermore, the links will be maintained and updated on the website as needed over time, and new sources may be added. Please email your comments, changes, and suggested additions to the author at heather@hedden.net.

Disclaimer

Introduction

After reading a case study of an enterprise taxonomy in which corporate research librarians were charged with the task of building the taxonomy,[1] it occurred to me that many people who get involved in creating taxonomies do so by accident. Even if this case study is not typical, it illustrates the point: The growing interest in taxonomies means that the people being asked to create taxonomies may not have done that work before, may not have sufficient training, and/or may not even have thought of pursuing such work before they were asked to. This hypothesis was borne out by responses to an online questionnaire I wrote, in which taxonomists explained how they got into the field.

Most of us first became familiar with the term *taxonomy* in high school biology when the concept was used in reference to the classification and naming of plants and animals. If you did not pursue a career in biology, you probably did not give the concept any further thought for quite some time after that. Although the term is also used to refer to nomenclature and classification of concepts in other academic disciplines, only since the late 1990s has it been understood to mean information organization in general. Taxonomy in this sense includes controlled vocabularies for document indexing and retrieval, subject categories in content management systems, navigation labels and categories in website information architecture, and standardized terminology within a corporate knowledge base. In some of these areas, such as websites, the application of taxonomy is relatively new, coinciding with the newer adoption of the term taxonomy. Other areas, such as controlled vocabularies and thesauri used in periodical indexing and literature retrieval, have been around for decades. Their publishers may continue to refer to a "controlled vocabulary," an "authority file," or a "thesaurus," even though the newer usage of the term taxonomy is also used for these purposes.

Today there are many meanings of the word taxonomy, which can complicate any research into the term. Although the original meaning, the *study* of classification, is rarely used, the term taxonomy continues to be used to designate classification systems of things. Originally used for the classification of things in nature, the term spread from the sciences to the social sciences and thus came to be used also for the classification of concepts. (One of the better known such taxonomies is the Taxonomy of Educational Objectives, also known as Bloom's Taxonomy.) Despite the recent popularity of the term taxonomy for generic knowledge organization, the majority of books and scholarly articles on taxonomies in print today are still about highly specific classification systems in the sciences or social sciences. Their taxonomists are experts in their academic disciplines rather than librarians or information architects.

Even as a generic system of knowledge organization, the term taxonomy presently has two different common usages. One meaning of taxonomy, reflecting the earlier usage for the classification of living organisms, is a hierarchical classification of things or concepts in what may be considered a tree structure. Terms within the taxonomy each have a "parent," or broader term, and a "child," or narrower term, unless the terms are at the very top or bottom levels of the taxonomy. Another, even more recent, usage of the term taxonomy is to refer to any controlled vocabulary of terms for a subject area domain or a specific purpose. The terms may or may not be arranged in a hierarchy, and they may or may not have even more complex relationships between each other. Thus the term taxonomy has taken on a broader meaning that encompasses all of the following: specific-subject glossaries, controlled vocabularies, information thesauri, and ontologies. Each of these will be explained in further detail in Chapter 1. For the purposes of this book, this second, broader definition of taxonomy is used. It is the simplest term, and it corresponds to the word taxonomist.

As the word taxonomy has different meanings, so does the designation of a taxonomist. It can still refer to a biologist who specializes in the field of naming and classifying organisms. The majority of people with the title of taxonomist today, however, are information specialists, librarians, or information architects and are not likely to be subject matter experts. They deal with taxonomies in the broader definition of knowledge organization systems (not limited to hierarchical trees of terms). They may be creators of controlled vocabularies, thesauri, metadata schemes, or website categorization systems. Taxonomist is a more practical and catchy job title than "controlled vocabulary editor," "thesaurus creator," or "nomenclature manager."

Yet for the scope of this book, taxonomists are not limited to people who have the word taxonomy or taxonomist within their job title. There are other job titles for essentially the same tasks, such as vocabulary developer, technical categorization analyst, and information classification specialist. There are many people who work on taxonomies as only one of several job responsibilities, whether as corporate librarians, information architects, or knowledge managers. Finally, there are those who serve in the role of taxonomist temporarily on a project, returning to other duties after completing the taxonomy.

In sum, a taxonomist is someone who creates taxonomies, either singly or as part of a team of taxonomists, and taxonomies are defined as any knowledge organization system (controlled vocabulary, synonym ring, thesaurus, hierarchical term tree, or ontology) used to support information/content findability, discovery, and access. This taxonomy work may be an ongoing job responsibility or a temporary project, and it may be a primary job responsibility or a secondary responsibility. These people, and those who are interested in getting into such work, are the primary audience of this book.

There is no undergraduate major or graduate degree in taxonomy and no department, program, concentration, or certificate in the field. Thus, people do not choose to be taxonomists when they decide what they want to study. Furthermore, the majority of graduate schools and programs of information science, or library and information science, do not have even a single course devoted to creating taxonomies (although it is often a topic within a course).[2] Therefore, even people with an education in information science are probably not thinking of working as a taxonomist. For this reason, too, we can say that many taxonomists become so by chance or by "accident."

Unlike working as a reference librarian or corporate librarian, working as a taxonomist does not usually require a degree in library and information science (although it is often preferred). For this reason, too, people with varied educational backgrounds may accidentally find themselves working as taxonomists. In fact, according to the results of an online survey of taxonomists in November 2008, not quite half had an MLS or MLIS degree. (The full survey questions and answers are reproduced in Appendix A of this book.)

Information taxonomies are relatively new and growing in terms of their applications. New web interactive technologies make taxonomies more usable and user friendly, and the exponential growth of electronic data increasingly calls for new means of organizing and accessing information. Since information taxonomies have been getting attention only since the late 1990s or around 2000, any experienced professional who is getting into taxonomies is doing so somewhat accidentally. As for entry-level taxonomy positions for the new MLIS or MIS graduate, I have yet to see such a position posted.

As for my story, although I came to developing corporate taxonomies via work on controlled vocabularies for periodical database indexing, I did come to the field of controlled vocabularies quite accidentally. I had started my career in writing and editing and responded to a job notice for an abstractor at the computer magazine publisher Ziff Communications, not realizing that Ziff, at the time, owned a large periodical indexing division called Information Access Company. It turned out that the abstractors did the indexing and other metadata application as well, so after intensive employee training on indexing, I got my first exposure to controlled vocabularies. After indexing for a couple of years, I decided to move onward and upward into the controlled vocabulary management group and soon forgot about abstracting. But I never completely gave up writing, as the production of this book will attest. When my position was eliminated in early 2004 and I had to look for new work, I had difficulty finding a job in a profession that I didn't know what to call. My previous title had been controlled vocabulary editor, but, alas, I found nothing by that name on the job board sites. Although publishers of aggregate periodical indexes are few and far between, it turned out that similar skills were in demand by large companies to organize and retrieve their internal documents. I then discovered *taxonomy* and *taxonomists* and realized that I could call what I had been doing for the previous 10 years "taxonomy work." With my prior taxonomist position, I soon landed new taxonomy contract work and then another full-time taxonomist position, this time at a software vendor.

While taxonomy may no longer be the latest, hottest topic, as it was around 2000, it has moved beyond being a buzzword to become a topic of more stable interest. The following illustrate the sustained interest in taxonomies:

- An online discussion group dedicated to taxonomies, Taxonomy Community of Practice (taxocop.wikispaces. com), gains new members every week (membership is now close to 1,000) and averaged a dozen postings per week over the period 2005–2009 (higher in more recent years).

- A two-day annual conference, Taxonomy Boot Camp (www.taxonomybootcamp.com/2010), which draws more than 200 attendees, has been growing since its inception in 2005.

- The terms taxonomy and taxonomies are now appearing in dozens of open job descriptions (160 on Monster.com in April 2008 alone).

- According to one researcher, the industry of taxonomy software and services grew on average 21 percent between 2002 and 2006.[3]

Although there are numerous articles and conference presentations on information taxonomies, books dedicated to the subject are rare. There have been several good books on thesaurus construction published in recent decades. While these might serve as useful guides for the practicing taxonomist, thesaurus construction books do not sufficiently cover other kinds of taxonomies, such as enterprise and website taxonomies and issues of automated indexing and search. The more recent books on taxonomies, on the other hand, are focused on enterprise taxonomies or take a more project management perspective on taxonomy creation. These may be good books for the manager or executive who is considering a taxonomy project, but they lack sufficient depth to instruct the practicing taxonomist, who needs advice on how to handle various situations in working with the taxonomy terms themselves. The primary audience of this book is the person actually creating and editing the terms within a taxonomy.

There has remained an unmet need for a practical book aimed at practicing taxonomists that goes beyond the introductory level. Introductory information on taxonomy creation abounds in articles, conference workshops, Taxonomy Boot Camp, and a few graduate school or continuing education courses. I teach such a continuing education course myself and have been asked by prospective students about offering an intermediate or advanced course, as nothing exists. Rather than teach a second course—an ongoing commitment—I decided to write a book. That is not to say that this book is purely at an advanced level. It is still appropriate for beginning taxonomists and includes all the content of my introductory course on creating taxonomies and controlled vocabularies. The currently practicing taxonomist will also find useful information, as additional content has been included based on various presentations and articles I have written the past two years and on some more recent research.

Because there are many different kinds of taxonomies—for human and automated indexing, for literature retrieval and website information categorization, for consumers and internal enterprises—a taxonomist's experience in creating one kind of taxonomy is not necessarily sufficient preparation for working on a different kind of taxonomy. Thus, this book also serves the purpose of cross-training existing taxonomists for different kinds of taxonomy projects. If we want to carry the label of *taxonomist* and move from one job to another, then a broader understanding of the types of work and issues involved is needed.

This book aims to explain what you need to know to be a good taxonomist rather than explain how to create a taxonomy, step-by-step. Therefore the chapters are arranged in order of importance in terms of what you need to know, rather than in the project sequence for building a taxonomy. Chapters 1 and 2 provide background on taxonomies and taxonomists. Chapters 3 and 4 present the basics of term and relationship creation in accordance with the ANSI/NISO Z39.19 standard, which may serve as a review for experienced taxonomists but is fundamental for the new taxonomist. Chapter 5 provides practical information on the various taxonomy management software options available. While some software tools have come and gone, others have been around for a long time and have staying power. The next four chapters move beyond the basics to focus on particular issues for different types of taxonomies. Chapter 6 deals with creating taxonomies or thesauri used by human indexers, whereas Chapter 7 discusses the issues involved with creating taxonomies used in automated indexing, auto-categorization, or search. Chapter 8 examines various taxonomy structures, and Chapter 9 presents various display options. Chapter 10 turns to broader issues of taxonomy planning and design, which often involve the taxonomist, and Chapter 11 deals with ongoing taxonomy work, such as the maintenance, merging, and translating of taxonomies. Finally, Chapter 12 returns the focus to the taxonomist: the nature of the work, what kind of work exists, and training and resources available.

I hope *The Accidental Taxonomist* will prove not just informative but practical and useful as well. While it covers most of what you need to know to create taxonomies, it does not address every detail. For additional specific instructions, I highly recommend consulting the ANSI/NISO Z39.19 standard, *Guidelines for the Construction, Format, and Management of Monolingual Controlled Vocabularies*. It has a wealth of information but is really too much for the newcomer to taxonomies to digest. That is where this book comes in. This book also discusses additional types of taxonomies and taxonomy features not addressed in the ANSI/NISO Z39.19 standard.

The quotations at the start of each chapter were proposed mottos for the Taxonomy Community of Practice discussion group, suggested by its various members in January 2009. (The quotation for Chapter 1 was the winning motto.)

Endnotes

1. Wendi Pohs, unpublished case study (2008).
2. American Library Association, "Alphabetical List of Institutions With ALA-Accredited Programs," www.ala.org/ala/educationcareers/education/accreditedprograms/directory/list/index.cfm (accessed January 21, 2009).
3. Darin Stewart, "(Why) Taxonomies Need XML. (Extensible Markup Language)." *EContent* (March 2007).

Chapter 1

What Are Taxonomies?

Taxonomies? That's classified information.
—Jordan Cassel

The first step in discussing the role and work of the taxonomist is to clarify what a taxonomy is. Even if you already have some understanding of the concept, there are multiple meanings and various types of taxonomies that require further explanation. The descriptions provided here are not strict definitions, and the range of knowledge organization systems should be thought of as a spectrum.

Definitions and Types of Taxonomies

The word *taxonomy* comes from the Greek *taxis*, meaning arrangement or order, and *nomos*, meaning law or science. For present-day information management, the term *taxonomy* is used both in the narrow sense, to mean a hierarchical classification or categorization system, and in the broad sense, in reference to any means of organizing concepts of knowledge. Some professionals do not even like to use the term, contending that it is too often ambiguous and frequently misused. Yet it has gained sufficient popularity, and a practical alternative term does not seem to exist. In this book, taxonomy will be used in its broader meaning and not limited to hierarchical structures.

In the broader sense, a taxonomy may also be referred to as a *knowledge organization system* or *knowledge organization structure*. This designation sometimes appears in scholarly discussion of the field and in course titles at graduate schools of library and information science. The designation *knowledge organization system* was first used by the Networked Knowledge Organization Systems Working Group at its initial meeting at the Association for Computing Machinery Digital Libraries Conference in Pittsburgh, Pennsylvania, in 1998. Gail Hodge further expanded on it in an article in 2000 for the Digital Library Federation Council on Library and Information Resources. In Hodge's words:

> The term *knowledge organization systems* is intended to encompass all types of schemes for organizing information and promoting knowledge management. Knowledge organization systems include classification schemes that organize materials at a general level (such as books on a shelf), subject headings that provide more detailed access, and authority files that control variant versions of key information (such as geographic names and personal names). They also include less-traditional schemes, such as semantic networks and ontologies.[1]

Although she does not mention taxonomies per se in this paragraph, Hodge goes on to list the various types of knowledge organization systems, which include[2]:

1. Term lists (authority files, glossaries, dictionaries, and gazetteers)

2. Classifications and categories (subject headings, classification schemes, taxonomies, and categorization schemes)

3. Relationship lists (thesauri, semantic networks, and ontologies)

Needless to say, the designation *knowledge organization system* has not caught on in the business world and is not likely to do so. We are even less likely to hear of a *knowledge organization system creator/editor*; that would be a good description of a taxonomist.

While this book uses the term taxonomy broadly (as a synonym for knowledge organization system), most of our discussion focuses on taxonomies that have at least some form of structure or relationship among the terms (types 2 and 3 in Hodge's list) rather than mere term lists. Indeed, people do not usually call a simple term list a taxonomy. Let us turn now to definitions and explanations of some of these different kinds of knowledge organization systems or taxonomies.

Controlled Vocabularies

The term *controlled vocabulary* may cover any kind of knowledge organization system, with the possible exclusion of highly structured semantic networks or ontologies. At a minimum, a controlled vocabulary is simply a restricted list of words or terms for some specialized purpose, usually for indexing, labeling, or categorizing. It is "controlled" because only terms from the list may be used for the subject area covered. If used by more than one person, it is also controlled in the sense that there is control over who may add terms to the list and when and how they may do it. The list may grow, but only under defined policies.

The objective of a controlled vocabulary is to ensure consistency in the application of index terms, tags, or labels to avoid ambiguity and the overlooking of information if the "wrong" search term is used. When implemented in search or browse systems, the controlled vocabulary can help guide the user to where the desired information is. While controlled vocabularies are most often used in indexing or tagging, they are also used in technical writing to ensure the use of consistent language. This latter task of writing or creating content is not, however, part of *organizing* information.

Because controlled vocabulary has this broader usage when applied to content creation, not merely information organization, the term *controlled vocabulary* should not be used as a synonym for knowledge organization system.

Most controlled vocabularies feature a *See or Use* type of cross-reference system, directing the user from one or more "nonpreferred" terms to the designated "preferred" term. Only if a controlled vocabulary is very small and easily browsed, as on a single page, might such cross-referencing be unnecessary.

In certain controlled vocabularies, there could be a set of synonyms for each concept, with none of them designated as the preferred term (akin to having equivalent double posts in a back-of-the-book index instead of *See* references). This type of arrangement is known as a *synonym ring* or a *synset* because all synonyms are equal and can be expressed in a circular ring of interrelationships. An example of a synonym ring, as illustrated in Figure 1.1, is the series of terms applications, software, computer programs, tools. Synonym rings may be used when the browsable list of terms or entries is not displayed to the user and when the user merely accesses the terms via a search box. If the synonyms are used behind the scenes with a search engine and never displayed as a browsable list for the user, the distinction between preferred and nonpreferred terms is thus moot. Though these types of controlled vocabularies are quite common, they are often invisible to the user, so the terminology (synonym ring and synset) is not widely known.

Sometimes controlled vocabularies are referred to as *authority files*, especially if they contain just named entities. Named entities are proper-noun terms, such as specific person names, place names, company names, organization names, product names, and names of published works. These also require control for consistent formats, use of abbreviations, spelling, and so forth.

Figure 1.1 Example of terms in a synonym ring

Controlled vocabularies may or may not have relationships among their terms. Simple controlled vocabularies, such as a temporary offline list created by an indexer to ensure consistent indexing or a synonym ring used behind the scenes in a search, do not have any structured relationships other than preferred and non-preferred terms. Other controlled vocabularies may have broader/narrower and related-term relationships and still be called controlled vocabularies rather than thesauri or taxonomies. This is often the case at periodical and reference index publishers, such as Gale, EBSCO, and H.W. Wilson, which maintain controlled vocabularies for use in their periodical indexes. In some cases, the publisher maintains multiple kinds of controlled vocabularies, some being more structured than others, and controlled vocabulary is the more generic designation for all of these.

Hierarchical Taxonomies

When we think of taxonomy, hierarchical classification systems are what typically come to mind. However, as explained in the previous section, we are using a broader definition of taxonomy that encompasses all kinds of knowledge organization systems. So taxonomies that are structured as hierarchies we will refer to specifically as *hierarchical taxonomies.*

A hierarchical taxonomy is a kind of controlled vocabulary in which each term is connected to a designated broader term (unless it is the top-level term) and one or more narrower terms (unless it is a bottom level term), and all the terms are organized into a single large hierarchical structure. Taxonomy in this case could apply to a single hierarchy or a limited set of hierarchies. This type of structure is often referred to as a *tree*, with a trunk, main branches, and more and more smaller branches off the main branches. Actually, if the taxonomy is displayed as a tree, it is an upside-down tree, with multiple smaller branches for narrower terms lower down on the page or screen. Another way to describe such structure is a taxonomy with *nested categories*. The expression *to drill down* is often used to describe how a user navigates down through the branches. An example of an excerpt from a hierarchical taxonomy appears in Figure 1.2.

The classic example of a hierarchical taxonomy is the Linnaean taxonomy (named after Carolus Linnaeus) of biological organisms, with the hierarchical top-down structure: kingdom, phylum, class, order, family, genus, and species. The Dewey Decimal Classification system for cataloging books can also be considered a hierarchical taxonomy (although, like the Linnaean taxonomy, it has the drawback that each item can be classified in only one place). Other well-known examples of hierarchical taxonomies are the Standard Industrial Classification (SIC) and North American Industrial Classification Systems (NAICS) codes for classifying industries. Hierarchical taxonomies are also common

Top Level Headings	Leisure and culture
Business and industry	. Arts and entertainment venues
Economics and finance	. . Museums and galleries
Education and skills	. Children's activities
Employment, jobs, and careers	. Culture and creativity
Environment	. . Architecture
Government, politics, and public	. . Crafts
administration	. . Heritage
Health, well-being, and care	. . Literature
Housing	. . Music
Information and communication	. . Performing arts
International affairs and defence	. . Visual arts
Leisure and culture	. Entertainment and events
Life in the community	. Gambling and lotteries
People and organisations	. Hobbies and interests
Public order, justice, and rights	. Parks and gardens
Science, technology, and innovation	. Sports and recreation
Transport and infrastructure	. . Team sports
Leisure and culture	. . . Cricket
	. . . Football
	. . . Rugby
	. . Water sports
	. . Winter sports
	. Sports and recreation facilities
	. Tourism
	. . Passports and visas
	. Young people's activities

Figure 1.2 Terms in an expandable hierarchical taxonomy;
top categories (left) and the expansion of one category (right) from
the Abridged Integrated Public Sector Vocabulary, Version 2.00

in geospatial classification, as for regions, countries, provinces, and cities. While hierarchical taxonomies tend be used mostly for generic things or concepts, they can be used for proper nouns that naturally fall into a hierarchy, such as place names, product names, government agency names, or corporate department names.

The structure of a hierarchical taxonomy often reflects an organization of nested categories. Some hierarchical taxonomies permit a term to have multiple broader terms, thus appearing in multiple places in the taxonomy, whereas other hierarchical taxonomies do not permit this "polyhierarchy" structure. Hierarchical taxonomies may or may not make use of nonpreferred terms. Finally, nonhierarchical related-term relationships may exist but usually are not present in such hierarchical taxonomies.

In contrast to the other types of taxonomies described subsequently in this chapter and this book, the hierarchical taxonomy is actually not a defined type of taxonomy. Rather, it is my designation for the narrower, standard definition of taxonomy: "A collection of controlled vocabulary terms organized into a hierarchical structure."[3] It is a kind of taxonomy that is commonly seen in countless real-world applications. And it is the type of taxonomy that the accidental taxonomist is probably most likely to create.

Thesauri

The classic meaning of a thesaurus is a kind of dictionary, such as *Roget's*, that contains synonyms or alternate expressions (and possibly even antonyms) for each term entry. A thesaurus for information management and retrieval shares this characteristic of listing similar terms at each controlled vocabulary term entry. The difference is that a dictionary-thesaurus includes all the associated terms *could potentially* be used in place of the term entry in various contexts; the user (often a writer) needs to consider the specific context in each case because in certain contexts some of the alternate terms would not be appropriate. The information retrieval thesaurus, on the other hand, is designed for use in *all* contexts within the domain of content covered, regardless of any specific term usage or document. The synonyms or near synonyms must therefore be suitably equivalent in *all* circumstances. An information retrieval thesaurus must clearly specify which terms can be used as synonyms (used from), which are more specific (narrower terms), which are broader terms, and which are merely related terms.

A thesaurus, therefore, is a more structured type of controlled vocabulary that provides information about each term and its relationships to other terms within the same thesaurus. National and international standards that provide guidance for creating such thesauri include the following:

- International Organization for Standardization
  (www.iso.org/iso/iso_catalogue.htm)

  - ISO 2788 (1986): Guidelines for the Establishment and
    Development of Monolingual Thesauri

  - ISO 5964 (1905): Guidelines for the Establishment and
    Development of Multilingual Thesauri

  - ISO 2788 and 5964 are to be replaced in 2011 by ISO
    25964: Thesauri and Interoperability With Other
    Vocabularies

- American National Standards Institute and National
  Information Standards Organization
  (www.niso.org/kst/reports/standards)

  - ANSI/NISO Z39.19 (2005): Guidelines for the
    Construction, Format, and Management of
    Monolingual Controlled Vocabularies

- British Standards Institution (www.bsigroup.com)

  - BS 8723-1 (2005): Structured Vocabularies for
    Information Retrieval: Definitions, Symbols and
    Abbreviations

  - BS 8723-2 (2005): Structured Vocabularies for
    Information Retrieval: Thesauri

  - BS 8723-3 (2007): Structured Vocabularies for
    Information Retrieval: Vocabularies Other than
    Thesauri

  - BS 8723-4 (2007): Structured Vocabularies for
    Information Retrieval: Interoperability Between
    Vocabularies

Although the ANSI/NISO standard refers to controlled vocabularies, a document created in accordance with these guidelines is usually called a thesaurus.

The standards explain in detail the three types of relationships in a thesaurus: hierarchical (broader term/narrower term), associative (related term), and equivalence (use/used for). Additional information about a term, such as a *scope note*, may be included to clarify usage. An example of a term and its details from a thesaurus is shown in Figure 1.3. The consensus is that if a controlled vocabulary includes both broader/narrower and related-term relationships between terms, along with nonpreferred terms that redirect to the accepted term, then it is called a thesaurus.

In comparing a thesaurus with a hierarchical taxonomy, a thesaurus typically includes the features of a taxonomy plus the additional feature of associative relationships, for a greater degree of structural complexity. However, while all terms must belong to a limited number of hierarchies within a hierarchical taxonomy, this is not a strict requirement for a thesaurus. Although most thesaurus

```
materials acquisitions
UF   acquisitions (of materials)
     library acquisitions
BT   collection development
NT   accessions
     approval plans
     gifts and exchanges
     materials claims
     materials orders
     subscriptions
RT   book vendors
     jobbers
     subscription agencies
     subscription cancellations
```

Figure 1.3 A term in the *ASIS&T Thesaurus* with its various relationships to other terms (BT: broader term. NT: narrower term. RT: related term. UF: used from)[4]

entries will list a broader and/or a narrower term, such relationships are not necessarily required for every term. If there is no appropriate broader term, that relationship may be omitted. In a thesaurus, the focus is more on the individual terms than on the top-down structure. Thus a thesaurus might include multiple small hierarchies, comprising as few as two or three terms, without the strong overarching tree structure typical of a hierarchical taxonomy.

If you had to force all the terms in a thesaurus into a single hierarchical tree, some of the hierarchical relationships would probably be imperfect. Thesaurus guidelines, however, mandate that each term's hierarchical relationships be accurate and valid. In addition, having multiple broader terms for an entry is never a problem in a thesaurus, whereas such "polyhierarchies" may be prohibited in a given hierarchical taxonomy. Some thesauri do in fact have a significant hierarchical structure, and thus the distinction between a hierarchical taxonomy and a thesaurus may be blurred. Finally, recursive retrieval by a broader term (explained in Chapter 9) is not as common in a thesaurus as in a hierarchical taxonomy.

The greater detail and information contained in a thesaurus, compared with a simple controlled vocabulary or a hierarchical taxonomy, aids the user (whether the indexer or the searcher) in finding the most appropriate term more easily. A thesaurus structure is especially useful for a relatively large controlled vocabulary that involves human indexing and/or supports a term list display that the end user (searcher) can browse. In contrast to a hierarchical taxonomy, which is designed for user navigation from the top down, a thesaurus with multiple means of access can more easily contain a greater number of terms. Thus, a thesaurus may be able to support more granular (specific) and extensive indexing than a simple hierarchical taxonomy can, especially if the hierarchical taxonomy lacks nonpreferred terms. As thesauri explain relationships among terms, they are more common in specialized subject areas, where the purpose is not merely to aid the user in finding information but also to aid the user in obtaining a better understanding of the terminology. In some cases, thesauri have even been published and printed as stand-alone works, separate from any indexed content.

Examples of thesauri include the Getty Art & Architecture Thesaurus, the ERIC (Education Resources Information Center) Thesaurus for education research, and the NASA Thesaurus of aeronautics and space terminology. The periodical and reference index publisher ProQuest also refers to its topical controlled vocabulary as a thesaurus.

Ontologies

An ontology can be considered a type of taxonomy with even more complex relationships between terms than in a thesaurus. Actually, an ontology is more than that; it aims to describe a domain of knowledge, a subject area, by both its terms (called *individuals* or *instances*) and their relationships and thus supports inferencing. This objective of a more complex and complete representation of knowledge stems from the etymology of the word *ontology*, which originally meant the study of the nature of being, or existence. Tom Gruber provides a current definition of ontology:

> An ontology defines a set of representational primitives with which to model a domain of knowledge or discourse. ... ontology can be viewed as a level of abstraction of data models, analogous to hierarchical and relational models.[5]

The relationships between terms within an ontology are not limited to broader/narrower and related. Rather, there can be any number of domain-specific types of relationship pairs, such as owns/belongs to, produces/is produced by, and has members/is a member of. The creator of the ontology also creates

these relationship types. Thus, not only do the terms have meanings, but the relationships themselves have meanings as well.
Relationships with meanings are called semantic relationships.

The terms within an ontology have not merely simple descriptions, such as scope notes in a thesaurus, but are also accompa-
nied by specific attributes in a more structured format, such as
properties, features, characteristics, or parameters. The terms also
have assigned classes, which the ontologist defines, as an additional kind of classification. All of these components of an ontology—semantic relationships, attributes (for each of the
terms/instances), and classes—contribute to making an ontology
a richer source of information than a mere hierarchical taxonomy
or thesaurus. A schematic representation of part of an ontology
dealing with retail management appears in Figure 1.4.

While not considered standards, there are guidelines of specifications for constructing ontologies in machine-readable format

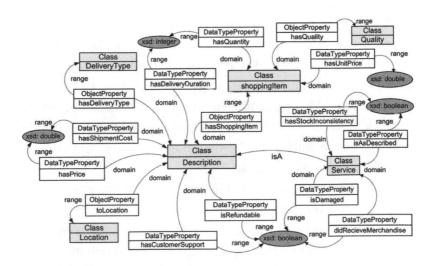

Figure 1.4 Example of a domain ontology dealing with
retail management (reproduced with permission of the creators,
Murat Sensoy and Pinar Yolum)[6]

for the web, which has become the most common implementation of this type of taxonomy. The World Wide Web Consortium (WC3) has published the RDF (resource description framework) Schema and the Web Ontology Language (OWL) recommendation. There is also a presentation format for ontologies called Topic Maps, which is the ISO 13250 standard. Topic Maps are implemented more in Europe than in North America. A looser structure of knowledge organization that does not attempt to adhere to such guidelines might be called a semantic network instead of an actual ontology.

Ontologies are suitable for any subject area, but a significant percentage of those currently published have been in the biological sciences, such as the Gene Ontology, Protein Ontology, Systems Biology Ontology, and Purdue Ontology for Pharmaceutical Engineering. It is an interesting irony that taxonomies, which got their start in biological classification, are now widely used for any form of knowledge, while ontologies, which originally applied to the broad scope of existence, are now used most often in the field of biology. As other scientists find a need to express more complex relationships among terms in their disciplines, the spread of ontologies to other subject areas, however, will likely increase. There is also a growing importance of ontologies in semantic search engine deployment in specialized industries, and building ontologies could be a growth area for experienced taxonomists. In 2009, a new organization for supporting ontologies, the International Association for Ontology and Its Applications (www.iaoa.org), was founded.

The designation given to a knowledge organization system—controlled vocabulary, taxonomy, thesaurus, ontology, and so on—depends largely on the complexity of the structure, but complexity is not the only factor to be considered. As all these designations have ambiguous meanings, the choice of what to call a set of terms also depends on what is most clear and understandable to the contributors, stakeholders, or end users. Depending on the display of the knowledge organization system, the end users may not even need to know what it is called. The confusion in terminology is why we default to using the single designation of taxonomy in most contexts.

Applications and Purposes of Taxonomies

As we have seen from the various definitions, there are different kinds of taxonomies or controlled vocabularies, based on their complexity. However, that is only one way to classify them. A more practical approach is to categorize taxonomies by their application and use. While one taxonomy can certainly serve multiple functions, there tends to be a certain emphasis in its design, use, and purposes. As such, taxonomies serve primarily one of the following three functions, although there certainly can be combinations of the different types:

1. Indexing support

2. Retrieval support

3. Organization and navigation support

Indexing Support

For indexing or cataloging support, a taxonomy, better known as a controlled vocabulary in this context, is a list of agreed-on terms for the human indexing or cataloging of multiple documents and/or for indexing performed by multiple indexers, to ensure consistency. If multiple documents, especially by different authors, will be indexed over time, the indexer is apt to forget exactly which index terms were assigned and perhaps inadvertently use different synonyms when the same topic comes up in a different document. Similarly, different indexers will also choose different index terms for the same topic if not forced to use a controlled vocabulary.

Thus, the taxonomy's initial purpose is to serve the people doing the indexing, although a second, equally important purpose is to serve the end users, who, of course, benefit from consistently indexed content and may also have access to the taxonomy. This type of controlled vocabulary is used for cataloging entire works and for indexes to periodical articles, image files, database records, multivolume printed works, webpages, etc. Because indexers must always choose the most accurate terms, they often use a more structured thesaurus type of controlled vocabulary. The broader, narrower, and related term relationships guide the indexer to the best term, and scope notes further clarify ambiguous terms. Named entities are often indexed, too, and these are managed in an authority file. An authority file lacks the interterm relationships of a thesaurus but may have many synonymous nonpreferred terms for each preferred term, such as variations on an individual's name.

Controlled vocabularies for indexing support have been around the longest, and their format may be electronic or print. Such controlled vocabularies are used by reference and periodical article database publishers, including H.W. Wilson, ProQuest, Gale, and EBSCO; in more specialized subject databases such as Chemical Abstracts and PsycINFO; and in the internal documents of large companies, especially those in the sciences. The fact that some of these controlled vocabularies are offered for sale/license illustrates the fact that they serve the purpose of indexing and not just specific content retrieval.

While controlled vocabularies for indexing are quite widespread, those that are publicly available on the web are limited and tend to be those published by public agencies. You may search or browse them, and in some cases, you may also access linked content. Library of Congress Subject Headings and Medical Subject Headings are two such examples.

Library of Congress Subject Headings (LCSH; authorities.loc. gov) contains both subjects and names, and covers all subject areas. LCSH was originally established for cataloging library materials but has also been adapted by various publishers for indexing articles. The terms are called *authorities*, as in authority file, even those that are not named entities. The purpose of the website is to aid catalogers of library materials in finding the approved subject heading in the Library of Congress controlled vocabulary. It is not aimed at the end user looking for a book, although consistently cataloged books will, of course, benefit the user. The subject headings can be searched and the results browsed alphabetically. Nonpreferred terms are included in the alphabetical list along with preferred terms. Nonpreferred terms are prefaced by a button labeled References, which provides a cross-reference to the preferred term. Preferred terms are called *authorized headings* (see Figure 1.5).

Medical Subject Headings (MeSH; www.nlm.nih.gov/mesh/MBrowser.html) is the thesaurus of the U.S. National Library of Medicine, which is considered the authority for medical terms. Users can search terms, or they can browse by selecting the button Navigate from Tree Top. The browse display is hierarchical rather than alphabetical. Clicking once on a term expands the tree and reveals its narrower terms; double-clicking on a term displays its details (see Figure 1.6).

Other examples of thesauri that aid indexing and are publicly available include the ERIC Thesaurus (eric.ed.gov), sponsored by the Institute of Education Sciences of the U.S. Department of Education, and the various controlled vocabularies of the Getty Research Institute of the J. Paul Getty Trust: the Getty Art & Architecture Thesaurus, Getty Thesaurus of Geographic Names, Cultural Objects Name Authority, and Union List of Artist Names (www.getty.edu/research/conducting_research/vocabularies).

Retrieval Support

A taxonomy that serves indexing also serves end-user retrieval. Searchers benefit from nonpreferred terms, as their search terms

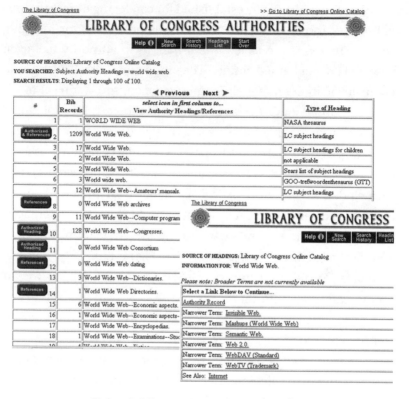

Figure 1.5 Two successive screenshots from
Library of Congress Subject Headings, searching on the term
World Wide Web and displaying its details

may be different from the terms used to index the document. For example, a user may type in **doctors** for articles that are about physicians. Users can also take advantage of broader and narrower term relationships or hierarchies to broaden or narrow their search. These relationships, and also the related-term relationships, may suggest to users other possible terms of interest. In such cases, the end-user searcher is seeing an explicit representation of the taxonomy to navigate.

There are also taxonomies designed to aid search retrieval without supporting human indexing. These taxonomies are typically

MeSH Heading	Arm Injuries
Tree Number	C21.866.088
Annotation	GEN or unspecified; consider also / inj with specific bones of arm; also available are FOREARM INJURIES; HAND INJURIES; FINGER INJURIES; WRIST INJURIES & many specific organ/fract precoords
Scope Note	General or unspecified injuries involving the arm.
Entry Term	Injuries, Arm
Allowable Qualifiers	BL CF CI CL CN CO DH DI DT EC EH EM EN EP ET GE HI IM ME MI MO NU PA PC PP PS PX RA RH RI RT SU TH UR US VE VI
Entry Version	ARM INJ
Date of Entry	19990101
Unique ID	D001134

MeSH Tree Structures

Disorders of Environmental Origin [C21]
  Wounds and Injuries [C21.866]
           Abdominal Injuries [C21.866.017] +
           Amputation, Traumatic [C21.866.062]
    ▶ Arm Injuries [C21.866.088]
                  Forearm Injuries [C21.866.088.268] +
                  Humeral Fractures [C21.866.088.390]
                  Shoulder Dislocation [C21.866.088.666]
                  Shoulder Fractures [C21.866.088.749]
                  Tennis Elbow [C21.866.088.890]
                  Wrist Injuries [C21.866.088.906]
           Asphyxia [C21.866.103]
           Athletic Injuries [C21.866.115]
           Back Injuries [C21.866.117] +
           Barotrauma [C21.866.120] +

Figure 1.6 Searching Medical Subject Headings
for the selected term *arm injuries*

mapping-tables of terms and their synonyms/variants designed to aid online retrieval. These might be synonym rings or synsets, especially if the terms are not even displayed to the user; or, if there is a display, it may designate preferred terms.

Depending on the user interface display, there may or may not be a hierarchical structure to the taxonomy. A hierarchical arrangement allows users to browse and locate narrower (more specific) subjects of interest. Thus, users find out what is included in the taxonomy and what is not, saving themselves the trouble of repeatedly typing in terms that yield no results. Users may also find related subjects of interest by browsing the hierarchies.

These types of controlled vocabularies are often used with site search engines, enterprise search systems (used internally within a large organization), online databases, and large commercial directories (such as online "yellow pages" or classified ads). The format is always electronic, and a form of automated indexing is usually involved.

Examples of taxonomies aiding retrieval include the Verizon SuperPages yellow pages directory site (www.superpages.com/yellowpages) and the Amazon.com ecommerce site (www.amazon. com/gp/site-directory), as shown in Figure 1.7. While a hierarchy can be selected for browsing in each, the synonyms in the case of Verizon SuperPages and the related subject links in the case of Amazon.com are not displayed to the user, although the links are evident in the display of results.

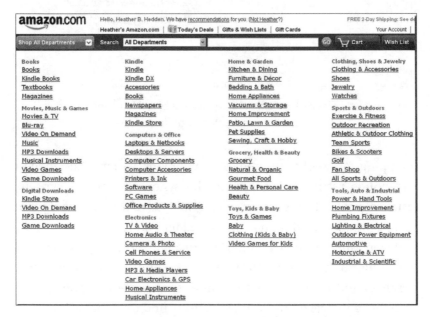

Figure 1.7 Top-level taxonomy of Amazon.com

Faceted Taxonomies for Retrieval Support

One way to better serve specifically the retrieval of data is to construct a controlled vocabulary that is divided into multiple subsets, lists of terms of different types representing different aspects of information. These aspects are often called *facets,* and this type of controlled vocabulary is therefore called a *faceted taxonomy.* Examples of facets might be people, places, events, products, and laws. Facets can also reflect metadata other than subject categories, such as document type, author, and audience. The search interface for a faceted taxonomy is designed for the user to search on a selected combination of multiple facets.

Faceted taxonomies are commonly used for online databases and ecommerce sites, such as the shoe-retailing site Shoebuy.com. In Shoebuy's advanced search (www.shoebuy.com/s.jsp/r_as), the facets are Brand, Category, Type, Size, Width, Color, Country, Price, and, additionally for women's shoes, Heel Height. Another example of a faceted browse interface is on the Microbial Life Education Resources site (serc.carleton.edu/microbelife/resources), where facets are Subject, Resource Type, Extreme Environments, Ocean Environments, and Grade Level (Figure.1.8).

Faceted taxonomies, or *faceted browse* systems, make use of the electronic format. Depending on the size of the vocabulary in each facet, these taxonomies may not make use of synonyms and may or may not have hierarchies within them. Some facets can be quite small. Facets will be discussed in more detail in Chapter 6.

Organization and Navigation Support

A taxonomy, as a hierarchy, can provide a categorization or classification system for things or for information. For the organization of information, we often see taxonomies applied in website information architecture (structural design), online information services, intranet content organization, and corporate content management systems. In such website or enterprise taxonomies,

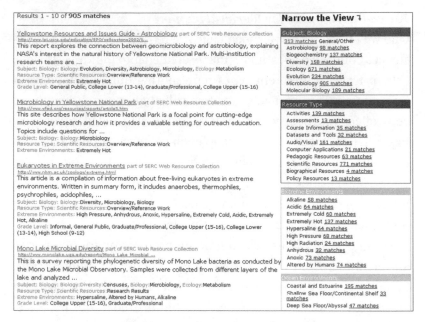

Figure 1.8 Faceted taxonomy in the margin
of the Microbial Life Education Resources search site

the emphasis is on classification and guided user navigation rather than on search and retrieval of specific information. *Navigation* means finding one's way around, whereas *retrieval* means going after specific information. The taxonomy for a website is a lot like a table of contents, organized by topic. It can be reflected in the navigational menu and in the site map. As such, it might be called a *navigational taxonomy*. These types of taxonomies tend to be relatively small and can coexist with additional, more detailed taxonomies elsewhere on the website.

An example of navigational website taxonomy that is present in both the site map and the navigational menu can be found on the Information Architecture Institute site map (iainstitute.org/en/site-map.php), where the top-level categories of the taxonomy and the navigation are Member Services, IA Network, Learning IA, and

About Us (Figure 1.9). Another example of a navigational taxonomy is MyFlorida.com, the State of Florida site map (www.my florida.com/taxonomy), where the top-level categories of the taxonomy, which also are the main navigation menu items, are Visitor, Floridian, Business, and Government. It is interesting to note that the file name for this site map page has been named taxonomy.

Enterprise taxonomies can be very large, but the top levels typically demonstrate some form of information organization for the enterprise. The purpose is not merely to retrieve documents but also to help users better understand the organization of the enterprise and its intranet and thus make better use of it.

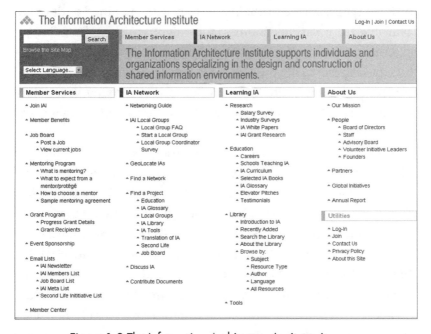

Figure 1.9 The Information Architecture Institute site map,
a navigational taxonomy

Taxonomies for License

Although the primary objective of this book is to provide instruction on building taxonomies, it is not always necessary to build an entire taxonomy from scratch. Some or all of a taxonomy could be acquired from another source. While navigation taxonomies for websites and intranets and taxonomies for enterprises and content management systems should be custom-created, a taxonomy for the indexing of documents or files in a given subject area could be purchased or licensed. Furthermore, taxonomies for license not only serve the purposes of indexing and content retrieval but may also provide an outline of a domain of knowledge. Many subject areas are already covered by existing published taxonomies. There are generic taxonomies for geographic places, industry types, product types, and so forth. In addition, lists of named entities are available from various sources. You might consider licensing an external taxonomy if the right taxonomy already exists or if creating one from scratch would be too great a task due to size, specialty subject area, and limited time. A licensed controlled vocabulary could be used for merely a single facet or for part of a larger set of taxonomies.

Taxonomies or controlled vocabularies that are available for license come from all kinds of sources: government agencies, professional associations, other nonprofit organizations, and a few commercial enterprises. Governmental published taxonomies available for license (or even without a license) include LCSH, Library of Congress Thesaurus for Graphic Materials, MeSH, USDA National Agricultural Library Thesaurus, and the U.K.'s Integrated Public Sector Vocabulary. The Getty Research Institute (part of the J. Paul Getty Trust) is a reputable nonprofit provider of controlled vocabularies, including the Art & Architecture Thesaurus, Getty Thesaurus of Geographic Names, and Union List of Artist Names. Commercial vendors of taxonomies, both pre-built and custom, include Dow Jones Client Solutions, which specializes in business and finance, and WAND Inc., which has strengths in products and services.

The largest (and the only multisource) directory of taxonomies available for use is Taxonomy Warehouse (www.taxonomyware house.com). The list was started by the taxonomy software vendor Synapse and is now managed by Dow Jones Client Solutions. The database includes hundreds of taxonomies, including most of those mentioned previously. Some are simple controlled vocabularies or glossaries, but others are full-featured thesauri. Although some are hosted on the web, the data files (usually in CSV or XML formats) can be obtained for most of them. Figure 1.10 shows the information that Taxonomy Warehouse provides for a specific taxonomy. A single source/publisher may also offer numerous taxonomies on different subjects.

Formats may vary, but typically, taxonomies or thesauri that are made available for other uses are formatted in some kind of XML whereby all terms, relationships, nonpreferred terms, scope notes, and so forth are retained when they are imported into other taxonomy management systems. The use of XML and other interoperable taxonomy formats is described in greater detail in Chapter 10.

If you acquire a taxonomy, however, you will likely want to modify or enhance it for your own needs, and in any case it will require some maintenance over time. The following is an example of how a generic taxonomy taken as-is may not be ideal. A large-scale historical digitization project that coded early American election results used the Getty Thesaurus of Geographic Names. Even though the thesaurus includes historical place names, it was still found to be insufficient for the project's needs. It does not include all the towns and boroughs that were named in the elections project and does not indicate exactly when various historical names were used or when boundaries were redrawn.

Licensing agreements may allow use of a taxonomy without a fee in some cases but may prohibit for-profit use or require statements

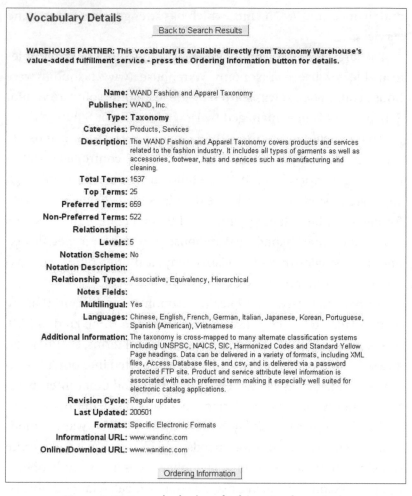

Vocabulary Details

Back to Search Results

WAREHOUSE PARTNER: This vocabulary is available directly from Taxonomy Warehouse's value-added fulfillment service - press the Ordering Information button for details.

Name: WAND Fashion and Apparel Taxonomy
Publisher: WAND, Inc.
Type: Taxonomy
Categories: Products, Services
Description: The WAND Fashion and Apparel Taxonomy covers products and services related to the fashion industry. It includes all types of garments as well as accessories, footwear, hats and services such as manufacturing and cleaning.
Total Terms: 1537
Top Terms: 25
Preferred Terms: 659
Non-Preferred Terms: 522
Relationships:
Levels: 5
Notation Scheme: No
Notation Description:
Relationship Types: Associative, Equivalency, Hierarchical
Notes Fields:
Multilingual: Yes
Languages: Chinese, English, French, German, Italian, Japanese, Korean, Portuguese, Spanish (American), Vietnamese
Additional Information: The taxonomy is cross-mapped to many alternate classification systems including UNSPSC, NAICS, SIC, Harmonized Codes and Standard Yellow Page headings. Data can be delivered in a variety of formats, including XML files, Access Database files, and csv, and is delivered via a password protected FTP site. Product and service attribute level information is associated with each preferred term making it especially well suited for electronic catalog applications.
Revision Cycle: Regular updates
Last Updated: 200501
Formats: Specific Electronic Formats
Informational URL: www.wandinc.com
Online/Download URL: www.wandinc.com

Ordering Information

Figure 1.10 Example display of information for a single taxonomy offered for sale through Taxonomy Warehouse

referring to the original copyright holder. If the taxonomy is treated as a published copyrighted work, whether free or for a fee, then there will also be restrictions on making changes to it. The policy for modifications to the Getty vocabularies is as follows:

The license for the Getty vocabularies, AAT, TGN, ULAN, and CONA (in development) does not restrict additions or alterations to the vocabulary, provided that—if the product is visible to the public or other end users—the terms and other information that come from the Getty vocabulary are labeled with a citation for the vocabulary and the copyright of the J. Paul Getty Trust. Likewise, any additions and alterations must be clearly indicated as NOT being from the Getty vocabulary. If the vocabulary is only used behind the scenes for retrieval and not visible to the end user, labeling which bits come from Getty vocabulary and which are added is irrelevant.[7]

The policy for using and modifying MeSH is as follows:

If the use is not personal, (1) the U.S. National Library of Medicine must be identified as the creator, maintainer, and provider of the data; (2) the version of the data must be clearly stated by MeSH year, e.g., 1997 MeSH; and (3) if any modification is made in the content of the file, this must be stated, along with a description of the modifications.[8]

Often you will want to make changes to the acquired taxonomy, so make sure the license permits changes. Also be aware that you are responsible for continued updating. Thus, a solid understanding of how to create terms and relationships, as discussed in Chapters 3 and 4, is still necessary to manage pre-built taxonomies. Therefore, acquiring a taxonomy from an external source does not eliminate the need for a taxonomist. Starting with a pre-built taxonomy, though, is much easier for the less experienced taxonomist. You can follow examples of term formats and relationships as you build out the taxonomy further. Licensed taxonomies, both those that prohibit and those that permit changes, typically offer updates through an annual subscription.

History of Taxonomies

Taxonomies are both new and old. "Both librarians and indexers were doing 'taxonomy' long before it became a hot topic in the 1990s," wrote taxonomy trainer Jean Graef of the Montague Institute.[9]

Taxonomies in Cataloging and Indexing

The earliest taxonomies were for classification, such as for organisms or for books, but each item could only go in one place in the taxonomy. For example, a book gets a single call number for its location on the shelf. In the field of library science, by the end of the 19th century more practical taxonomies emerged that supported supplemental descriptive cataloging, which is not limited to one descriptive term per book. The leading controlled vocabularies for cataloging books have been the American Library Association Subject Headings (1895), LCSH (1898), and the Sears List, published originally as the List of Subject Headings for Small Public Libraries (1923). These were simple controlled vocabularies lacking broader/narrower and related term relationships. LCSH used *See also* references for every kind of relationship and began to introduce broader term, narrower term, and related term references only in 1985.[10]

The LCSH, still in its simpler form, was adopted by various periodical index publishers for the indexing of articles from multiple newspapers, magazines, and journals. These publsihers include the H.W. Wilson Company, which is as old as the LCSH, and in the 1970s Information Access Company (now Cengage Learning) and ABI Inform (now ProQuest). H.W. Wilson still uses modified LCSH, whereas Cengage's and ProQuest's controlled vocabularies have diverged over the years based on the work of their taxonomists.

Meanwhile, professional societies developed their own controlled vocabularies for indexing periodical literature in their fields since at least the early 1900s. These included the American Chemical Society's Chemical Abstracts Service founded in 1907. The word *thesaurus* was first used to refer to a controlled vocabulary for information retrieval purposes by Peter Luhn at IBM in 1957. Early published thesauri included the Department of Defense's *ASTIA Descriptors* in 1960 and the American Institute of Chemical Engineers' *Chemical Engineering Thesaurus* in 1961.[11] Standard thesaurus relationships emerged over time, and guidelines were developed that reinforced them, including UNESCO's 1967 guidelines, which formed the basis of the ISO 2788 standard of 1986.[12] Since the 1960s, various companies, government agencies, and professional associations have published dozens of specialized thesauri. In 1972, the new company Dialog began offering the first publicly available online research service, providing access to multiple bibliographic citation databases indexed with controlled vocabularies.

Corporate Taxonomies

Up through the 1980s, however, taxonomy (thesaurus) development was mostly limited to large index or literature-retrieval database publishers and to a few large companies, especially in the sciences (such as DuPont), or government agencies. The companies and government agencies that developed taxonomies did so mostly within specific subject areas. Taxonomies for an entire organization, that is, enterprise-wide taxonomies, first began to appear in the late 1970s, but their adoption was limited. According to taxonomy and knowledge management consultant Lynda Moulton, it was not so much a lack of interest but simply the limitations of software tools at the time that hindered a wider adoption of enterprise taxonomies.

Moulton recalls teaching a number of thesaurus construction workshops during 1982–1984, attended by librarians and indexers from such companies as Liberty Mutual, John Hancock, Fidelity, MITRE, and Digital Equipment Corp.[13]

Contemporary library automation began to emerge in the late 1970s and systems for "special libraries" (corporate libraries and information management) as early as 1980. Although dedicated taxonomy management systems had not yet appeared on the market, these earlier systems included taxonomy management features. These included BiblioTech by Comstow (acquired in 1999 by Inmagic), which was first installed at Polaroid in 1981, and TechLib, released in 1984, which was built on BASIS and acquired by OpenText in 1998. Comstow Information Services held a number of workshops that were devoted to thesaurus development for corporate libraries in the early 1980s.[14]

It was only in the late 1990s that a broader interest in taxonomies, and the corresponding tools to support them, developed. For example, the taxonomy consultancy Earley and Associates started working on classification, categorization, and metadata projects (essentially taxonomy, but not called that yet) to help their clients make the most out of the Lotus Notes application, by building classification structures, forms, and navigation. In 1998, IBM introduced its Lotus Discovery Service, which "really called out the need for a taxonomy," according to Seth Earley, so he and other consultants at the time provided services in creating taxonomies for Lotus Notes.[15]

The Growth of Enterprise and Web Taxonomies

The emergence and growth of the web in 1990s was a major contributing factor in the growing interest in taxonomies, for several reasons. The web enabled smaller publishers to offer online information services. Companies started developing intranets that quickly expanded in size and required better navigation and search. "With growth of the internet, there was a lot of interest in building to improve search results," explained Synapse co-founder Trish Yancey regarding the start of the company.[16] The proliferation of search engines, and then site search or enterprise search, also led to an interest in taxonomies as it became apparent that search alone was not sufficient. According to Jean Graef, "Taxonomy became hot when IT realized that search engines by themselves couldn't solve the whole retrieval problem."[17] Finally, attention to site design and navigation through the new field of information architecture also put value on taxonomies. Indexer, information architect, and taxonomist Fred Leise wrote, "As the field of information architecture and the influence of Louis Rosenfeld's and Peter Morville's *Information Architecture for the World Wide Web* grew, the knowledge of library science-related information such as faceted browsing classifications and the use of synonym rings as search improvements spread more widely."[18]

The growing interest in taxonomies in the 1980s and 1990s was also reflected in the growth of taxonomy management software. Software for creating and maintaining taxonomies was originally developed internally within the few large organizations that had already developed taxonomies. In 1980 Comstow released BiblioTech, its fully integrated library system for corporate and government libraries, which included a module for thesaurus creation, fully integrated with the cataloging and indexing module. Battelle Columbus Laboratory released similar functionality in TechLib soon after.[19] In the mid-1980s commercial PC software for thesaurus creation became available, including the desktop tools MultiTes, Term Tree, TCS (later a part of WebChoir), and several others that have not survived. Larger-scale client server systems became available in the 1990s, reflecting the growing demand. Synapse Corp. had developed software to maintain taxonomies it was creating for others as a consulting service but soon found a market for the software itself and began selling the Synaptica taxonomy management system in 1999. Similarly, Access Innovations had been offering indexing services since 1978 but then found demand for its taxonomy management tool and has commercially offered its Data Harmony Thesaurus Master since 1998. Wordmap, another major taxonomy software vendor, was founded in 1998. Content management systems and enterprise search solutions, which only really entered the market in the 1990s, have also begun to offer taxonomy management components or features.

The 1990s also saw the establishment of commercial vendors of taxonomies, including Synapse Corp. and WAND, both of which were founded in 1995, and the automatic taxonomy generator company Intellisophic in 1999.

The rise of the term taxonomy paralleled this growing interest in taxonomies. Taxonomy consultant Ron Daniel, now a partner of Taxonomy Strategies, got his start in the field working for the Department of Energy on its thesaurus. He recounts how around 1997, it was starting to use the word *taxonomy* interchangeably with *thesaurus* and another term that hasn't become quite as popular, *synonymy*.[20] Earley recalls starting to use the word *taxonomy* with clients around 1996 or 1997. Moulton recalls the adoption of the term taxonomy:

> Throughout my professional career, first as a technical librarian, then as a software developer and consultant, the operative terminology for my work was thesaurus. … I first heard the term taxonomy applied to "organization maps," in the early 1990s. … In the late 1990s I began to see the term "taxonomy" routinely used to describe "terminology maps," "topical hierarchies," and "terminology relationships." Before long, taxonomy became the de facto label for topical navigation schemes on commercial websites that had a focus on text content retrieval. … At some point I recognized that the term

thesaurus was not understood by IT and business management professionals. So, about 2000, I adopted taxonomy to cover any controlled vocabulary being developed or applied in any indexing, metadata management or retrieval situation. ... To this day, I use thesaurus and taxonomy interchangeably depending on which word will most likely resonate with my audience.[21]

Our online survey completed by 65 taxonomists in November and December 2008 also confirmed the recent trend toward increased use of the term taxonomy. Whereas 17 (26.2 percent) of the respondents had been involved in taxonomy work as we define it (taxonomies, controlled vocabularies, metadata for classification or tagging, thesauri, or authority files) for more than 15 years, only four of them, or 6.3 percent of the total, reported that their work was specifically called taxonomy as long ago as 1993 (15 years prior to the survey). This response contrasts with the answers of those who had been working in the field less than a year: Six out of nine of these respondents call their work taxonomy (see Appendix A, Questions 3 and 4).

Another way to track the growing popularity of taxonomies is to count the magazine and trade journal articles (excluding scholarly journals) in literature retrieval databases with the plural word *taxonomies* appearing in their texts. While many of these articles may be about specific-subject taxonomies, rather than information taxonomies in general, searching on the word *taxonomies* (rather than *taxonomy*) focuses the results more on the creation of generic information taxonomies. Looking at Gale's InfoTrac PowerSearch of 12 databases of magazine and newspaper articles and at HighBeam Research's database of journals, newspapers, and press releases, occurrence of the word *taxonomies* shows a marked increase especially in the period of 1998 to 2002, as shown in Table 1.1. (HighBeam's numbers are higher because High Beam includes

Table 1.1 Number of periodical articles including the word *taxonomies*

Year	Gale InfoTrac	HighBeam
1997	6	88
1998	14	74
1999	31	128
2000	67	242
2001	85	269
2002	205	413
2003	134	382
2004	171	401
2005	151	506
2006	127	504
2007	125	613

scholarly journals, which occasionally mention scientific nomen-clature taxonomies.) Although the periodical collections in both database services also grew over time, the collection did not grow at such a fast rate.

A similar more focused search on the truncated string *taxonom** in the industry journals of Information Today, Inc. (specifically *ONLINE Magazine, EContent, Information Today, KM World, Computers in Libraries,* and *Searcher*) shows a similar trend: 0 results through 1989, a significant increase in articles on the subject just before and after 2000, and then a more recent slight decline (Figure 1.11).

The turning point came around 2000. In the summary of the European Business Information Conference (EBIC) conference in 2000, Tom Koulopoulos, president of the Delphi Group and renowned writer and public speaker on knowledge management, declared, "Taxonomies are chic." Since then taxonomies have been a popular topic in conference presentations and workshops. The Montague Institute held its first taxonomy roundtable in 2000. A

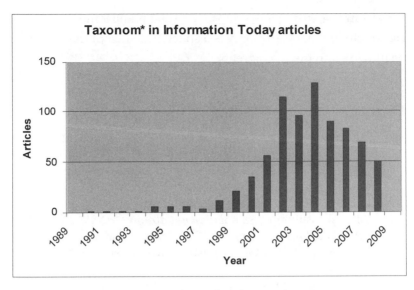

Figure 1.11 Numbers of trade journal articles
returned by the search string *taxonom**

significant number of taxonomies had become available publicly
(usually for licensing), so in 2001 Synapse Corp. launched its
Taxonomy Warehouse website directory of taxonomies. Taxonomy
consultant Marcia Morante recalled:

> The year 2000 was probably the very beginning of the
> commercial taxonomy wave. That was the year that I
> started with Sageware, and we still had to do a lot of
> explanation. But by that time, there were definitely a
> few companies whose business was built around
> taxonomies.[22]

Although newer buzzwords, such as *folksonomy, social networking*, and *Web 2.0*, have superseded taxonomy in the 2000s, a sustained interest in taxonomy and taxonomists continues. Search
industry analyst Steve Arnold analyzed web traffic on Google from
2002 to 2008 on the term *taxonomy* and found it continuing to

remain strong, stronger than *CMS* (content management systems). He concluded that "taxonomy is a specialist concept that seems to be moving into the mainstream."[23]

Endnotes

1. Gale Hodge, *Systems of Knowledge Organization for Digital Libraries: Beyond Traditional Authority Files* (Washington: The Digital Library Federation Council on Library and Information Resources, 2000), 1, www.clir.org/pubs/reports/pub91/pub91.pdf
2. Ibid. 4–7.
3. National Institute of Standards Organization, *ANSI/NISO Z39.19-2005 Guidelines for Construction, Format, and Management of Monolingual Controlled Vocabularies* (Bethesda, MD: NISO Press, 2005), 166.
4. Alice Redmond-Neal and Marjorie M. K. Hlava, eds., *ASIS&T Thesaurus of Information Science, Technology, and Librarianship*, 3rd ed. (Medford, NJ: Information Today, 2005).
5. Tom Gruber, "Ontology," tomgruber.org/writing/ontology-definition-2007.htm
6. This image, reprinted with permission of the authors, first appeared in Murat Sensoy and Pinar Yolum, "Ontology-Based Service Representation and Selection," *IEEE Transactions on Knowledge and Data Engineering* 19, no. 8 (2007). It is also available at mas.cmpe.boun.edu.tr/project/AgentBasedSemanticWebServices.htm
7. Patricia A. Harpring (Managing Editor of the Getty Vocabulary Program, Getty Research Institute), email to author, August 20. 2009.
8. MeSH Memorandum of Understanding, www.nlm.nih.gov/mesh/termscon.html
9. Jean Graef, email to author, November 21, 2008.
10. Alva Stone, "The LCSH: A Brief History of the Library of Congress Subject Headings, and Introduction to the Centennial Essays," *Cataloging & Classification Quarterly* 29, no. 1–2 (2000),1.
11. Jean Aitchison and Stella Dextre Clarke, "The Thesaurus: A Historical Viewpoint With a Look to the Future," in *The Thesaurus: Review, Renaissance, and Revision*, eds. Sandra K. Roe and Alan R. Thomas (Binghamton, NY: Haworth Press Inc., 2004), 7.
12. Ibid. 8.
13. Lynda Moulton, telephone interview with the author, October 19, 2009.

14. Lynda Moulton, email to author, October 19, 2009.
15. Seth Earley, telephone interview with author, November 22, 2008.
16. Kimberly S. Johnson, "International Information Provider Buys Franktown, Colo., Taxonomy Company," *Denver Post*, June 30, 2005.
17. Jean Graef, email to author, November 21, 2008.
18. Fred Leise, email to author, December 2, 2008.
19. Lynda Moulton, email to author, October 19, 2009.
20. Ron Daniel, telephone interview with author, December 1, 2008.
21. Lynda Moulton, email to author, November 9, 2009.
22. Marcia Morante, email to author, November 21, 2008.
23. Steve Arnold, "Taxonomy: Silver Bullet or Shallow Puddle," *Beyond Search* blog, September 27, 2008, arnoldit.com/wordpress/2008/09/27/taxonomy-silver-bullet-or-shallow-puddle

Chapter 2

Who Are Taxonomists?

Taxonomists: Classy people
—Harry A. Pape

Taxonomists, as we define them, are people who work on taxonomies. Just as there are various kinds of taxonomies, there are various kinds of taxonomists. Among those who identify themselves as taxonomists, taxonomy work is as frequently their secondary job responsibility as it is a primary one. Although most people who work on taxonomies are employed full-time, there are also a significant number of independent contractors and consultants. As for when taxonomists entered this field of work, the times are evenly distributed over the past 20 years or so, although it is more recent that the work has been called taxonomy.

These characteristics of taxonomists—and the others described in this chapter—come from our own online survey conducted November–December 2008. Self-described taxonomists were solicited as survey participants from among members of an online discussion group, Taxonomy Community of Practice (finance. groups.yahoo.com/group/TaxoCoP), and a total of 65 people responded. A larger survey of 184 self-described taxonomists conducted by Patrick Lambe in mid-2009 shows similar responses to the same kinds of questions; these survey respondents already identify themselves as taxonomists. For each of these professionals, there are undoubtedly several more who, probably by accident, find themselves doing taxonomy work from time to time but do not consider themselves taxonomists.

Backgrounds of Taxonomists

Taxonomists have varied backgrounds. The largest number have training or experience in library science, but this group makes up only about half of today's taxonomists. In our survey only 31 (48.4 percent) of 64 of the self-described taxonomists had a master's of library science (MLS) or master's of library and information science (MLIS) degree, and only 18 (28.1 percent) described their prior professional background as "librarian," (which includes those without even an MLS degree). The professional backgrounds of the others included: eight in software/IT, six in miscellaneous other fields, including science or engineering; five each in indexing and knowledge management; four in database development or administration; three each in content management, document/ records management, information architecture, and writing/editing/publishing; and two in project management. Additionally, five respondents came to taxonomy work directly from being a student. (Most taxonomist positions, though, are not entry level.) These statistics correlate with Lambe's survey finding that 46 percent of taxonomists hold an MLIS, master's of information management, or master's of knowledge management.[1] Another informal survey of taxonomists, by a simple show of hands at a general session at the Taxonomy Boot Camp conference attended by this author in 2007, indicated that approximately half of the attendees had a background in library and information science. Most others had business or technology backgrounds.

Library Science Backgrounds

Although there is no certificate or degree in taxonomy creation, the degree programs that provide the best preparation for this kind of work are the MLIS or master's in information studies/science (MIS). These programs all tend to have courses on knowledge organization and classification in general; some also offer a course more focused on thesauri, controlled vocabularies, and taxonomies. Nevertheless, although 31 survey respondents said they had an MLS or MLIS degree, fewer reported having taken courses on taxonomies. Just nine of our 65 taxonomists had been in some kind of concentration or specialty program within their degree program that was specifically taxonomy-related, 11 had taken two or more college/university courses on taxonomy-related subjects, and two reported taking only one such course. Indeed, a number of the taxonomists with an MLS or MLIS degree reported that their only specific training in taxonomy or classification was on the job.

While some MLS/MLIS graduates had already taken an interest in taxonomies as students, others came to the field through other work first. Cataloging and metadata design are common prior career paths to taxonomy work. In our survey of taxonomists, we asked them how they first got started doing taxonomy work. Several of their responses refer to cataloging:

- "Worked in library cataloging for many years. With advent of web resources, moved to creating internal taxonomies."

- "I started as a cataloger, then got pulled into controlled vocabulary, thesaurus, and taxonomy development and management … A pretty natural development for me."

- "Changed from cataloging to taxonomy, as the company I work for does not have a traditional catalog."

Digital asset management, which involves the cataloging, storage, and retrieval of specifically digital content, is also a background of a number of taxonomists, especially since taxonomies have become more common in the digital medium. These taxonomists explain how they got started:

- "Through work in the digital asset management field."

- "National Archives Still Pictures branch digitization project in the 90s then building Digital Asset Management systems for libraries, corporations, agencies, and historical foundations."

- "Nonprofit consultancy for digital library development."

People with a library science background may work on any kind of taxonomy: indexing support, retrieval support, or navigational support. However, as the fields of user experience design and human factors engineering are playing a larger role in navigational design and information architecture in general, fewer taxonomists are called on to work on navigational support taxonomies.

Indexers

Indexing, as it is related to cataloging, is another common background for taxonomists. While cataloging is done on the material or document level and follows prescribed rules, indexing is done on an article, page, or even paragraph level and thus involves greater subject analysis and gives greater decision-making power to the individual indexer. Periodical article indexing or other "database" indexing typically requires the indexer to look up terms in a controlled vocabulary and assign each document one or more such terms that best describe the document's content. These controlled vocabularies need to be maintained and updated. It is natural that those who have used controlled vocabularies for indexing might transition into the role of managing the controlled vocabulary.

Another kind of indexing is involved in creating indexes at the back of books. Although indexers of books generally do not use controlled vocabularies, some of the skills used in creating indexes and taxonomies are similar, so book indexers, too, may be attracted to taxonomy work. Relevant skills include:

- Deciding what is important and likely to be looked up

- Deciding how best to word a concept

- Structuring hierarchical relations among terms, as main entries and subentries in a book index, or as broader and narrower terms in a taxonomy

- Determining variant terms, as double-posts or See references in a book index, or as nonpreferred terms (used for) in a taxonomy

- Creating related-term relationships, as See also relationships in a book index or associative relationships in a taxonomy

The majority of book indexers work as freelancers, and a considerable amount of taxonomy work can also be done on a freelance basis. Taxonomists who previously worked as indexers recounted the transition as follows:

- "Used to be a freelance indexer, did some work in medical cataloging … taxonomy seemed to be a natural progression!"

- "Original cataloging, indexing, authority controls in traditional library setting (along with reference and management responsibilities) provided the on-the-job experience that led to taking a newly created position creating and managing a taxonomy and metadata model for a new digital asset management system."

- "I started by taking the indexing course with Candy Schwartz at Simmons. I indexed her book, *Records Management and the Library*."

- "As part of my work as an information architect, because of my background in indexing."

When people with a background in indexing move into taxonomy work, they usually start out working on taxonomies that support human indexing, as just described. They then may move on to work on other kinds of taxonomies.

Information Technologists

Professionals with a more technical background in software, information technology, or database development may also work on taxonomies. Some have both a software/IT and a library/information science background. This combination of skills makes them especially suited for taxonomy work and its technical implementations. Jean Graef of the Montague Institute, which provides taxonomy and knowledge management training, explained her role:

> I'm in the business of covering gaps between corporate information cultures and technologies. … I got interested in it when I realized that there was an opportunity for a boundary-spanner like me to help bridge the gap between the way IT staff viewed taxonomy (a browsable hierarchy on a website), the way librarians viewed it (a subject index to a collection of books), and the way editors viewed it (a topical hierarchy at the beginning of a book and a topic index at the back). … The technologists didn't understand how to create semantic relationships, and librarians and indexers didn't understand how to translate their semantic structures and skills into internet-based technologies.[2]

Taxonomy consultant Marcia Morante also had a combined background of library science training and work experience with software companies. She wrote:

> Although I have an MS in library and information science, I never worked in a library. All of my jobs out of graduate school were with search engine companies. Two of them are no longer in business or were bought

out—Infodata and Information Dimensions. Several are still around: Fulcrum (taken over by a company that was taken over by OpenText), Verity, and Autonomy. In those days, the focus was on text searching (Boolean and/or "natural language") and very little on metadata. However, given my educational background, controlled vocabularies were never far from my mind.[3]

Others with a more technical background have explained how they got started in taxonomy work:

- "Via text mining, auto-categorization, and visualization of unstructured information."

- "It became clear there were likely 'better' ways and opportunities to access, push, and display information online, so I began discussing with colleagues, and one of them identified a project opportunity to do taxonomy work, so I jumped at the chance and tried to amass as much training and knowledge as I could before I first began the project."

- "Hired as a domain expert for an engineering search engine [and] moved from project management of domain taxonomy areas to manager of entire taxonomy."

- "I started as a formal ontology modeler in AI. The taxonomy work came later as a byproduct, depending on company needs."

Taxonomists with a software or information technology background typically work on taxonomies that aid retrieval and rely on automated rather than human indexing, since they may have been, or are still, involved in developing and improving the search and auto-categorization software. Because of the data modeling aspect of ontologies, they may also be designed by people with a software development background and who are often interested in the web development aspect of the semantic web. Math or logic (philoso-phy) backgrounds are also suitable for ontology work as relations in ontologies are sometimes based on set theory.[4]

Information Architects

Skill in taxonomy is increasingly being required of information architects, the professionals who design the structure and naviga-tion for websites or intranets, especially large and complicated ones, and the user interfaces of online information retrieval sys-tems. Information architecture focuses on the structure and organization of content, leaving graphic design to the artistically talented. Information architect–taxonomists generally work on organization/navigation types of taxonomies rather than those supporting indexing or search retrieval, but a few have branched out to work on retrieval support taxonomies especially when a search engine is integrated into a website. The first information architects, in fact, had backgrounds in library and information sci-ence, and some graduate programs of library and information sci-ence now offer courses in information architecture. In more recent years, however, there has been a slight shift in the profession toward an emphasis on user experience, user centered design, and human–computer interaction. Thus, the most qualified informa-tion architects now combine expertise in information organiza-tion/design with a focus on serving user needs.

Several taxonomists with an information architecture back-ground explained how they got into taxonomies:

- "Ecommerce web design—now I do process-based taxon-omy work for a strategic content management consulting company."

- "I was asked to do the taxonomy for the new portal, a new technology and the foundation for the company's intranet. Found out months later that the portal use of the word 'taxonomy' was different from the librarian use

of the word. Turned around and used the work that was
wasted on the portal project for the new search engine
project. Much better fit!"

- "As part of website design and management, I had to
organize and maintain a subject taxonomy, first for an HR
intranet for a multinational company."

- "Looking for a role in information management, and my
current information architect position focuses on the use
of controlled vocabularies."

Today the word *taxonomies* appears in job descriptions most
often in the field of information architecture or user experience
design, due primarily to the large number of open positions in
these fields. The role of taxonomy in these jobs could still be relatively small.

Subject Matter Experts

Another possible route to taxonomy work— less common now
than it used to be—is for a taxonomist to start out as a subject
area specialist, such as a scientist or healthcare industry professional. Knowing a subject area very well is an important qualification for building a technical subject taxonomy. Those with a
science or engineering background explained how they got into
taxonomy work:

- "National Agricultural Library funded a special mono-
graph series cataloging project to the Agriculture Library
at University of Illinois at Urbana-Champaign. I was hired
as a graduate student and worked with a project team
consisting of one [full-time] librarian, one staff, and five
grads to provide article-level access to the collections
with subject terms using LCSH, and classification number using National Agricultural Library call number

(USMARC 070) and Subject Category Code (USMARC 072) during the period 1990–1992."

- "Hired as a domain expert for an engineering search engine, moved from project management of domain taxonomy areas to manager of entire taxonomy."

An interesting story is that of Marti Heyman, currently a knowledge manager at Deloitte. She explained how she got into indexing/taxonomy work with a scientific background (a BS in chemistry), accidentally got into a different subject area, and then realized that she enjoyed the taxonomy work in general, regardless of the subject area:

> I started using and developing controlled vocabularies in corporate settings in 1991 when I joined DuPont's Indexing and Abstracting Group. … As a former polymer chemistry researcher at DuPont, I was one of a few indexers responsible for the indexing and abstracting of said polymer chemistry research reports.
>
> However, I made the mistake of many junior staff, and I actually took vacation, thus missing a critical meeting. Of course, during that meeting the senior staff resolved how they would reduce the significant backlog of research materials about electronic materials. Their solution was simple: assign the work to the junior staff member not present at the meeting! … Well, it was obvious I was closer to being technically qualified to index these reports than any of the agricultural science or life science folks, so I went off to do my best. What I quickly discovered was that given a basic understanding of physics and mathematics, one really could do a pretty decent job indexing and abstracting these technical reports by using the technical thesaurus as the knowledge map to the company's view and understanding of

the domain. I was floored and I was hooked; truly an accidental taxonomist.

Actually, a BS degree may not be sufficient to pursue a high-level career in taxonomy management. Heyman went on to earn both an MLIS and an MBA later in her career.

Taxonomists with expertise in a particular subject area more often work on the larger taxonomies for indexing or retrieval support, rather than on smaller taxonomies supporting website navigation. Ontologists are also typically subject matter experts, with perhaps some additional background in linguistics.

Accidental Taxonomists

Many taxonomists have come to their work, not by applying for a taxonomy job, but because a need arose within an organization where they were working in another capacity. Responsibilities were redefined, or what started out as project eventually became a job. Occasionally a taxonomy job is created because an individual sees a need and pursues an initiative. Some of these accidental taxonomists explained how they got into the profession as follows:

- "The company needed the ability to find content better. Therefore I was tasked with delivering a solution that enabled us to find content more easily, which led to the development of a taxonomy/metadata approach."

- "Was working as Data Entry Clerk. Someone needed to create the terms in one of the taxonomies, and I got picked for the task. It went from there as no one else wanted to do it!"

- "We needed it as part of an asset management strategy and also for our documents management project."

- "My career started in a federal government library. I was asked to take on the responsibilities for the organization's corporate website (in the mid nineties). I then worked to acquire a content management system. The system we use requires metadata and controlled vocabularies (which are evolving to become taxonomies) to dynamically generate webpages for the corporate website within a content management system. I now manage the team that does the metadata, information architecture, controlled vocabularies, and search engine work for the department."

- "Need to manage growing training content, need for some level of reuse."

- "Saw the need in my corporate library for managing digital information, and after some reading I realized that taxonomy was the way."

- "Through a digital asset management project—the company needed a taxonomy to manage photos, illustrations, etc."

Taxonomy work, especially when it involves building a new taxonomy rather than ongoing maintenance, is very often project-oriented work. Thus, the project might pull in additional people for a temporary period. Some of these people then return to their previous duties, others may end up staying on with taxonomy maintenance duties added to their job description, while still others truly enjoy the experience and their new skills and seek out such jobs and projects in the future.

Taxonomist Skills

The main task of a taxonomist is to create taxonomies, namely, the terms and their structured relationships or categories. Although the next chapters will address this in detail, let us first consider the basic skills required of a taxonomist. The skills discussed here are based on this author's own experience rather than on any job descriptions.

Familiarity with the principles of knowledge organization structures. The core skill of a taxonomist is to have a solid under-standing of the relationships between terms—broader/narrower, related, and equivalent—and to implement these relationships accurately and consistently according to standards and best practices.

Analytical skills. Survey results and feedback from users or potential users must be analyzed to determine user needs and how they should be met. Content must be analyzed to determine what concepts should make up the taxonomy. Concepts themselves need to be analyzed in terms of meanings and usage to determine whether a given concept is better left as one or broken into two. Writing rules for taxonomy terms in an auto-categorization system also requires analytical skills.

Organization/categorization skills. The taxonomist needs to determine how concepts, subjects, or entities are to be classified or categorized for creating hierarchical relationships. It is worth not-ing that organizing concepts is not necessarily the same as organ-izing things or one's environment—even a person with a messy desk can work as a taxonomist.

Language skills. Taxonomies deal with words and phrases. A solid understanding of grammar is important to ensure that terms are created in a consistent style and relationships between terms are correctly constructed. Strong language skills also aid the tax-onomist in compiling comprehensive lists of synonyms as nonpre-ferred terms. Thus, there is a creative language component to taxonomy work.

Research skills. Taxonomists often need to research the mean-ings and usage of terms to make the proper term choices, deter-mine their scopes, and relate them correctly to other terms.

Search skills. Taxonomies usually support searching, so it is imperative that the taxonomist be a capable online searcher in order to understand the taxonomy's implementation and use. The taxonomist should be familiar with both the basic and the advanced features common in online search systems and search engines, including complex Boolean searching, wildcards, and truncation. It may also be important for a taxonomist to know how to manipulate search results. Although searchers of all levels use taxonomies, the taxonomist needs to fulfill the expectations of the advanced searcher. Taxonomists also need search skills to conduct research on potential terms, as previously mentioned.

Technical skills. While taxonomists do not need to be software developers, they must have competence in using different kinds of software. Basic skills in using a spreadsheet program are fundamental as it is common to create simple taxonomies this way. Taxonomists should also have experience using various database management systems as taxonomies, metadata, and content are organized and stored in some form of a database structure. Taxonomists should have experience with (or be able to learn quickly and independently) at least one taxonomy/thesaurus management software program. Basic familiarity with XML, and possibly also RDF and OWL tagging formats, is highly desirable. Experience with specific content management systems, document management systems, and/or enterprise search systems is desirable and sometimes requested but not always necessary.

Subject matter expertise. Depending on the position, specific subject matter knowledge may or may not be required. For publicly accessed taxonomies, it is usually not necessary. For internally used taxonomies, however, especially in the fields of pharmaceuticals, healthcare, financial services, legal services, science, and engineering, subject matter knowledge is important.

Attention to detail. Taxonomy work requires accuracy and consistency in creating terms. For example, capitalization and abbreviations should be consistent. Some taxonomy tools do not even have a spell checker, so careful checking on the part of the taxonomist is required.

Attention to user needs. While a taxonomist need not be a professional in the area of user experience, an understanding of user needs, expectations, and behaviors in the online environment is very valuable, so some exposure to the field of user-centered design is helpful. The taxonomist might have input into the design of the search/browse user interface.

Ability to work independently. In many cases an organization has only one taxonomist, and a taxonomist may report to someone who does not know taxonomies very well. Thus, the taxonomist needs to be able to make decisions independently, set priorities, determine requirements, and plan timetables.

Ability to work with diverse people. The taxonomist will likely need to work with those in other specialties: software developers, interface designers, and product or project managers. If the taxonomy will be used for an external product or service, then the taxonomist may also need to work with people in marketing, sales, or customer support.

Communication skills. Taxonomists need to write down the policies and procedures involved in creating the taxonomy and the instructions for its use. Additionally, taxonomists may contribute to user documentation. Taxonomists also need to be able to communicate well orally with different groups in order to convey the purpose, function, and best use of the taxonomy. As taxonomies are generally not widely understood, good communication skills are important.

Related Duties

Although the primary task of a taxonomist is creating terms and their relationships, there are numerous additional related responsibilities.

The extent to which the taxonomist is involved in the following tasks depends on the type of taxonomy, its implementation, and the project management:

- Project planning
- Researching concepts and names
- Developing and documenting policies
- Taxonomy use/search testing
- Indexing support or supervision
- Interface design
- Metadata design

If available at the time, taxonomists are often included in the planning process, even if others make project and market decisions. All kinds of taxonomies require some degree of user studies or research in order to guide the design of the taxonomy, and taxonomists are often involved at this stage. The main reason for not including a taxonomist in designing and implementing user studies would be simply because that person may not have been hired or assigned to the project yet.

Creating taxonomy terms involves some research to scope and define the terms and their relationships. Certain terms, especially named entity terms, may have additional attributes that require further research—for example, latitude and longitude coordinates for place names, headquarters location for company names, birth dates for person names, and various specifications for products.

As the taxonomy is developed, those involved in the project will be called on to make decisions and refine policies. As a result, the taxonomist must document the taxonomy creation policies in order to guide future development and use of the taxonomy. The taxonomist will also likely need to develop and document policies for the continued maintenance of the taxonomy. In addition to policies, if the project relies on an internally developed or cus-tomized taxonomy management system, the taxonomist may need to document the basic procedures for creating terms and relationships. The taxonomist might even be asked to perform user testing of taxonomy management software.

After a taxonomy is created, it needs to be tested. Taxonomists typically perform at least some of the testing themselves, espe-cially if it involves sample searches rather than site navigation. A navigational taxonomy, however, should also be tested by sample user groups. Evaluating the user test results, and possibly setting up the user tests in the first place, is the role of the taxonomist.

The taxonomist will undoubtedly also get involved, to an extent, in any indexing that uses the taxonomy. If there is human indexing, then the taxonomist may perform some sample test indexing and will probably be responsible for writing the indexing guidelines. The taxonomist may train and monitor indexers and will need to check indexers' work, adjusting the taxonomy to improve accurate use. Even if the indexers have a supervisor to train them and check their work, the taxonomist needs to inform indexers of new and changed terms and to solicit their suggestions for new terms. If the taxonomy is used in a form of automated indexing or auto-categorization, the taxonomist is involved, but in a different way. Tasks may include writing rules for rules-based auto-categorization or selecting sample training documents for fine-tuning an algo-rithm-based auto-categorization system. Chapters 6 and 7 cover these related indexing tasks in detail.

A taxonomy is usually a part of something larger, and whatever that something is, the taxonomist may work on it as well. In many cases, the taxonomy is integrated into a web interface. In such implementations, the taxonomist needs to evaluate the interface and provide input into its design.

In content management, document management, or records management systems, taxonomies provide input into certain metadata fields, so the taxonomist may also be involved in defining the overall metadata architecture. Patrick Lambe analyzed how members of the largest online taxonomy community described themselves in their introductions (367 self reports in introductions from April 2005 to September 2009 on the Taxonomy Community of Practice Yahoo! group) and found that "metadata work" was the biggest area of application for taxonomy, with "findability/discovery/search" coming in second.[5] In other words, metadata work is not merely related to taxonomy work; the two are often inseparable. There are a number of books on the topic of metadata, significantly more than on taxonomies, so there is no need to discuss metadata design at any length in this book.

Employment of Taxonomists

According to our limited survey, the largest number of taxonomists (44 percent, or 28 out of 63) are employees in organizations that use taxonomies primarily internally, for their website or in ecommerce. Another 19 percent are employees of organizations that incorporate taxonomies into a marketed information product or information service (information providers, software vendors, etc.), and 11 percent are employees of companies or agencies that provide taxonomy services or custom taxonomies to clients. The rest, about 25 percent, are self-employed as business owners, independent consultants, or freelancers. In Lambe's survey of 184 taxonomists, aside from the taxonomists who are independent contractors, consultants, or involved in the professional services industry (26 percent), leading sectors are publishing news and media (13 percent), information and communications technology (13 percent), government (9 percent), education (7 percent), and finance/banking (5 percent).[6] We will look at where taxonomists are employed in this section and address the nature of freelance and consulting work in Chapter 12.

Where Taxonomists Work

Full-time and temporary taxonomists are employed by the following kinds of organizations, with the sectors that employ more taxonomists listed toward the top:

- Large corporations in any industry
- Government agencies
- Publishers and the media industry
- Information providers and database vendors
- Web search engines and online advertisers
- Retailers
- Agencies and consultancies
- Software vendors
- Taxonomy vendors

In addition, people who would not consider themselves taxonomists but who occasionally work on taxonomies as a secondary activity work in:

- Libraries
- Museums
- Academic institutions

Let's examine each of these sectors more closely. Specific companies that are mentioned in the following paragraphs either have advertised taxonomy positions on job board websites or through the Taxonomy Jobs Yahoo! list (finance.groups.yahoo.com/group/taxonomy-jobs) or employ people with position titles containing the word *taxonomy* or *taxonomist,* as indicated in employee profiles on the professional networking site LinkedIn (www.linked in.com).

Large Corporations

Taxonomists may work in any industry as long as the company is large enough to have significant information management needs. Industries employing taxonomists include, but are not limited to, finance, healthcare, pharmaceuticals, engineering, consulting, computers, software, manufacturing, and entertainment. The taxonomies in these industries, which are often enterprise taxonomies, contribute to content management or document management systems and are primarily for internal use. If the company has a knowledge management team, this is where the taxonomist might belong, but a taxonomist might also be a part of other departments, such as research or IT or even editorial. Companies that have advertised positions for taxonomists in the past year include Dell, Motorola, Deloitte, and the Mayo Clinic. Other corporations that have at least one taxonomist on staff include Walt Disney Company, Caterpillar, General Motors, Novell, Kaiser Permanente, ConocoPhillips, PricewaterhouseCoopers, and Hoffmann-La Roche. Many other corporations hire temporary contract taxonomists from time to time.

Government Agencies

Government agencies and legislative offices manage massive amounts of information, and many state and federal agencies employ someone in a taxonomist role. The taxonomies in these agencies organize information both for internal access and for public access via the web. The federal government also outsources some taxonomy and related services, so some taxonomists work for government contractors. For example, a management services agency recently posted an opening for a taxonomy and metadata librarian in Washington, DC, to support its Environmental Protection Agency contract. For some federal government jobs, a security clearance is a requirement, even for a contractor. Large international agencies such as the United Nations and the World Bank also employ taxonomists.

Publishers and the Media Industry

Publishers, especially of newspapers and periodicals such as the *New York Times,* have long employed taxonomists to create and maintain their own thesauri, used by their own indexers to support retrieval of their articles or books. Taxonomist jobs announced in 2009 included positions at the Associated Press, John Wiley and Sons, and Wolters Kluwer Health (a publisher of professional, reference, and textbooks in healthcare). Other media/publishing companies with taxonomists include Time, Hearst, and Elsevier. Directory publishers, whether of consumer yellow pages or more specific business directories, also employ or contract taxonomists to create and manage their categories of industries, products, and services. Finally, as other forms of content, such as images, sound recordings, and video, are digitized, media companies involved in television, film, and image publishing have also begun to employ taxonomists. For example, HBO and History.com each advertised positions for taxonomists in 2009, and the vendors of stock photos and images, Getty Images, Corbis, and Veer, also make use of taxonomists.

Information Providers and Database Vendors

A separate class of publishers is the online information vendors that index published content, usually from multiple sources, for databases sold primarily to libraries and researchers and sometimes to consumers over the web. In this type of publishing, taxonomies are part of the information product/service being marketed. Since information retrieval is their core business, these companies may have not just one taxonomist (more likely called a thesaurus editor or controlled vocabulary editor) but a staff of several. Traditional information vendors that have employed taxonomists for decades include H.W. Wilson, ProQuest, Cengage

Learning (formerly Gale) and EBSCO. In addition to these companies, some professional associations and nonprofit organizations publish specialized, academic, or technical information databases, such as the American Psychological Association (PsycINFO) and the American Chemical Society (Chemical Abstracts). Their taxonomists need to be subject matter experts as well.

A new kind of online information provider that has been seen recruiting taxonomists is the dot-com startups, which usually specialize in niche information areas, such as job search (OneWire and MatchTheChallenge) and business-to-business product marketing (JAZD Markets).

Web Search Engines and Online Advertisers

Although the major web search engines (Google, Yahoo!, and Bing) do not utilize taxonomies in their primary search functions, these companies do provide other specialized search-related services that may involve taxonomies, such as the Yahoo! Directory (dir.yahoo.com). Furthermore, these companies earn revenues from online advertisements, so a taxonomy that can link search queries to advertising clients' profiles is particularly important to them. Microsoft employs taxonomists for this function, and Google has at least sought a contract taxonomist in the past. In addition to these major companies, there are numerous smaller, niche search engines. Some of these (e.g., ChaCha and Goby) have hired taxonomists to create their initial taxonomies.

Retailers

Both traditional retailers and online-only retailers use taxonomies to categorize their products on their websites, especially to make it easier for customers to find what they want to purchase. The internal organization of products is also useful to the employees, especially of the large retailers. Retail companies with taxonomists on staff include Sears, Amazon.com, and Home Depot. Online-only vendors with taxonomists include eBay, Zappos.com, and Etsy.

Agencies and Consultancies

There is a continuum of different kinds of agencies and consultancies dedicated to helping clients organize and present information. While some web design and user experience firms have little interest in taxonomies, other information architecture and design agencies, such as Razorfish, Molecular, and Roundarch, that serve clients with especially large website projects employ information architects specializing in taxonomies. There are also consultancies that specialize in enterprise taxonomy services. These tend to be small and do not have many employees, but they often hire taxonomists as contractors if a large project requires it.

Software Vendors

Some automatic indexing software includes integrated taxonomies, so these software companies may employ or contract taxonomists to build generic and possibly customized taxonomies. Some taxonomists also work for companies that develop vertical-market search software. Vendors of taxonomy or thesaurus software, such as Access Innovations (Data Harmony), SchemaLogic, WordNet, Synaptica, and Nstein, also have taxonomists on staff to provide taxonomy consulting services for their software clients. Employment, however, is less secure in this industry, which is characterized by rapid change, mergers, and unsuccessful startups.

Taxonomy Vendors

Although taxonomy vendors are a natural employer for taxonomists, there are very few such enterprises. They comprise the companies, organizations, and government agencies mentioned among the sources of licensed taxonomies in Chapter 1, such as the Library of Congress, National Library of Medicine, Getty

Research Institute, Dow Jones, and WAND. Depending on whether they are creating new taxonomies or merely maintaining existing ones, these organizations may have one to several taxonomists on staff.

Libraries, Museums, and Academic Institutions

While repositories of knowledge might seem like the most natural kind of employer for taxonomists, this is not necessarily the case, simply because taxonomies in some form have already existed for decades, and creating new ones is not necessary. Libraries have the Library of Congress Subject Headings (LCSH) and the Sears List of Subject Headings. Museums often use the *Revised Nomenclature for Museum Cataloging* by James R. Blackaby.

The trend we are seeing, however, is that libraries and museums are digitizing their collections (especially smaller, special collections), putting them into databases, and making them accessible in various electronic formats, including the web. Smaller, more specialized collections both require and permit taxonomies different from the traditional cataloging vocabularies, and web access similarly changes the parameters for retrieval. Academic libraries in particular have numerous small special collections, each of which would benefit from its own taxonomy rather than fitting into a general vocabulary such as LCSH. Thus, librarians and museum archivists find themselves (accidentally perhaps) taking on taxonomy projects. For libraries, this work typically falls under the responsibility of "technical services."

In addition, some of the larger academic libraries employ taxonomists, particularly if the institution has its own publications or has created its own online information service to serve students, faculty and researchers. An example is Harvard Business School Baker Library, which has engaged in taxonomy projects.

Job Titles

Employed taxonomists work under various job titles. The simple title *taxonomist* is seldom used, perhaps to avoid any ambiguity with biological taxonomists (which also exist today) and perhaps due to conventions that job titles need to be longer than one word. Titles such as lead taxonomist, chief taxonomist, senior taxonomist, and assistant taxonomist are not unusual. More often, there are hyphenated or slashed double titles that have *taxonomist* as one of components, or there are two-word titles containing word *taxonomy*. The following titles have appeared on job listing websites and on LinkedIn profiles for employed positions.

Examples of two-word taxonomist titles include:

- Information taxonomist

- Enterprise taxonomist

- Nomenclature taxonomist

- Web taxonomist

Combined titles (which could also appear in reverse order) include:

- Content manager/taxonomist

- Taxonomist and content architect

- Taxonomist/business semantics lead

- Taxonomist/cataloger

- Taxonomist/information architect

- Taxonomist/project manager

- Taxonomist/program manager

However, about twice as common as titles with the word *taxonomist* are titles with the word *taxonomy* in them. These include:

- Director of taxonomy
- Manager, search and taxonomy
- Taxonomy analyst
- Taxonomy architect
- Taxonomy consultant
- Taxonomy developer
- Taxonomy manager
- Taxonomy specialist

Additionally, there are a number of titles qualified with the word *taxonomy*, such as:

- Information architect, taxonomy
- Information scientist, taxonomy
- Senior editor, taxonomy
- Senior records and information analyst, taxonomy

There are also many jobs in which taxonomy development and management is the main responsibility, but whose titles do not contain the words *taxonomist* or *taxonomy*. These include:

- Content strategist
- Controlled vocabulary editor
- Controlled vocabulary design specialist
- Data and information strategist
- Director of content classification
- Enterprise vocabulary specialist
- Information classification specialist
- Information specialist

- Knowledge engineer

- Search engine project analyst

- Search vocabulary editor

- Technical categorization analyst

- Thesaurus developer

- Thesaurus editor

- Vocabulary developer

- Vocabulary editor

- Vocabulary specialist

Finally, there are many more positions that may involve some taxonomy work, although perhaps not as the primary responsibility. Such positions include the following job titles:

- Business analyst

- Digital asset librarian

- Digital asset manager

- Enterprise architect manager

- Information architect

- Information management coordinator

- Knowledge manager

- Metadata architect

- Metadata librarian

- Ontologist

- Search analyst

- User experience architect

Even though the word *taxonomy* occurs more frequently than the word *taxonomist* in job titles, we will continue to refer in this book to taxonomists because it is the simplest one-word designation.

Endnotes

1. Patrick Lambe, "Taxonomists: Evolving or Extinct? The Future of Taxonomy Work," presentation delivered at the Taxonomy Boot Camp conference, San Jose, CA, November 19, 2009.
2. Jean Graef, email to author, November 21, 2008.
3. Marcia Morante, email to author, November 21, 2008.
4. Irene Pappas, email to author, July 29, 2009.
5. Patrick Lambe, "Taxonomists: Evolving or Extinct? The Future of Taxonomy Work."
6. Ibid.

Creating Terms

Taxonomies: Not as boring as you think.
—Seth Earley

While different kinds of taxonomies may have different structures and different kinds of relationships between terms, they are all made up of terms. Therefore, we will begin our discussion on creating taxonomies with the details of how to create terms.

Concepts and Terms

Just as there are various types of taxonomies, so are there various designations for the terms—the controlled and defined words or phrases that make up the taxonomy. Fundamentally, a taxonomy comprises distinct concepts, which are things or ideas; a term, on the other hand, is a label for a concept, and a single concept may be described by multiple, somewhat synonymous terms. Although in a very simple hierarchical taxonomy you may decide to have just a single term per concept, most controlled vocabularies accommodate multiple terms for each concept. In a synonym ring or synset type of taxonomy, all the terms for a concept have equal standing. In other taxonomies, however, the taxonomist designates a single term as preferred, and the rest are nonpreferred terms, which serve as cross-references pointing to the preferred term. Even in the case of a synonym ring, each concept needs to have a single name, at least for internal administration purposes, although it does not matter so much what name it is.

You may find any of the following designations used to refer to terms or components of a taxonomy.

A *concept* is a thing, idea, or shared understanding of something. A set of synonymous terms could describe it. It is therefore the combination of both a preferred term and its various nonpreferred terms, if any, or all the linked synonyms within a synonym ring. Nevertheless, a concept has to be called something, so if there are also nonpreferred terms, the concept is typically referred to by its preferred term name (a convention that may lead to confusion between a concept and its label), even though every concept is more than just a term. A concept may also be called any one of the following:

- Node: A concept as expressed within a hierarchical taxonomy. If a hierarchy is like a tree, then the nodes are places where new branches or leaves connect. A node may refer to the preferred term alone, especially if there are no nonpreferred terms, or to the preferred term plus its nonpreferred terms.

- Object: A concept especially in an object-oriented database structure. An object comprises any nonpreferred terms and also its definition, notes, and any other attributes. Information on relationships to other terms/objects may be part of an object as well.

- Individual: A concept in an ontology.

- Entity: Sometimes used for a concept in an ontology or semantic network.

- Instance: May refer to (1) an individual in an ontology; (2) a named entity as it relates to a broader topical term, in an instance-type of broader/narrower relationship; or (3) the most specific concept at the narrowest, bottom-level of a taxonomy.

- (Term) Cluster: A concept that comprises multiple equivalent terms.

- Wordset: A concept that comprises multiple equivalent terms.

- Taxon: A concept usually only in biological taxonomies.

A *term* is a label for a concept—the most common, generic designation, which can be in any controlled vocabulary. It can refer to any kind of term, both preferred terms and nonpreferred terms. However, it sometimes refers to just the preferred term, so the designation may be somewhat ambiguous in practice. Other designations for terms, used to avoid ambiguity, include:

- Vocabulary term
- Subject term

A *term record* is the complete information regarding a term, especially as stored and displayed in taxonomy management or indexing software. It includes all of a term's relationships, notes, categories, and any additional attributes, along with administrative information such as approval status, creation and modification dates, etc., in other words, the metadata for a single term. Not all of these details need to be included, though, for it to be called a term record. Since most taxonomy management software is based on some kind of database management software, a term record is thus a database record. A term record may also be called *term details*.

A *preferred term* is the official displayed word or phrase for the concept. Nonpreferred terms are the various synonyms, variants, or other sufficiently equivalent words or phrases used as cross-references pointing to the preferred term. Other names for a preferred term include:

- Descriptor: A preferred term, especially when nonpreferred terms are called nondescriptors.

- Subject descriptor: A preferred term, especially one that is a subject or common noun, not a named entity or proper noun.

- Authorized term: A preferred term, especially if nonpreferred terms are called unauthorized terms.

- Node name: A preferred term when the designation "node" is used for concepts. This is more often an internal, rather than an end user, designation.

A number of other designations often used in taxonomies are ambiguous, as they might refer either to concepts or to preferred terms. These include:

- Categories

- Subjects

- Subject areas

- Topics

As there are many ways to refer to the terms or concepts in a taxonomy, one of the first tasks in creating a new taxonomy is to decide what to call its components. It is not unusual to use one designation internally, because it appears logical to you, the taxonomist, or to the software developers responsible for the search software or the user interface, and to display a different designation in the user interface because it makes sense to the end users. Indeed, you might even need to create a mini controlled vocabulary to describe the taxonomy. At the very least, a glossary is helpful. In the following pages and chapters, we will refer to concepts and terms specifically and to preferred terms only when needed.

In creating terms, the taxonomist actually has two tasks:

1. Identify the concepts that make up the taxonomy

2. Choose the preferred terms for each of the concepts

Identifying Concepts

Deciding what concepts should go into a taxonomy involves gathering information on what *could* be included and then further evaluating these concepts to decide what *should* be included. In gathering information, the taxonomist should use two sources:

1. Documents/files representing the content to be searched with the taxonomy

2. People, including the taxonomy owners, subject matter experts, and sample users

Content as a Source of Concepts

Obviously, the primary source for concepts should be the content or material that will be indexed or categorized with the taxonomy. These materials could be almost anything: articles, reports, book chapters or sections, white papers, product specifications, brochures, transcripts, legal documents, website or intranet pages, image files, video files, presentation files, and so forth. The taxonomer's task is to look for significant concepts contained in or associated with these documents. Reading the full texts is neither practical nor even always possible, as in the case of multimedia files. Rather, the taxonomist should look for concepts within any of the following text sources that may be associated with the documents or files:

- Titles of the documents or articles

- Subdocument-level section headings

- Abstracts or summaries

- Image or illustration captions

- Website navigation menu labels, site maps, and webpage titles

- Tables of contents and chapter names in longer documents

- Items within directory listings, especially products, names, and so on.

- Existing metadata (keywords, titles, short descriptions)

There could also be significant concepts that are mentioned only within the body of a text, but a quick skim of the lead paragraph and the lead sentences of additional paragraphs should be sufficient for identifying these concepts. Additional sources for a content audit specifically for enterprise taxonomies are listed in Chapter 10.

To keep track of the potential concepts at this stage, it is probably easiest to enter them into a spreadsheet table (such as Excel), along with information pertaining to the concept and its source. Of course, to record them, you will need to name the concepts, so even at this stage each concept requires some sort of term. The term you choose at this point is not final, and you can change it later. Usually the term used in the content text is sufficient unless it is vague and needs clarification. Writing down two or three terms for a concept, separated by slashes, is also fine.

There are different methodologies for recording the concepts at this stage of taxonomy preparation, sometimes referred to as a content audit or a content inventory. There could be a new row for each concept, with the source document noted in one of the columns, as illustrated in Figure 3.1.

Alternatively, there could be a new row for each source file with multiple concepts, as found in each source file, recorded in one of the columns, as illustrated in Figure 3.2. This latter method might

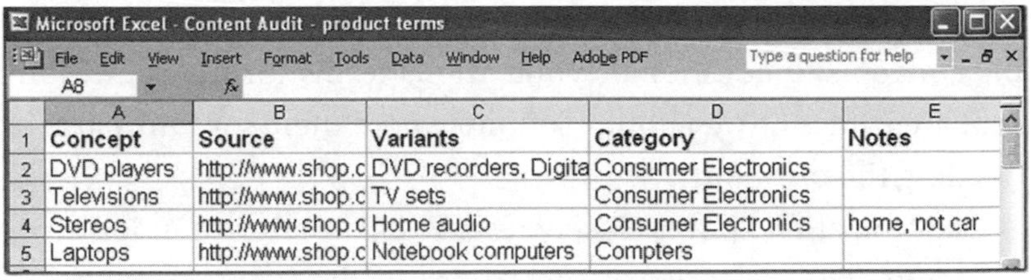

	A	B	C	D	E
1	**Concept**	**Source**	**Variants**	**Category**	**Notes**
2	DVD players	http://www.shop.c	DVD recorders, Digita	Consumer Electronics	
3	Televisions	http://www.shop.c	TV sets	Consumer Electronics	
4	Stereos	http://www.shop.c	Home audio	Consumer Electronics	home, not car
5	Laptops	http://www.shop.c	Notebook computers	Compters	

Figure 3.1 Example of how a spreadsheet can be set up for a content audit, with a unique row for each concept

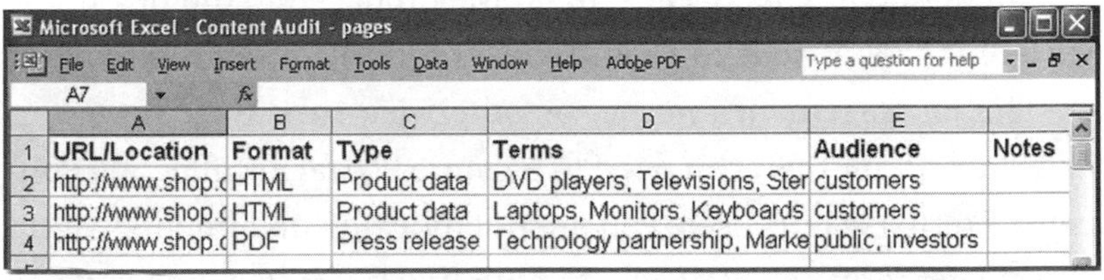

	A	B	C	D	E	
1	**URL/Location**	**Format**	**Type**	**Terms**	**Audience**	**Notes**
2	http://www.shop.c	HTML	Product data	DVD players, Televisions, Ster	customers	
3	http://www.shop.c	HTML	Product data	Laptops, Monitors, Keyboards	customers	
4	http://www.shop.c	PDF	Press release	Technology partnership, Marke	public, investors	

Figure 3.2 Example of how a spreadsheet can be set up for a content audit, with a unique row for each source file or document

be preferred if you want to make sure you include every source page/document.

If the content to be indexed is in the form of a stream of incoming files, such as periodical articles, then only a sample of the content can be analyzed for concepts. This is better described as a content survey than an audit. If, on the other hand, the content is relatively stable, as on a website, then ideally you should conduct a complete content inventory, as long as the number of pages is not too many to look at individually (hundreds instead of thousands of pages). If the number of pages is too great, you should still conduct an audit of representative pages. In the case of a complete content inventory, such as of a website or intranet, it is best to record the unique file name and directory in the first column of the table and then enter concepts into a subsequent column, thus ensuring that every page, or at least every representative page type, is inventoried. In addition to a concept and its source file, other information to record may include additional synonyms for the concept, content type, file format, and audience. Although the focus at this stage is the concepts, if additional synonymous terms for the same concept are evident, you should definitely note them for future use in building the taxonomy.

The task at this point closely resembles descriptive indexing or cataloging. In a sense, you are test indexing the content to see what concepts might be useful for indexing. This approach makes most sense if you are preparing a taxonomy primarily for indexing a collection of documents or files. If, on the other hand, the taxonomy is to organize a website or intranet, support a search engine or content management system, or otherwise constitute an enterprise taxonomy, then you need to be more liberal in collecting concepts. For these purposes, you are not indexing documents; rather you are gathering all concepts of potential interest, which you will weed through later.

There are also automated methods for extracting terms from sample content. Simple text analytics programs can generate lists of words or phrases occurring in the text and sort those lists by frequency or generate statistical graphs (histograms). Examples are the World List Expert from MechanicWords (www.mechanicwords. com) and Disk Bee developed by Prakash Govind.[1] Most programmers can also write scripts to extract single words, although extracting useful phrase terms is more complicated. With the right tools, unstructured text can quickly produce useful lists of candidate terms.[2]

If the content already has metadata, there are additional software tools that are useful for extracting the metadata. For example, some taxonomists have used Metalogix for this purpose. It is designed to support migration of content to SharePoint, but its inventory feature captures a lot of metadata that can be useful for analyzing the content.[3]

People as a Source of Concepts

The various people who contribute ideas for the concepts within the taxonomy usually include the owner or manager of the taxonomy, subject matter experts, users or test users, and finally you, the taxonomist.

The owner, manager, or sponsor of the taxonomy (who may be a product manager, project manager, or executive in an organization) often has a significant stake in the taxonomy and may want to suggest at least some concepts, based on the owner's understanding of strategic or business needs, the search database design, or perceived customer or user needs. These suggestions are more likely to be the top-level concepts in a hierarchical taxonomy but often include other miscellaneous sample terms. Concept suggestions from the taxonomy owner are welcome, but usually the taxonomist should decide the term names.

If a specialty subject area is to be covered, subject matter experts should also be consulted to ensure that all the basic concepts within that subject area are included, although these experts are of greater importance during the stage of determining term names rather than concepts. For a hierarchical taxonomy, subject matter experts can recommend the inclusion of concepts that would fill in any gaps in the hierarchy.

Users are an important source of ideas for taxonomy concepts. If the taxonomy is part of a product or service marketed to external clients or is part of an external website, then you can pose questions pertaining to the taxonomy to focus groups or test-market users. If the taxonomy is for internal use, as an enterprise taxonomy, then you should conduct interviews to find out the needs of employees of various departments who will contribute to and search for the content. Usually some form of online searching has already been taking place before a taxonomy comes along. Search engine logs of user queries and feedback forms can provide ideas for both concepts in general and specific terms.

Finally, you, the taxonomist, can contribute concepts to be included in the taxonomy. Especially if the taxonomy is general in nature, you may rely on your general knowledge. If you have built hierarchies or facets before, you can draw on your previous experience. If charged to build a hierarchical taxonomy, for example on news categories, industries, or occupations, you can establish a good basic structure on your own, especially if you are familiar with well-known classification systems in these areas, such as industry SIC or NAICS codes. In some cases, it is better to start out with your own ideas of concepts before consulting outside reference sources lest the outside sources influence you too much.

Evaluating Concept Inclusion

Inevitably, there will be more concepts than practical for a taxonomy, especially when including concepts gathered from a content audit. A potential concept should become a term only if the following questions can be answered affirmatively.

1. Is the concept within the intended subject-area scope of the taxonomy?

A taxonomy needs to have a defined subject area scope; otherwise, it can get out of hand. This is especially the case for a hierarchical taxonomy because hierarchies work best when confined to a specific area. This contrasts with an alphabetical back-of-the-book index, which can easily accommodate off-topic entries.

2. Is the concept important and something users are likely to look up?

Trivial subjects should not be included. Any analysis of document content will reveal numerous concepts that are relatively insignificant. If these concepts do not come up in user studies or interviews, then you can probably omit them.

3. Is there enough information on the concept?

Just because a concept appears in the text does not mean that it should be indexed. A given concept may come up only once and with little substantive information about it. This is another reason a taxonomy or a human-created index provides more useful information than a mere keyword search. If creating a taxonomy for periodical-types of content (i.e., if new content is added over time), you also need to determine whether there will be recurring future occurrences of the concept. Will there be a sufficient number of documents on the topic over time? For websites, a content survey thus needs to be large enough so that you can recognize whether a given concept is indeed rare or may appear more frequently.

4. Do users want and expect the concept to be covered?

If a concept appears only marginally in the content, and user questionnaires and search logs never reveal any interest in that concept, then perhaps it should not be included in the taxonomy. Conversely, a marginally covered concept that is repeatedly a topic of interest among users should be included in the taxonomy as long as there is at least some content or anticipated content on the topic.

Choosing the Preferred Term

Unless the taxonomy is of the synonym ring type, the taxonomist must select a preferred term to describe each concept; the other possible terms for a concept can then become nonpreferred terms. In general, the preferred term should reflect the language of the taxonomy's users. If you decide to include a concept in the taxonomy but are not ready to finalize its preferred term name, you may still enter a temporary term name into the taxonomy as a *candidate term*. Most commercial taxonomy management software supports the designation of candidate versus approved terms.

Candidate terms cannot be used for indexing, and the software flags them as requiring further review.

Choosing Among Synonyms

Selecting the preferred term often involves choosing between two or more synonyms, such as:

> **doctors** vs. **physicians**
> **movies** vs. **motion pictures**
> **cars** vs. **automobiles**

In choosing the preferred term from two or more synonyms, the taxonomist needs to consider the following:

1. *The wording the intended users will most likely look up.* This is especially the case in a displayed, browsable taxonomy. For example, if the users are the general public, they are more likely to look up **doctors** than **physicians**. Healthcare professionals, on the other hand, will more likely look up **physicians**.

2. *The subject focus or scope of the taxonomy and its indexed content.* The content and scope are closely related to audience. For example, if the scope is travel services, then **cars** is probably more appropriate than **automobiles**. If, instead, the focus is on selling vehicle parts, then **automobiles** is likely the more appropriate term.

3. *Enforcing an organizational/enterprise controlled vocabulary.* This consideration applies especially if the taxonomy is for internal use or is a public agency taxonomy. For example, an intranet for a company may require the term **employee development** instead of **employee training**.

4. *Conforming to academic, cultural, political, or trade/industry standards.* This includes taking into consideration cultural sensitivities and what is "politically

correct." For example, it has become more common to
use the term **Middle East** instead of **Near East**. If a taxonomy has a scholarly or academic focus, then the preferred
terms will reflect those accepted by the discipline.

5. *Consistency in style throughout the taxonomy.* A taxonomy should use a similar level of wording throughout,
   either informal or formal/technical, to make it more predictable for the user. For example, names of occupations
   should be either consistently formal, such as **physicians**,
   attorneys, and **law enforcement officers**, or consistently
   informal, such as **doctors**, **lawyers**, and **police officers**,
   but not a mixture of both levels.

6. *The wording of terms within the documents/content
   indexed by the taxonomy.* This will depend, of course, on
   the degree of consistency within the body of content. If
   the content has multiple authors, then wording is likely
   to be inconsistent in some areas. Where it is consistent,
   though, the content can be a guide for choosing the preferred term, but as just mentioned, this factor is secondary to the needs and expectations of the users.

The relative importance of these different criteria will vary, but
in general, the wording that is most likely to be looked up by the
intended users/audience—in other words, the preferred language
of the taxonomy's target population—should take precedence over
the other criteria.

Choosing Among Near Synonyms

At times, the taxonomist needs to choose which of two similar, but
not synonymous, concepts will be the preferred and which the nonpreferred. When two concepts have overlapping meaning, maintaining a distinction may be important for the nuances within a
specialized subject area, but it is often not practical when it comes
to indexing and organizing content. Without clear distinctions

between concepts, users may become confused, and content will not be consistently indexed, whether by humans or by auto-categorization methods. Examples of closely related terms, which might require the taxonomist to select one as nonpreferred, include:

> **foreign policy** vs. **international relations**
> **colleges and universities** vs. **higher education**
> **books** vs. **literature**

Naturally if the taxonomy has a narrow focus, and there is a significant volume of content on each related subject, then perhaps the two concepts should be maintained as distinct terms. Both **foreign policy** and **international relations** could exist as separate terms in a single taxonomy focused on international affairs, both **colleges and universities** and **higher education** could exist as terms in a taxonomy focused on education, and both **books** and **literature** could exist in a taxonomy focused on the humanities. However, even with specialized content, maintaining accurate indexing quality would require a great deal of effort (see Chapter 6), so it may still be simpler to choose one term as preferred and the other as nonpreferred. If the taxonomy does include terms with overlapping meaning, it tends to work best if they are used in different facets. For example, **colleges and universities** could be in an institutions/organizations facet while **higher education** could be in a topic/subject facet

A similar dilemma arises in choosing between different grammatical forms of a word, such as terms describing a topic or an action. For example:

> **contracts** vs. **contracting**
> **investments** vs. **investing**
> **manufacturers** vs. **manufacturing**

Even in a specialized taxonomy, it is nearly impossible to maintain the distinction between two single-word terms differentiated only by their morphological form, and the taxonomist must choose one over the other. Again, a possible exception would be in a faceted taxonomy. For example, **contracts** could be in a subject facet while **contracting** could be in an actions facet, but the indexing would need to follow clearly written rules and policies in order to distinguish the two. In any case, terms within the same hierarchy should adhere to the same morphological form for consistency of style. Determining the overall style is the taxonomist's decision but may require input from other people.

Sources for Preferred Term Choice

Content is the primary source for concepts, but not necessarily for preferred term names. If the content is consistent and the same terms appear throughout the content to be indexed, then the terms from the content should be primary candidates for the preferred term names. Far too often, however, term usage is inconsistent within a diverse collection of content, and the taxonomist needs to rely on other sources in choosing the preferred terms.

While content is the determining factor in choosing concepts, in general people play a more important role in determining the preferred terms. You should consult subject matter experts, if available, to choose the preferred term for any specialized or technical concepts. The experts understand the terminology better and can advise you on the most appropriate term for specific circumstances and audiences. Taxonomy owners or sponsors play less of a role in determining term names than they do in suggesting some of the top-level concepts, but in certain circumstances, their input into the choice of preferred term names is important. This is particularly the case for internal nomenclature used in enterprise taxonomy.

User expectations and needs are also very important in settling on the preferred term for each concept. Access to information on user expectations varies greatly depending on the type of taxonomy and its use. If the taxonomy is to be part of an information product or service that offers licenses or subscriptions, then the company's marketing department will likely conduct user studies, and the taxonomist may be only marginally involved in designing these studies. If the taxonomy is to be implemented primarily on a website that is freely accessed by the public, then the user-experience or user-centered design staff will likely be the ones conducting user research, and the involvement of the taxonomist in this research will depend on the degree to which the taxonomist is integrated into the user-experience team.

If the taxonomy is part of an internal content management system, document management system, or intranet, then the users are internal employees. This means that the marketing department will not bother to research user needs, thus leaving more of this responsibility to the taxonomist. On the other hand, gathering information from users who are employees is much easier in a practical sense because the users are identifiable and can be contacted. Nevertheless, in a taxonomy of hundreds or thousands of terms, it is not always feasible to gather user opinions regarding the preferred term for every concept. Gathering input from potential users and other stakeholders will be discussed in more detail in Chapter 9.

External Sources for Preferred Terms

Finally, there are external published sources that can provide valuable input in determining your preferred terms. These include industry standards, specialized glossaries, and the publications or websites of regulatory agencies and trade and professional organizations. Especially interesting are other existing taxonomies or controlled vocabularies. You may utilize those taxonomies that are publicly accessible, but only on term-by-term basis if you do not have a license. In some cases, it is also possible to purchase a license to an entire taxonomy, as described in Chapter 1, which allows you to use as much of the taxonomy as you wish.

Publicly available taxonomies or controlled vocabularies for browsing include the Library of Congress Subject Headings (LCSH), Library of Congress Thesaurus for Graphic Materials, and those of government agencies, such as NASA, the U.S. Department of Education (ERIC thesaurus), the National Agricultural Library, and the National Library of Medicine. United Nations agencies maintain multilingual thesauri, such as the UNESCO Thesaurus. Longer lists of online thesauri are available on the Online Thesauri and Authority Files webpage of the American Society for Indexing (www.asindexing.org/site/thesonet.shtml) and the Thesaurus Sites webpage of Queensland University of Technology Faculty of Information Technology (www.imresources.fit.qut.edu.au/vocab/thes_sites.jsp). The latter is longer but less up to date.

There are other sources for determining the preferred term for a named entity (person, company, organization, creative work, place, etc.). These include the Library of Congress Name Authorities (along with the LCSH, part of the Library of Congress Authorities), government websites, and the websites of companies or organizations. For the correct forms of names of people in current events, you can consult websites of reputable newspapers. Finally, for names that have variant forms or spellings, checking the total number of results from a Google search on each variation, restricted by language (English), will indicate which form or spelling is the most common. You will also need to develop consistent policies for certain kinds of names; for example, whether to spell out, abbreviate, or omit company designators in company names.

Term Format

When it comes to the format of the terms, there are guidelines in the published taxonomy standards. *ANSI/NISO Z39.19-2005*

Guidelines for the Construction, Format, and Management of Monolingual Controlled Vocabularies (www.niso.org/kst/reports/ standards) addresses the issue of single word versus multiword terms (section 6.3); grammatical forms of terms (section 6.4); singular and plural nouns (section 6.5); abbreviations, slang and jargon, popular or scientific names, foreign or loan words, and variations in spelling (section 6.6); capitalization (section 6.7); and compound terms (section 7).[4] Rather than repeat the entire contents of ANSI/NISO Z39.19, we will discuss only some of the points of formatting here. It is important to remember that these standards are guidelines only, and there can certainly be flexibility in their application, especially for an internally used taxonomy.

Lowercase or initial capitals, but not title caps. Although the guidelines recommend all lowercase, initial capitalization is also common. Using title capitalization, however, could cause confusion between proper nouns and generic terms. For example, **Business services** or **business services** are both fine, but not **Business Services.** There is a tendency to use initial capitalization for terms in hierarchical taxonomies to represent a view of hierarchical category labels, whereas all lowercase terms more commonly appear in less hierarchical thesauri or controlled vocabularies. (Examples in this book demonstrate both styles.)

Single words or multi-word terms. The preferred length of terms will largely be determined by your software system, the user interface, and what makes sense for usability. Except for proper nouns, which must appear in complete form regardless of length, terms are usually one to four words long.

Nouns or noun phrases. Terms are usually nouns or adjective + noun phrases. Prepositional phrases are acceptable if they are commonly phrased concepts, such as **prisoners of war.** Terms may be verbal nouns, such as **teaching**, but not verbs, such as **teach.** Adjectives alone, such as **educational,** are generally not used except in a faceted taxonomy in which a feature or characteristic is a facet, in which case the facet comprises a short list of adjectives, such as a list of colors. Adjectives can also serve as subdivisions in precoordinated indexing, discussed at the end of this chapter.

Common nouns or proper nouns. Common nouns and proper nouns (named entities or unique entities) may be kept separate in individual taxonomies or authority files, or they may be integrated so as to link proper nouns (narrower terms) to their corresponding common noun terms, such as **Golden Gate Bridge** and **bridges**.

Countable nouns. Countable nouns used as terms are in the plural when possible in order to reflect the fact that there are multiple records indexed or multiple occurrences of the topic in the content. However, abstract concepts, substances, and collective nouns are not plural, and neither are body parts, according to the standards. For example, preferred formats are **hospitals**, **healthcare**, and **ear**. Be aware that countable and noncountable forms of some nouns have slightly different meanings, such as **finance** and **finances**. Both are correct forms, depending on the meaning required, and software should support this distinction.

Parenthetical qualifiers. There are different ways to handle multiple concepts in a taxonomy that have the same term name, also known as homographs. Usually parenthetical qualifiers are an option for disambiguation, although certain software systems may preclude this. An example is **French (language)** and **French (people)**. It may not even be necessary to have parentheses in both of the terms. For example, you might have **walnut (wood)** and **walnuts; walnuts** in the plural is unambiguous and must mean the nuts, whereas **walnut** in the singular might be ambiguous.) The form of the qualifier could be of the subject *domain*, as in **Saturn (astronomy)** and **Saturn (mythology)**, or of the term *category*, as in **Saturn (planet)** and **Saturn (god)**. Choose a single format, either domain or category, and stay consistent with it. Do not use parentheses to modify a term with an inverted qualifying adjective, though, such as **schools (elementary)**. Instead, **elementary schools** is the preferred format.

Acronyms, if well known. Use an acronym instead of a spelled out form if the acronym is better known. For example, **DNA** is preferred over **Deoxyribonucleic acid**. Be sure that the acronym is not ambiguous: If the scope of the taxonomy is broad, **CDs** could mean either compact discs or certificates of deposit, in which case you should use the full form as the preferred term.

No term inversions. Inverted terms with a noun followed by an adjective, such as **loans, commercial**, were common in controlled vocabularies in printed formats and in the older LCSH used in physical card catalogs because they aided the user when alphabetical browsing was the only option. Now that taxonomies exist in electronic formats and users can search them in addition to browsing them, these awkward inversions are no longer necessary. Thus, **commercial loans** would be the preferred term. If you know that there will also be a browse option for the taxonomy, then you may include inverted terms as nonpreferred terms, but avoid them as preferred terms in all cases.

Precoordinated Terms

When coming up with concepts, especially from analyzing content sources, it may be difficult to discern whether a complex idea should be expressed as a single concept or a combination of two or more concepts. Take, for example, the idea of foreign relations between the United States and Mexico.

This could be a single term:

United States–Mexican relations

It could be two terms:

United States foreign policy and **Mexico,** OR
United States foreign relations and **Mexican foreign relations**

It could also be three terms:

United States and **Mexico** and **international relations**

The terms **United States–Mexican relations, United States foreign policy, United States foreign relations,** and **Mexican foreign relations** are all combinations of two or more concepts and are called precoordinated terms. Precoordinated means that two or more concepts are put together (i.e., coordinated) prior (thus pre-) to indexing and searching. Other examples of precoordinated terms are:

Hispanic actors instead of the separate concepts **Hispanics** and **actors**
software testing instead of **software** and **product testing**
sales force training instead of **sales force** and **employee training**
plastic motor vehicle parts instead of **plastic parts** and **motor vehicles** OR **plastics** and **motor vehicle parts**

Sometimes precoordinated terms are very obvious, with the word *and* joining two concepts to create one term. This format appears in LCSH and other thesauri based on it, but the standards today discourage this practice. Examples are:

business and politics
computers and children

Another kind of precoordination of terms involves a main heading term and a subdivision term that limits the scope of the main heading. In this case, the two terms remain distinct but are tied together and used in combination, both at the indexing stage and in retrieval. This is the format used in the LCSH and in other cataloging systems, and it is still commonly used in catalogs of library materials. An example is:

Massachusetts—History

This type of structured indexing or second-level indexing is discussed further in Chapter 6.

Advantages of Precoordination

The justification for creating a precoordinated term is that, if the scope of the content provides sufficient coverage of the combined concept and the audience is sufficiently interested in the concept, precoordination makes it easier for the users to find that specific information. Use of a precoordinated term retrieves content about the combined concept more reliably than merely combining the terms at the search stage, which is referred to as *postcoordination*. Postcoordination, even if done correctly, as in Boolean searching, may not always retrieve the desired results, as the following examples illustrate.

Precoordinated term: **Hispanic writers**
Postcoordinated alternative: **Hispanics** and **writers**
But this could also retrieve content about **writers who write about Hispanics.**

Precoordinated term: **Russian foreign policy**
Postcoordinated alternative: **Russia** and **foreign policy**

But this could also retrieve content about **foreign policy toward Russia.**

Precoordinated term: **software testing**
Postcoordinated alternative: **software** and **product testing**
But this could also retrieve content about **software used for testing various products.**

If the content being indexed is very limited, consistent in its type and focus, then such unpredictable results from Boolean-type searching are less likely, and postcoordination is fine. If, however, the content is varied, there is a greater chance of unreliable results with postcoordinated searching. Thus, a broad scope of content benefits from precoordination to avoid ambiguity. Precoordinated terms are also common, though, in specialized subject taxonomies, where there are a greater number of narrower, specific topics. Finally, precoordination is desirable when users are likely to employ a high level of phrase searching to target specific complex topics—in other words, subject expert users.

Considerations in Precoordination
Precoordinated terms do have their disadvantages, however. Using precoordinated terms requires a larger, more complex taxonomy, which then requires more time and effort—and consequently cost—to maintain. The user, whether a human indexer or end-user searcher, may not expect precoordinated terms and thus may overlook them or may use them inconsistently. Thus, it is more difficult to index content correctly with a larger, more complex taxonomy comprising precoordinated terms.

You are not as likely to create precoordinated terms for a taxonomy accessed through a faceted search/browse, as facets naturally enable postcoordination. This does not mean that a faceted taxonomy should never contain precoordinated terms. Rather, any precoordinated terms would likely be limited to certain subject areas. For example, if you have a *place* facet of geographical names, then you would probably not also include *place names* as a precoordinated term. Furthermore, a small, simple taxonomy, which faceted taxonomies usually are, is simply less likely to have precoordinated terms. A website navigation taxonomy can be an exception: although relatively small, it may be describing very specific and often precoordinated concepts, such as **meeting room reservations policy.**

In conclusion, you should consider creating precoordinated terms whenever:

- Postcoordination cannot reliably retrieve the desired content of a subject of relative importance.

- The subject area is focused and thus deep, as in a relatively specialized controlled vocabulary.

- There is a significant amount of anticipated content for the precoordinated concept.

- The types of documents making up the content vary greatly, a factor that contributes to unreliable results with postcoordinated searching.

- You are creating a hierarchical navigation taxonomy.

Notes and Attributes

As mentioned previously, a concept is more than just a term. It comprises a preferred term and its equivalent nonpreferred term(s) with a single definition and possibly additional information. Depending on how you manage the taxonomy, the concept's definition may be merely implied, or you may write it down and store it with the concept. Supplemental information pertaining to the concept, such as notes regarding its use, foreign language equivalent preferred terms (in a bilingual or multilingual taxonomy), and designated concept types or categories, is also sometimes stored with the concept and might also be searchable.

Scope Notes and Other Term Notes

Except in technical subjects, it is best to avoid dictionary-type definitions of concepts in taxonomies. Usually users of a taxonomy understand the meaning of its concepts, so including obvious definitions is a waste of everyone's time. Furthermore, copyright law prohibits you from copying a definition found in a published dictionary, so trying to think up original definitions for each concept would require additional effort.

What may be necessary, however, is a note of clarification as to the use of the concept, or more precisely its preferred term, within the context of the taxonomy. As this refers to the term's scope of usage, this note is commonly called a *scope note* (often abbreviated as SN). Scope notes serve any one of the following purposes:

1. To restrict or expand the application of a term

2. To distinguish between terms of overlapping meaning (the terms involved may have reciprocal notes)

3. To provide advice on term usage

The following two examples illustrate different ways in which a scope note can restrict the use of a term:

> From the ProQuest Controlled Vocabulary:
> **inequality**
> SN: Socioeconomic disparity stemming from racial, cultural, or social bias

From the NASA Thesaurus:

analyzers

SN: Excludes devices for performing mathematical analysis

The following example from the NASA Thesaurus illustrates how a pair of reciprocal scope notes distinguishes between terms of overlapping meanings:

aramid fiber composites

SN: Aramid fiber utilization in composites. For properties of aramid fibers themselves use "aramid fibers."

aramid fibers

SN: Properties of aramid fibers themselves. For aramid fiber utilization in composites use "aramid fiber composites."

The following example, taken from the ERIC thesaurus, illustrates advice on term usage:

school organization

SN: Do not confuse with "School District Reorganization."

A scope note ought to be viewable to all: the taxonomy editors, any human indexers, and the end users. Keep scope notes concise to facilitate quick reading by the user and to save space in the user interface display. Keep in mind that users may not have the patience to read the notes, however, or may not even know that scope notes exist, so do not use a scope note as the only means to disambiguate otherwise identical terms or homographs. Also, at some point in the future the taxonomy could be implemented in a different user search interface or a third-party vendor's interface that does not support scope note display. For this reason, too, you cannot rely on scope notes to clarify ambiguity. What is more critical, though, is that human indexers have access to the scope notes for correct, consistent indexing.

Although scope notes will most likely be accessible to the users, you may also choose to create other kinds of term notes that are not necessary for the end user and will display only in the taxonomist and indexer interfaces. These would include notes pertaining to the history of a term, such as a change from a previous preferred term name, or the splitting or merging of concepts. It may also be desirable to include a field noting the source of the term. The source can be a reference to a periodical article, another thesaurus, or even web usage according to search engine (such as Google) results. A source note can refer to the concept and/or to the preferred term name.

In summary:

- If term notes are included, not all concepts need notes (except perhaps in a technical subject thesaurus).

- Notes should be concise.

- There may be multiple types of notes serving various purposes (scope, history, source, etc.).

- Notes may be intended for the end user, indexer, or other taxonomists. You can designate different levels of access for different note types.

Descriptive Attributes

If you are maintaining the taxonomy in a kind of database system, and each concept is a database record, it is technically very simple to store various types of additional information for each concept or preferred term. Thus, the taxonomy not only serves to retrieve indexed files or documents but also organizes relatively static data for each concept. This structure makes most sense for named entity (proper noun) types of terms, such as people, companies, organizations, brand-name products, places, laws, and events. Examples of possible extended attributes for various kinds of concepts include:

- Named persons: birth date, occupation/title, affiliation, address

- Companies: industry code(s), headquarters location, ticker symbol

- Places: latitude and longitude

- Events: dates, location

The values for the extended attributes themselves should be restricted if possible. For example, you might have a controlled vocabulary of cities for company headquarters location and a standard format for entering dates and latitude/longitude. If the search interface supports it, end users can then limit searches according to the extended attributes, thus providing a more powerful means to execute and narrow a search. Most commercial thesaurus management software offers the ability to store some additional data with each concept, under various labels: attributes, additional data, term characteristics, term info, and so forth. In the user interface, the information may have various labels, depending on the term type.

Administrative Attributes

Finally, a concept or term can be assigned various administrative attributes, including identifier numbers, approval status, and creation/update data. Supporting such data is a standard feature in commercial taxonomy/thesaurus management software. If your organization is developing software for taxonomy maintenance internally, you should ensure that it supports administrative attributes.

In some cases, assigning each concept a unique *identifier number* allows you to easily manage multiple taxonomies in which the same term name may occur more than once. It also provides an added measure of security when changing term names. Multi-digit numeric identifiers may be assigned sequentially to denote the order in which the concepts or terms were added.

A *term approval status* attribute is an important feature. It allows the taxonomist to create a candidate term and then research it further for possible modification or even elimination before allowing it to go live. This feature is especially practical for a taxonomy that is in active use for indexing. Term approval may also be an issue if there are junior-level taxonomy editors whose additions of new terms need approval from a taxonomy manager.

Standard administrative statistics that any taxonomy management software ought to record include each term's creation date, date last modified, and the user ID/initials of the taxonomist who made the changes. It is often useful to be able to call up or determine how many terms you modified within the past week or month. For example, you may want to review a batch of work you did recently, such as offline batch spell checking, in cases where the thesaurus software lacks a spell checker.

Considering the various notes and attributes that a taxonomy term may have, we see how taxonomy and metadata can come full circle. While a taxonomy or controlled vocabulary provides descriptive metadata for a file or document, a single term in the taxonomy can itself be described by a large amount of metadata.

Endnotes

1. Prakash Govind, email to author, November 12, 2009. There is no website or company for Disk Bee, but the developer can be contacted directly at prakash@earley.com.
2. Lynda Moulton, email to author, November 9, 2009.

3. Layne Foit, Taxonomy Community of Practice group post, "Subject: Content Inventory tools—Mac or PC," November 15, 2007, finance.groups.yahoo.com/group/TaxoCoP/message/2341

4. National Institute of Standards Organization, *ANSI/NISO Z39.19-2005 Guidelines for Construction, Format, and Management of Monolingual Controlled Vocabularies* (Bethesda, MD: NISO Press, 2005).

Chapter 4

Creating Relationships

A day without taxonomies is not found.
　　　　　　　　　　　　　　　　—Jared Spool

What makes a taxonomy more useful than a mere term list or glossary is the presence of relationships between its terms. Relationships between pairs of terms are bidirectional (reciprocal). Broadly speaking there are three kinds of relationships:

1. Equivalence: between preferred and nonpreferred terms

2. Hierarchical: between broader and narrower terms

3. Associative: between related terms

The most basic controlled vocabularies and authority files have at least the equivalence relationship. Classification and categorization schemes, thesauri, and nearly all taxonomies have hierarchical relationships and usually (but not necessarily) associative relationships as well. Thesauri, ontologies, and semantic networks additionally have associative relationships. Thesauri have all three kinds, but ontologies may lack the equivalence relationship. In fact, the kinds of relationships in a given knowledge organization system are often the defining feature. (Decisions regarding which kinds of relationships to include and what kind of knowledge organization system to have are covered in Chapter 10.) Even if you have decided that your taxonomy will include all three kinds of relationships, it is not required that every single term have all three kinds. Each individual relationship should provide some value or purpose. Although hierarchical taxonomies have hierarchical relationships for all terms, a thesaurus might not. It is unusual, however, for a term in a taxonomy or thesaurus to have no relationships to other terms. Such a term is called an *orphan*. An individual taxonomy's policy may specify whether orphan terms are permitted.

Relationship types are often denoted by labels, with their corresponding abbreviations or codes, between pairs of terms or preceding the various related terms for a selected term. The following is a list of the most common such labels, although you may choose a different designation in each case:

- Equivalence: USE/UF (use/use[d] for)
- Hierarchical: BT/NT (broader term/narrower term)
- Associative: RT (related term)

All relationships are reciprocal, meaning that they function in both directions between a pair of terms. For example, *Term A* has a relationship with *Term B*, and *Term B* has a relationship with *Term A*. Depending on the relationship type, the relationships may or may not be identical in both directions. If the relationship is not identical in both directions, it is asymmetrical. The equivalence and hierarchical relationship types are asymmetrical. If the relationship is the same in both directions, it is symmetrical. The default associative relationship type is symmetrical.

Equivalence Relationships and Nonpreferred Terms

An important feature of controlled vocabularies, except for those that are small enough to browse through on a single page, is to have synonymous or equivalent nonpreferred terms pointing, as a kind of cross-reference relationship, to the desired preferred terms. These guide the searcher, either visibly or invisibly, to the preferred term that is linked to the content. The equivalent nonpreferred terms also support the indexing, whether manual or automatic.

As we have seen in the previous chapter, concepts and preferred terms may have various designations. Not surprisingly, the same is true of nonpreferred terms. You do not have to call them nonpreferred terms, but can take your pick from the following list:

Aliases
Alternate terms
Entry terms
Equivalent terms
Lead-in terms
Nondescriptors
Nonpostable terms
Nonpreferred terms
NPT
See references
Use for terms
Use references
Used for terms
Variant terms
Variants

Additionally, you might run across the following designations for nonpreferred terms, but you should avoid using them due to ambiguity:

- Synonyms: However, nonpreferred terms are not just synonyms.

- Keywords: However, keyword can also mean a significant term used for indexing or searching that is not in the taxonomy.

- Cross-references: However, cross-references can mean either *See* references or *See also* references, the latter being an associative relationship rather than a nonpreferred term.

When it comes to the style and format of nonpreferred terms, you have more freedom than when creating preferred terms. After all, there is no need to maintain consistency in style, as you are trying to anticipate all the possible formats of terms that users might possibly search for or enter.

The Equivalence Relationship

When compiling nonpreferred terms that refer to a preferred term, it may not seem as though you are creating a relationship, because a preferred term and a nonpreferred term do not have the same standing in the controlled vocabulary. In fact, it might have been perfectly logical to address nonpreferred terms in Chapter 3, Creating Terms. However, the standards describe equivalence as a kind of relationship, thesaurus/taxonomy management software handles nonpreferred terms as relationship types, and thesauri usually display them as relationship types. Thus, it is important to understand that the connection between a preferred term and its corresponding nonpreferred term(s) is a relationship type. Creating nonpreferred terms uniquely combines the tasks of term-creation and relationship-creation.

The notion of equivalence does not imply that the terms have to be equal or that they are synonyms. First, it is the concepts, not the terms themselves, that are equivalent. Second, the two terms merely need to be sufficiently similar with respect to the content being indexed that trying to maintain them as distinct terms would lead to too much redundancy, ambiguity, and confusion, and thus for the purpose of indexing the content, they should be treated as the same.

The equivalence relationship between a preferred term and a nonpreferred term is asymmetrical. Thus, a different label for the relationship is used depending on the direction. A nonpreferred term instructs the indexer or searcher to *use* a preferred term, whereas a preferred term is *used for* a nonpreferred term. The expression of the relationship is "nonpreferred term use preferred term," and the reciprocal is "preferred term use(d) for nonpreferred term." (There is no difference between *use for* and *used for*.) In standard thesaurus notation, the relationship is represented by USE/UF. For example:

inundations	**floods**
USE **floods**	UF **inundations**

As the taxonomist, you may choose to use a different name for your equivalence relationship, such as *see* and *seen from*, if that makes more sense to your users.

Typically, multiple nonpreferred terms refer to a single preferred term. In other words, a preferred term may have multiple nonpreferred terms, as in the following example:

Oil and gas industry
UF **Oil and gas industries**
UF **Oil companies**
UF **Oil industry**
UF **Oil producers**
UF **Petroleum companies**
UF **Petroleum industry**
UF **Petroleum sector**

In the other direction, each nonpreferred term typically refers to only a single preferred term; that is, there are no multiple *use* references. However, this is not always the case. Some thesauri permit a one-to-many use reference, whereby a nonpreferred term may refer to two (but no more) preferred terms under certain conditions. Typically in this situation, the nonpreferred term would be a precoordinated type of term, and the two preferred terms would be the constituent terms coming from breaking apart this precoordinated term. Both preferred terms must be used in combination, in both indexing and in searching, to achieve the desired results. In other words, there is an implied AND, not OR, combination of the two preferred term. For example:

> **folk drama**
> > USE **drama** AND **folk culture**

To convey the concept of **folk drama**, the indexer must assign both the term **drama** and the term **folk culture** to the document, and to properly retrieve documents on folk drama, the searcher must enter both the terms **drama** and **folk culture**. This multiple *use* relationship is often known as *used for and* or *used for plus*. It appears only in more structured thesauri, not in simple taxonomies, and the nonpreferred terms must display to both the indexers and the end users. The multiple *use* relationship occurs in many traditional printed-only thesauri, but not all electronic/database-driven controlled vocabularies support this feature. You might choose to allow for multiple use relationships if you have decided to create a controlled vocabulary with few or no precoordinated terms, or if the content available on a particular precoordinated concept is rather minimal, yet research indicates that users want to search with the precoordinated term.

Types of Nonpreferred Terms

The most typical kind of nonpreferred terms are synonyms, but there are many other types as well. Table 4.1 lists the various kinds

Table 4.1 Types of nonpreferred terms

Type of Nonpreferred Term	Example
synonyms	**cars** USE **automobiles**
near synonyms	**junior high schools** USE **middle schools**
variant spellings	**defence** USE **defense**
lexical variants	**hair loss** USE **baldness**
foreign language terms	**Luftwaffe** USE **German Air Force**
acronyms/spelled out forms	**UN** USE **United Nations**
scientific/technical names	**neoplasms** USE **cancer**
phrase inversions	**buses, school** USE **school buses**
antonyms	**misbehavior** USE **behavior**
narrower terms	**hand drills** USE **hand tools**

of nonpreferred terms and an example of each. (The actual choice of preferred term in most of these sample pairs is arbitrary.)

Near Synonyms

Near synonyms, also called quasi-synonyms, can be tricky, and your choice to use a given nonpreferred term will depend on the scope of the content. In the example in the table, using **middle schools** for **junior high schools** (or vice versa) will be fine in most cases, but not for a thesaurus dedicated to the field of education, where the nuanced differences are important. In other cases, two terms may be synonymous only within a limited scope, and if that is the scope of the thesaurus, then there is no problem. The following example of nonpreferred terms may or may not be acceptable depending on the content:

    aviation
      UF **flight**
      UF **flying**

The terms **flight** and **flying** are acceptable as equivalent terms for **aviation** if the content or database is focused on careers, skills, industries, services, engineering, and so on, but they are not acceptable as nonpreferred terms in a broader, general-interest database that may contain information on birds. When trying to determine whether a term will work as a nonpreferred term, ask yourself this: Given the scope of the content covered, can the preferred term *always* be used to mean this nonpreferred term?

Variant Spellings

Spelling variations may include British/U.S. spellings and acceptable variations that you would find in a dictionary. Avoid including incorrect spellings as nonpreferred terms unless they (1) are common, (2) unambiguously have the meaning of the preferred term, and (3) are not displayed to the end user so as not to be confusing. Incorrect spellings as nonpreferred terms are more common for proper nouns.

Foreign Language Terms

Foreign language terms are typically used for native-language names of organizational or corporate entities or for rare cases of foreign words that are sometimes used in English discourse (such as **sharia** USE **Islamic law**), if not chosen as the preferred term in the first place. Foreign organizational names are usually nonpreferred terms only in the case of Latin-script-based languages (French or German, for example, but not Russian, Arabic, or Chinese). Otherwise, transliterations would be necessary, and then even more variations would come into play. In a bilingual or multilingual taxonomy, the different language terms are *not* treated as nonpreferred terms but rather have a specially designated foreign language relationship. Each language's preferred term then has additional nonpreferred terms in its own respective language.

Acronyms

Acronyms, if used as nonpreferred terms, need to be unambiguous. Therefore, you need to take into consideration the scope of the taxonomy and content. For example, **CDs** can refer to either compact discs or certificates of deposit, so for a general news/information service, such an acronym should not be used as a nonpreferred term and without some kind of qualifier.

Phrase Inversions

Phrase inversions typically involve putting an adjective after a noun. Only add them if you expect them to display in a browsable alphabetical list to the user, either the end user or the indexer. Otherwise, there is no need for them. Browsable alphabetical (as opposed to hierarchical) displays are more common for indexers than for end users. It is rare for end-use displays to consist of alphabetical lists of terms that are not proper nouns, unless the thesaurus is published in print form.

If phrase inversions are used, they should begin with a word that is likely to be looked up for the concept. They may be an inversion of the preferred term or an inversion of nonpreferred term, such as **pants, dress** USE **trousers** (in addition to **dress pants** USE **trousers**). Avoid creating phrase inversions as nonpreferred terms for prominent preferred terms that have multiple narrower terms. For example, you should not create **industry, computer** USE **computer industry**, since **industry** is likely a term in the taxonomy with numerous narrower terms. If users choose to look up the word **industry** first, they will find specific industries listed as narrower terms, which is easier to browse than a list of inverted nonpreferred term industries.

Antonyms

Antonyms generally work as nonpreferred terms for concepts that are limited to characteristics or attributes. Examples include the following pairs: **rigidity/flexibility**, **softness/hardness**, **obedience/disobedience**, and **literacy/illiteracy**.

Narrower Terms

Narrower or more specific terms (discussed in detail in the next section, Hierarchical Relationships) can be acceptable as nonpreferred terms for their corresponding broader preferred terms. The broader term can logically be used for the narrower concept that it includes. This is known as *upward posting* or *generic posting* and is done when there is too little content on the narrower subject to justify the term but there is reason to believe that people will look it up. On the indexing side, if a document discusses a very specific topic for which there is no preferred term in the taxonomy, such as tidal power energy, then the corresponding broader term of **alternative energy** should be used to index it. On the user search side, narrower terms may be used as nonpreferred terms only if the relationship is displayed so that the user is made aware of the fact, as in **tidal power energy** USE **alternative energy**. Otherwise, if a search on **tidal power energy** retrieved documents on all forms of alternative energy, the majority of which were not about tidal power, the user would end up with many undesired results to sift through and would assume the search was not functioning properly. If the end-user interface does not support the display of nonpreferred terms pointing to preferred terms, it may be possible to designate the nonpreferred term for indexing use only and not for end-user application. Otherwise, you should generally avoid upward posting except in unique circumstances when documented search behavior seems to warrant it.

In any case, if you designate narrower terms as nonpreferred terms, do so with discretion. Often a narrower concept is narrower to more than one broader preferred term, which would result in an unintended *used for and* or *used for plus* relationship. Furthermore, many end-user search interfaces will offer the additional option to search by keyword (words or phrases *not* in the taxonomy, but rather in the titles or texts) anyway. If such keywords were nonpreferred terms to a broader preferred term, then instead of getting the desired results through a keyword search, the user would get a much larger set of results, including many undesired records that match the broader term. Finally, you will want to consider narrower concepts as candidates for preferred terms if sufficient usage over time warrants it. If, however, such narrower terms were labeled as nonpreferred terms, then their frequency in keyword searches may not (easily) be tracked, and it would not be clear whether there was sufficient usage to reclassify a given term as a preferred term.

How Many Nonpreferred Terms to Create

Since each preferred term can have multiple nonpreferred terms, you may wonder how many nonpreferred terms to create for each. Considerations include whether the nonpreferred terms will be used for indexing only or also for end-user retrieval, whether the indexing is by humans or automated, whether the end user can browse the taxonomy or has access to a search box, and whether and how a search system matches entered keywords to taxonomy terms.

Nonpreferred terms may be displayed to the user or may not actually be displayed but function in the background to match a user-entered term to the preferred term. The user can be either the indexer or the thesaurus end user/searcher. In a controlled vocabulary that is implemented online, it is common to have the nonpreferred terms visible to the indexer but not to the end user. If there is a desire to educate the user on what the preferred term is, however, then nonpreferred terms, along with their corresponding preferred terms, would be displayed. This is especially common in academic thesauri.

If the taxonomy is small and easily browsable within a single page or through pulldown/dropdown term lists, then nonpreferred terms may not be needed for the user search and may only be implemented on the indexing side (whether human or automated), if at all. This may be the case for term lists in the examples of the Shoebuy.com and the Microbial Life Education Resources sites mentioned in Chapter 1.

If users can input search strings into a search box (instead of or in addition to browsing the taxonomy), more nonpreferred terms are needed because the users cannot see the terms to choose from and must guess what the search terms should be. Keep in mind that whenever a search box exists alongside a browsable taxonomy, a significant number of end users will ignore the taxonomy display and simply use the search box.

Even if the taxonomy is displayed for browsing, the type of display may affect the need for certain nonpreferred terms. Taxonomies that are displayed for end-user browsing may be arranged hierarchically, alphabetically, or both, although alphabetically is less common. Typically, only the alphabetical arrangements of taxonomies can logically show nonpreferred terms interspersed among the preferred terms; it is simply not practical to intersperse nonpreferred terms within a hierarchical display. If a browsable alphabetical display is the only means of accessing the taxonomy, then you may omit nonpreferred terms that are very close alphabetically with their corresponding preferred terms. This is because the user would find the preferred term in that part of the alphabetical display anyway if searching for the same start of a nonpreferred variant. An example of alphabetically close nonpreferred terms is as follows:

> **ethnic groups**
> > UF **ethnic minorities**
> > UF **ethnicities**

In a taxonomy that is displayed alphabetically only, you would not need these two nonpreferred terms, **ethnic minorities** and **ethnicities**. If a search box were present, though, the additional nonpreferred terms would be quite useful.

If a search system was programmed to match user-entered keywords or phrases with taxonomy terms and then to present the user with multiple matching taxonomy terms from which to select, then these keywords or phrases may not be needed as nonpreferred terms. The keywords would need to be somewhat unique, however, to be effective in this way. For example, if the user entered **nonverbal learning**, the matched term **nonverbal learning disorder** would be retrieved, which was probably the desired result. However, if the user entered **United States**, not only would the preferred term **United States of America** be retrieved, but so would the names of dozens of United States federal agencies and companies. In this case, finding the desired term within the list of retrieved terms would be time consuming. It would be preferable simply to designate **United States** as a nonpreferred term for **United States of America**, to take precedence over any partial term phrase matching.

If indexing is being done automatically, a greater number of nonpreferred terms might be needed to facilitate automatic matching of appropriate words and phrases in the various texts, depending on the method of automatic indexing used. Chapter 7 covers automated indexing in detail.

Finally, the nature of the end users may affect the need for nonpreferred terms. A narrow, limited, and uniform group of users, such as members of a certain profession, is likely to look up concepts consistently and thus not need many nonpreferred terms. The general public, on the other hand, is very diverse in the ways they think of concepts, so numerous nonpreferred terms are needed in order to serve everyone.

In summary, a greater number of nonpreferred terms is needed in the following circumstances:

- The taxonomy is too large to be browsed on a single page.

- Users can look up content via a search box.

- Automated indexing, which matches terms to words and phrases in text, is involved.

- The users are diverse.

Even for a relatively static taxonomy, the number of nonpreferred terms should be permitted to grow as needed. The taxonomist cannot be expected to fully anticipate all nonpreferred term needs from the beginning.

A final note of caution regarding nonpreferred terms: You should not rely on a dictionary-type thesaurus, such as *Roget's*, to suggest equivalent terms. Not only is it limited in that it contains only individual words, not phrases (and only a minority of the words are nouns), but because it serves a very different purpose. It provides all the *possible* equivalent words for a given entry term, and the appropriateness of any given equivalent would depend on the specific context. Nonpreferred terms, on the other hand, must be equivalent in *all* circumstances of usage for the preferred term. For example, in *Roget's Thesaurus*, a synonym for **performer** is **player**. However, players are not always performers, so in a taxonomy, **players** is not an acceptable nonpreferred term for **performers**.

Hierarchical Relationships

The presence of hierarchical relationships among terms is what makes a simple controlled vocabulary into what is best known as a taxonomy. Hierarchical relationships indicate subordination among concepts. Subordinate concepts are members, parts, examples, or instances of a broader concept, class, or category. The presence of a hierarchy facilitates the navigation of the taxonomy and the location of a concept or clarifies the scope of a concept in relation to others.

The hierarchical relationship, like the equivalence relationship, is asymmetrical or directional; that is, the relationship is not the same in each direction between a pair of terms. According to the standards for controlled vocabularies, a hierarchical relationship pair consists of a broader term and a narrower term. *All* members of a narrower term's category must be contained within the broader term, but a broader term is not limited to containing the members of a single narrower term. Thus, only *some* members of a broader term constitute the members of a given narrower term. The following diagram illustrates this directional relationship:

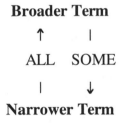

Broader Term

↑ |

ALL   SOME

| ↓

Narrower Term

As the hierarchical relationship is asymmetrical, a different label for the relationship is used depending on the direction. A broader term refers to its narrower term with the label NT, and a narrower term refers to its broader term with the label BT. The expression of the relationships is: "broader term NT narrower term," and "narrower term BT broader term." For example, with the terms **fruits** and **apples**, all apples are fruits but only some fruits are apples.

    fruits   **apples**

       NT **apples**   BT **fruits**

The all/some rule for creating hierarchical relationships ensures that a user navigating from a broader term down to a narrower term will find content that is indeed completely within, yet more specific than, the broader term. Similarly, if navigating from a narrower term up to a broader term, the user will find content that includes all of the narrower term and more. The following example of a hierarchical relationship is incorrect:

> **breakfast dishes**
>   NT **egg dishes**

Although egg dishes are most often for breakfast, they are not *always* for breakfast.

Adhering to the all/some rule also supports inclusive retrieval results of multiple narrower terms. A nested approach to retrieval allows a user to select a term that has narrower terms and retrieve not only content that was indexed with the selected term, but also all content that was indexed with each of its narrower terms. This feature, sometimes called *recursive retrieval,* may or may not be desired in the search interface, and you, as the taxonomist, may not know whether the taxonomy will ever be used this way. However, if you build hierarchical relationships correctly following the all/some rule, then there is no problem if recursive retrieval is implemented. (Recursive retrieval is discussed in more detail in Chapters 8 and 9.)

The designations BT and NT are the most common for the hierarchical relationship, but as the taxonomist, you can choose to use other labels for your hierarchical relationships, such as *parent* and *child*, if that makes more sense to your users or system developers. In accordance with the family metaphor, terms that share the same broader term are then called *siblings*. A child/narrower term in a sense "inherits" the additional broader meaning of its parent/broader terms, and it also may "inherit" certain properties, such as types of descriptive attributes (explained in Chapter 3), category or facet designations (explained in Chapter 8), and administrative and editorial policies.

Types of Hierarchical Relationships

Although determining whether a given concept is subordinate to another is often intuitive, sometimes it is not. To ensure that you create a hierarchical relationship only when appropriate, it helps to understand the different types. According to thesaurus standards, there are three kinds of hierarchical relationships:

1. Generic–specific

2. Instance

3. Whole–part

Generic–specific refers to a category or class and its members or more specific types. You can think of it as expressed by the wording *is, a,* or *are* in the following construction: "narrower term is a (kind of) broader term" or "narrower terms are a (kind of) broader term." Examples are:

computers NT **laptops**	Laptops are a kind of computer.
financial services NT **investment services**	Investment services are a kind of financial service.
engineers NT **software engineers**	Software engineers are a kind of engineer.

If it is desirable to distinguish between the different types of hierarchical relationships in a taxonomy, the standard notation used here is BTG/NTG, which stands for broader term (generic)/narrower term (generic). Here is an example:

libraries   academic libraries
   NTG **academic libraries**   BTG **Libraries**

Instance refers to a unique named entity, a proper noun, which has a narrower term relationship to the class to which it belongs. Instances include named individuals, companies or organizations, brand-name products, specific geographic places, published works, laws, etc. This relationship is not much different from the generic–specific type and also fits the "is a" phrase construction of "narrower term is a (kind of) broader term," or more specifically, "narrower term is a specific instance of broader term." Examples are:

national parks   Grand Canyon is a specific
   NT **Grand Canyon**   instance of national parks.

children's writers   J.K. Rowling is a specific instance
   NT **Rowling, J.K.**   of children's writers.

holidays   Thanksgiving is a specific instance
   NT **Thanksgiving**   of holidays.

If you are distinguishing between the different types of hierarchical relationships, the standard notation used here is BTI/NTI, which stands for broader term (instance)/narrower term (instance). Here is an example:

automobiles   Toyota Corolla
   NTI **Toyota Corolla**   BTI **automobiles**

In some organizational systems, however, named entities are kept in separate taxonomies or facets, in which case the instance hierarchical relationship cannot be created, as relationships between separate taxonomies may not be supported.

A *whole–part* relationship refers to something that is not more specific but rather is a part of a whole, where the part is the narrower term and the whole is the broader term. You can test the relationship by constructing a phrase with *is within* or *is a constituent part of*: "narrower term is within (the) broader term" or "narrower term is a constituent part of (the) broader term." The whole–part type of hierarchical relationship is much less common than the generic–specific type, as it occurs only within systems (including anatomical), organizations, geographic places, or disciplines/fields of study. Other kinds of whole–part relations, such as nonpermanent placement in (e.g., **automobiles** and **garages**) or manufactured things (e.g., **automobiles** and **automotive parts**), should be treated as associative and *not* hierarchical. Examples of whole–part hierarchical relationships are:

U.S. Congress NT **U.S. Senate**	The U.S Senate is a part of the U.S. Congress.
Colorado NT **Denver**	Denver is within Colorado.
biology NT **marine biology**	Marine biology is a part of biology.

If you are distinguishing between the different types of hierarchical relationships, the standard notation used here is BTP/NTP, which stands for broader term (partitive)/narrower term (partitive). Here is an example:

digestive system
   NTP **stomach**
	stomach
	   BTP **digestive system**

In summary, to decide whether the relationship between a pair of terms is indeed hierarchical and not merely associative, remember to think of the concepts behind the terms and then try formulating a sentence according to one of the following models:

- Narrower term is a (kind of) broader term.

- Narrower terms are a (kind of) of broader term.

- Narrower term is a specific instance of broader terms.

- Narrower term is within (the) broader term.

- Narrower term is a constituent part of (the) broader term.

If any one of these sentences holds true for a term pair in *all* cases, not merely sometimes or often, then the hierarchical relationship is valid.

Polyhierarchies

Sometimes a term may have more than one broader term. This is called a *polyhierarchy* or multiple broader terms (MBT). Polyhierarchies may occur within each type of hierarchical relationship—generic–specific, instance, or whole–part—or may even be a combination of types. An example of a generic–specific polyhierarchy is:

> **school librarians**
> BT **educators**
> BT **librarians**

An example of a whole–part polyhierarchy is:

> **Egypt**
> BT **Africa**
> BT **Middle East**

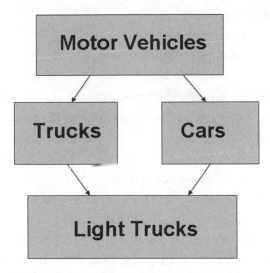

Figure 4.1 Polyhierarchy for the term *light trucks*

Polyhierarchies can involve terms that are in the same larger hierarchical structure and share the same ultimate parent, as in the case of **light trucks** in Figure 4.1.

Polyhierarchies can also be based on two different methods of categorization, or in other words, two different hierarchical types. For example, **Great Salt Lake** is narrower to **lakes** as an instance and also narrower to **Utah** in a whole–part hierarchy, as illustrated in Figure 4.2.

When creating a polyhierarchy with two (or more) broader terms, make sure that none of these terms has a direct hierarchical relationship with the other, in which one is the broader term of the other. To use the parent–child metaphor, a term cannot be designated as a narrower term to both a parent term and a grandparent term. For example, the following pair of broader terms would be incorrect:

genetic engineering
> BT **biotechnology**
> BT **technology**

Technology is already the broader term of **biotechnology**, so it should not also be an immediate broader term of **genetic engineering**.

Finally, remember that the all/some rule for hierarchical relationships applies to polyhierarchies. All members of a narrower term must belong within/be a part of each of its broader terms in a polyhierarchy, just as in a simple hierarchy.

Although the published thesaurus standards provide specific guidelines on when to create polyhierarchies, the ultimate determining factors for whether you create polyhierarchies are the user interface design and the technical capabilities of the search/browse software.

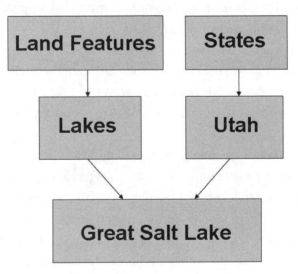

Figure 4.2 Polyhierarchy for the term *Great Salt Lake*

Associative Relationships

Associative relationships, also known as related-term relationships, are created between terms in a taxonomy to provide the indexer or searcher with useful information. Often a related term associated with the original search term is in fact a better match to the concept that the user was trying to locate. In addition, a list of related terms can be useful information in itself because it outlines the subject area of a concept. Finally, related terms allow a searcher who is merely browsing a subject area to branch out and discover related topics of interest. The associative relationship functions in a similar manner to *See also* cross-references in a book-style index. Associative relationships are generally not used in simple hierarchical taxonomies, but they are a required feature of standard thesauri. Unlike hierarchical relationships, simple associative relations are symmetrically bidirectional by default. The standard designation of RT (related term) applies in either direction. For example:

Cameras	Photography
RT **Photography**	RT **Cameras**

Creating associative relationships is generally more subjective than creating hierarchical relationships. Not everyone shares the same belief as to what constitutes "related," although differences of opinion usually depend on context. The taxonomist's task is to determine whether the terms are conceptually related, regardless of the circumstances. Furthermore, rules for creating associative relationships are not as strict as for hierarchical relationships. Associative relationships may exist between terms within the same hierarchy or between terms of different hierarchies.

Associative Relationships Across Different Hierarchies

It is more common to create associative term relationships between terms belonging to different hierarchies than between sibling terms. This is because the sibling terms already have an implied similarity relationship by being siblings under the same broader term, and this relationship is usually clear in the display of the hierarchy. Since the purpose of the associative relationship is to inform the indexer/searcher that other terms exist, it is the associative relationship indicating related terms in *other* hierarchies that is most helpful. A different hierarchy in this case means that the terms do not share a broader (parent) term or a broader term of a broader term (grandparent). Whether they have a shared ultimate top term depends on the structure of the taxonomy. In the example in Figure 4.3, the two terms **engineering** and **engineers** are located in different hierarchies but are clearly related.

There are many circumstances when establishing an associative relationship between terms of different hierarchies is desirable. Table 4.2 lists various possibilities. This list is not exhaustive, and taxonomists are free to add other related term types.

An index or a thesaurus that is displayed only in an alphabetical browse, such as in print only, would not designate related terms (or *See also* cross-references) between terms that lie next to or very

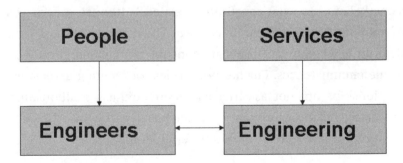

Figure 4.3 Associative relationship between terms in different hierarchies

Table 4.2 Types of associative relationships

Process and agent	research RT researchers researchers RT research
Process and counter-agent	infections RT antibiotics antibiotics RT infections
Action and property	environmental cleanup RT pollution pollution RT environmental cleanup
Action and product	programming RT software software RT programming
Action and target/patient	auto repair RT automobiles automobiles RT auto repair
Cause and effect	hurricanes RT coastal flooding coastal flooding RT hurricanes
Object and property	plastics RT elasticity elasticity RT plastics
Object and origins	petroleum RT oil wells oil wells RT petroleum
Raw material and product	timber RT wood products wood products RT timber
Discipline and practitioner	physics RT physicists physicists RT physics
Discipline and object/phenomenon	meteorology RT weather weather RT meteorology
Part and whole (which are not systems, geographic places, etc.)	office furniture RT offices offices RT office furniture

near each other in the alphabetical list, such as **physics** and **physicists**. However, if the users access the taxonomy via a search box, they would not see such neighboring terms that are obviously related alphabetically. Therefore, in a searchable taxonomy, it is important to create the associative relationship consistently regardless of whether the terms begin with the same letters or words. Even if a browsable display version of the taxonomy exists, whenever a search box is also present, a significant percentage of users will choose to access the taxonomy via the search box rather than take advantage of the alphabetical browse.

Associative Relationships Within the Same Hierarchy

The associative relationship can be created between two terms that share the same broader term (known as siblings) and also have overlapping meaning or usage. In fact, according to thesaurus standards, the associative link is required under these circumstances. In the example in Figure 4.4, the two terms **local taxes** and **property taxes** both share the same broader term, **taxes**, so they are considered sibling terms to each other. They also both have overlapping meaning (inasmuch as local taxes are largely property taxes, and most property taxes are local).

Other examples of sibling terms with overlapping meaning that should have the associative relationship between them are:

> **children's books** RT **picture books**
> **Middle East** RT **North Africa**
> **communications industry** RT **media industry**

For simplification and to avoid ambiguity, remember that in controlled vocabularies it might be preferable to combine concepts with overlapping meanings to create a single term. You may even have the word *and* within the term, such as **communications**

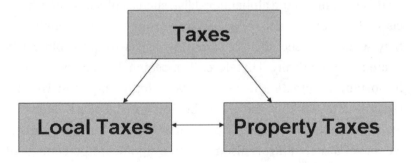

Figure 4.4 Associative relationship between sibling
terms with overlapping meaning

and media industry. In general, it is better to avoid having pairs of terms for concepts if their meaning overlaps too greatly.

If sibling terms do *not* have overlapping meaning (i.e., they are mutually exclusive), then the associative relationship is not required nor expected. It is not incorrect, according to standards, to have all sibling terms related, but since it is not necessary, in this case you should avoid creating such a relationship. Besides being a waste of the taxonomist's time, it creates needless information, which gets in the way of efficient thesaurus browsing. In the example in Figure 4.5, the two sibling terms **radios** and **TV sets** need not have an associated relationship created between them.

How Many Associative Relationships to Create

The extent to which you create associative relationships is, to a certain degree, a judgment call. It requires a keen sense of what would aid the user. Ask yourself if the searcher (or indexer) would get helpful information from a reminder that a particular term has a link to another term in the same general concept area. Keep in mind that the relationship needs to be close to be useful.

As with hierarchical relationships, you should create associative relationships between a term and its nearest relationships but not also to broader terms or narrower terms of those related terms. For

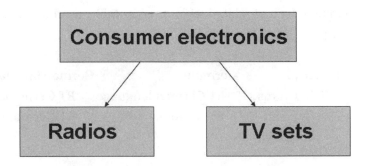

Figure 4.5 No associative relationship between sibling terms with no overlapping meaning

example, suppose you have in a thesaurus the following two sets of terms and relationships:

computers
    RT **computer peripherals**

computer peripherals
    NT **keyboards**
    NT **monitors**
    NT **printers**

You should then *not* also have:

computers RT **keyboards**
computers RT **monitors**
computers RT **printers**

Similarly, you should not create associative relationships between all the related terms of a related term. For example, you may have **engineers RT engineering** and **engineering RT CAE software**, but you should *not* also have **engineers RT CAE software**. Of course, selected related terms of related terms may be related to each other, if appropriate. Unlike hierarchical relationships, a close circle or web of related terms *is* acceptable, as in the following example:

Germany	**Germans**	**German language**
RT **Germans**	RT **German language**	RT **Germans**
RT **German language**	RT **Germany**	RT **Germany**

If you are unsure whether two terms are closely enough related to have an RT relationship, ask yourself, Would *most* of the people looking up the first term also be interested in information on the second term *most* of the time? The answer should not be only some people some of the time. For example, **Germany** RT **World War II**, is *not* appropriate, despite an obviously close tie. Most people looking up Germany are interested in issues other than World War II. The decision may depend on the scope of the content covered by the taxonomy, however. It might be acceptable to have an associative relationship between Germany and World War II in a specialized history resource.

Simple hierarchical taxonomies, especially those that are relatively small, may not have any associative relationships at all. However, creating just a few associative relationships is never a good compromise. A taxonomy should either have fully developed associative relationships or none at all—it should not go part way. It would be confusing or misleading to the user to find related terms only sporadically. The application of associative relationships should be logical and consistent for all types of terms.

Hierarchical/Associative Ambiguities

Despite the detailed nature of the taxonomy standards in distinguishing between hierarchical and associative relationships, there are still some gray areas, which various taxonomies may handle differently.

One area of ambiguity is the relationship between companies and their industries. While the generic–specific hierarchy is clear within industry groupings, opinions differ over whether to treat companies as instances of an industry. If you use the "is a" wording test, then a company is not an industry. For example, it is not correct to say: "Ford is an Automobile industry." However, if the industry were named differently, then companies could be instances. For example, if the **automobile industry** were called **automobile companies** or **automobile manufacturers**, then the companies would be valid instances of such broader terms. Thus, if you want to display companies as instances of industries in your taxonomy, it would be better to name your industries with words ending in *companies, manufacturers, producers, providers*, or the like, so that the relationships appear logical to the users. Otherwise, the relationship is associative.

A similar questionable area is whether members constitute narrower terms of the organization of which they are affiliated, as a whole–part relationship, since one can argue that the members are part of an organization. However, according to the ANSI/NISO Z39.19 guidelines, a whole–part hierarchical relationship exists when "one concept is inherently included in another, regardless of the context."[1] Applying this standard, it is clear that such a relationship is not hierarchical but rather associative, because membership status can change. If it is important to your taxonomy display to designate members as narrower terms to an organizational affiliation, you could do this through the instance rather than the whole–part relationship, provided that you use appropriate wording for the broader term organization. For example, instead of the organization **OPEC** having a narrower term relationship with its country members, which would be incorrect, you could use **OPEC countries** or **OPEC members** as the broader term, and then its member countries would be correctly linked as narrower terms. Needless to say, you probably do not want both terms—**OPEC** and **OPEC countries**—in your taxonomy, and maintaining both could be complex and confusing. So in most cases, the associative relationship is preferable for member-organization relationships.

Ambiguity can also occur when it is not clear whether terms of an apparently whole–part relationship are indeed within a "system." To qualify as a whole–part hierarchical relationship, the narrower term must be a constituent part of a broader term that comprises a *system*, which can be anatomical, administrative, political, or corporate. Whole–part constructions that are put together and can be taken apart again, such as **office furniture** and **offices** or **soccer goals** and **soccer fields**, are not hierarchical but associative. Since one may remove furniture from an office or soccer goals from a field, the inclusion is not inherent regardless of the context. Manufactured systems, however, can be more difficult to discern. A good example would be **automobile engines** and **auto-mobiles**, Some taxonomists will consider such a relationship to be hierarchical while others will consider it associative. In fact, the relationship depends on the context. If your content is an automobile user's manual, then the whole–part hierarchical relationship might be acceptable because the user of an automobile considers its parts to be a system. If, on the other hand, your content covers the automobile manufacturing industry, in which different automotive components are manufactured by different companies in different facilities and locations, then the relationship between **automobiles** and any automotive parts, including **automobile engines**, should be associative.

In all these ambiguous cases, the existence of more specific, semantic relationships would eliminate the ambiguity.

Semantic Variations for Relationships

You might wish to customize the relationships between certain terms by including more meaning than simply related or broader/narrower. *Semantic* refers to meaning, so more complex, customized relationships that have added meaning are often called semantic relationships. Commercial taxonomy/thesaurus software provides the ability to designate your own customized relationships to varying degrees. Although semantic relationships alone do not make an ontology, they are one of the key features that distinguish ontologies from other taxonomies.

Creating customized relationships in a taxonomy can result in an enhanced user experience. Semantic relationships between terms allow the user to access content in more ways, rather than just drilling down through a hierarchical tree or jumping across to related terms. If semantic relationships are implemented in a relational database, users can explore how different categories relate to each other and then access the desired content. For example, a movie database with semantic relationships among various types of terms (genres, themes, actors, producers, production companies, directors, countries, years, etc.) allows the user to obtain more customized retrieval results. These may include lists of actors who performed in certain genres in given years and countries, countries where certain subjects were the theme of movies in certain years, or production companies for which a given actor worked.

Even when you designate your own relationships, you should still base each one on a standard type: equivalent, hierarchical, or associative. Doing this will ensure that the relationships comply with standards and thus are logical. Additionally, most taxonomy software systems distinguish among the three different relationship types in their display, regardless of how you might customize the relationships names. Thus, for example, when generating a hierarchical display, the software knows to include relationships that are fundamentally hierarchical. Terms in a hierarchical relationship may branch out in a tree display. Therefore, most thesaurus software that supports semantic relationships requires that you choose a basic relationship type (equivalent, hierarchical, or associative) for any custom relationship.

When you define your own relationship types, they will still be reciprocal between the members of a pair of terms, that is, they will function in both directions. Users may approach the relationship from either term in a pair, and they need to link from one term to the other. Any customized semantic relationship is not, however, symmetrical. The only symmetrical relationship that exists is the generic associative type: the related term (RT). Customized relationships are inherently asymmetrical, or directional, as a consequence of the richer meaning they contain. You can compare this with relationships between people. For example, a generic associative relationship that is symmetrical is as follows: "Tom is related to David" and "David is related to Tom." A semantic version of this relationship might be: "Tom is the uncle of David" and "David is the nephew of Tom." This relationship designation is not identical in both directions. Thus, when you create a new kind of semantic relationship, you need to give distinct names and abbreviation codes to the relationship in both directions.

When designating your own relationships, they need to be specific enough to convey the desired meaning but not so specific as to be restrictive. Remember, the relationship needs to apply to multiple term pairings, not just a single pair. You also want to limit the set of relationships so that you or other people editing the controlled vocabulary can easily keep track of what the relationship choices are and not overlook any when creating relationships between terms. Two or three kinds of relationships based on each of the RT and BT/NT types, for a total of four to six, are often sufficient, although complex databases use more.

Hierarchical Semantic Relationships
The following are sample variations based on the hierarchical (BT/NT) relationship. There is nothing standard about them; the all-caps codes are merely examples of relationship labels that have been created by taxnonomists. Some are more general (closely following the standard variations of hierarchical types of relationships), and some are more specific.

Based on whole–part geographic: Located in (LOC)/Contains Location (CONT)

Empire State Building LOC **New York, NY**
New York, NY CONT **Empire State Building**

Based on whole–part organizational: Has parent organization (PAR)/Has sub-organization (SUB)

Internal Revenue Service PAR **Dept. of the Treasury**
Dept. of the Treasury SUB **Internal Revenue Service**

Based on instance: Is of the profession (PROF)/Has individuals (IND)

Smith, Joe PROF **biomedical engineers**
biomedical engineers IND **Smith, Joe**

Associative Semantic Relationships

Given the opportunity to customize relationships, you are more likely to customize associative relationships than hierarchical relationships. This is because there are so many kinds of associative relationships, such as those illustrated in Table 4.2. The following are sample variations based on the associative (RT) relationship. Again, there is nothing standard about them. The type and specificity of the relationship depend on the scope of the content indexed or tagged with the controlled vocabulary.

Produces the product (PRD)/Is manufactured by the company (COM)

Apple Inc. PRD **iPod**
iPod COM **Apple Inc.**

Has member affiliation with (AFF)/Has members (MEM)

Saudi Arabia AFF OPEC
OPEC MEM Saudi Arabia

For treating (TRE)/Can be treated with the drug (DRUG):

ACE inhibitors TRE **hypertension**
hypertension DRUG **ACE inhibitors**

Has patent (PAT)/Invented by (INV)

Smith, Joe PAT **Patent #7,501,419**
Patent #7,501,419 INV **Smith, Joe**

You may designate any code abbreviation you wish, as long as it is unique to the taxonomy. When creating the relationship names and their abbreviation codes, you should make them logical with respect to the type of term that follows the code in the expression, that is, the direction of the relationship "from–to."

The relationship names and codes will be visible to the taxonomists, indexers, and systems administrators but not necessarily to the end users. Semantic relationships can link various types of data in ways that are not obvious to the end user, functioning "under the hood." If the semantic relationships do in fact display to the end user, they should be designated by their full relationship names and not just the codes. Relationship names that will be displayed to the end users should be carefully chosen to be simple yet unambiguous, to make navigating the taxonomy as easy and user friendly as possible.

Semantic Equivalence Relationships

There are various situations in which you may want to distinguish between different kinds of nonpreferred terms. For example, you may want certain nonpreferred terms to display to the user and other nonpreferred terms (such as incorrect or misspelled terms) not to display. Thus, in addition to USE and UF, you might have something such as COR (Correct term) and CORF (Correct for), as in the following example.

> **Millenium** COR **Millennium**
> **Millennium** CORF **Millenium**

All the various equivalence relationships function as nonpreferred terms, but only those you designate with the standard USE will display, and those with COR will not display.

In these cases, a different relationship name allows you to manage the nonpreferred terms so that they are implemented only where and when appropriate. You might designate common abbreviations or acronyms this way, especially if the user can also search specifically by abbreviation or acronym. This can reduce ambiguity, especially for two-letter abbreviations, such as for states. Such standardized variants are also common in scientific fields. You might also use semantic equivalence relationships to give slang or jargon terms a designated status because this kind of nonpreferred term might be used only for certain audiences or in certain geographic regions or may change over time.

Sometimes specific kinds of nonpreferred terms are maintained for administrative purposes. Examples include a former or obsolete name for a term or the term name used by a third-party vendor or content provider's taxonomy. You might also want to have a nonpreferred term function on the indexing side but not on the end-user search side. As explained previously, a narrow concept can always be used as a nonpreferred term for its corresponding broader concept from the point of view of indexing, for it is logical to retrieve a document on a specific topic under the term for a slightly broader concept. However, it can be problematic on the search side to have a narrow concept function as a nonpreferred term, because a user who searches for a specific topic using the nonpreferred term would not be pleased to retrieve documents on other topics that merely share the same broader concept. You can solve this problem by designating a specific type of equivalence relationship that only operates on the indexing side. You could call it *USE-I* and *UF-I*, where *I* stands for indexing, and instruct the programmers to implement it only on the indexing side.

Endnotes

1. National Institute of Standards Organization, *ANSI/NISO Z39.19-2005 Guidelines for Construction, Format, and Management of Monolingual Controlled Vocabularies* (Bethesda, MD: NISO Press, 2005), p. 49.

Chapter 5

Software for Taxonomy Creation and Management

Taxonomy, thesauri, ontology, oh my!
—Julie Martin

A simple controlled vocabulary, such as a synonym ring, or a small, unified hierarchical taxonomy that lacks nonpreferred terms, could be created on paper (or in Word or Excel). Creating and maintaining a more typical larger taxonomy or a more complex thesaurus, however, with equivalence, hierarchical, and associative relationships, and perhaps also scope notes and term attributes, requires a specialized kind of database software. In fact, the indexing thesaurus as we know it did not exist prior to the computer age of the late 1950s. Database software designed specifically for the creation and maintenance of thesauri originally existed primarily in the form of in-house custom-developed software used on mainframe or minicomputers. Commercial thesaurus development software for mainframes and minicomputers first appeared in the early 1980s, embedded in such products as BiblioTech (VAX/VMS), TechLib (IBM and VAX/VMS), and Cuadra STAR (AlphaMicro), which were the forerunners of current content management systems. These modules also provided early navigation frameworks for browsing content by exposing the thesaurus to users.[1] Later in the 1980s, a few single-user desktop PC thesaurus software packages were introduced. These were followed in the 1990s by client-server-based distributed thesaurus software systems and then web-based systems. Most recently, taxonomy management components have been incorporated into some content management and enterprise search software. Today all of the following software options exist:

1. "Home-grown" programs developed in-house, especially within large organizations

2. Software not designed for creating taxonomies

3. Single-user desktop thesaurus software (mostly Windows based)

4. Larger-scale, multiuser client-server or web-based thesaurus systems

5. Taxonomy creation and editing components of larger systems that focus on capabilities for searching, indexing, content management, or document management

6. Industry-specific (vertical market) software for creating classification structures

Our survey of taxonomists conducted in November–December 2008 asked broadly what kind of software they used for creating and managing taxonomies. The largest number, although less than half, used licensed commercial dedicated thesaurus management software. Close to a quarter of those responding used internally developed software, and close to 20 percent used software not intended for taxonomies, such as generic database or spreadsheet software. A lesser but significant number of respondents used software in which taxonomy management is a component or module. The detailed breakdown from 64 respondents appears in Table 5.1.

Software Not Designed for Creating Taxonomies

The fact that close to 20 percent of taxonomists surveyed used software not designed to create taxonomies is significant, especially

Table 5.1 Survey responses for types of software used
for creating and managing taxonomies

Type of Software Used	Number	Percent
Licensed commercial dedicated thesaurus/taxonomy management software	24	37.5%
An internally developed thesaurus/taxonomy management system	15	23.4%
Other commercial software that is not intended for taxonomy creation (such as a word processor, spreadsheet, or database management software)	12	18.8%
Licensed commercial software, of which taxonomy management is a feature, module, or component	10	15.6%
Licensed open-source ontology/taxonomy development software	3	4.6%

since the survey allowed for only a single answer. We can probably assume that these people are creating very simple taxonomies. Additionally, there are many taxonomists who create the first steps of a taxonomy in software not designed for a taxonomy and then expand and manage the taxonomy further in dedicated taxonomy management software. Two types of software commonly used by taxonomists in the early stages of taxonomy development are 1) spreadsheet software, to record lists of terms within categories or facets, and 2) mind mapping, concept modeling, or ontology software, to develop a structure for a taxonomy. You may use one or both of these tools, depending on the nature of the taxonomy and the way you approach the project. Some people also use ontology software for designing taxonomies.

Spreadsheet Software

Although the assertion by one writer on taxonomies that "the vast majority of taxonomies are still created and maintained in Microsoft Excel"[2] is most likely an exaggeration (especially with respect to the maintenance of the taxonomies), the prevalence of this tool in taxonomy creation should not be underestimated. The accidental taxonomist is especially likely to use Excel, due to lack of experience with taxonomy software or perhaps due to lack of time, skills, or budget to evaluate different software alternatives. Even organizations intending to purchase taxonomy software or already owning such software often start building their taxonomies in Excel because it provides an easy way for various contributors, both in-house and external, including subject matter experts who might not be taxonomists, to quickly build up lists of terms and perhaps some simple hierarchy. When the taxonomy gets too complex or too big, such as when it contains several hundred terms, it is time to move it into taxonomy software.

If you are creating an extremely small taxonomy, such as for website navigation, it is possible to represent each of various hierarchical levels of the taxonomy through individual columns on a spreadsheet worksheet. The first column contains terms at the top level, the second column contains terms at the second level, etc. For each term, its broader term (if any) is in the column to its left, and its narrower terms are in the column to its right. Each row is unique by its narrowest term (column filled in to the right). Broader terms appear repeatedly, but initially you may leave cells empty and later fill them in with repeated references to a broader term. This makes it easier to visualize a form of indenting narrower terms under their broader terms. You may use a column to the far right for nonpreferred terms, but it is difficult to indicate more than one nonpreferred term in a systematic way. Another column can be used for notes, whether scope notes or something else. Figure 5.1 illustrates how you might use Excel to indicate three levels of a small taxonomy.

If there are separate categories, hierarchies, or facets, you could create a separate Excel worksheet for each hierarchy or facet. Each worksheet can be saved as a CSV (comma separated values) file, a format that can easily be imported into another system with relationships across rows preserved. The drawbacks to this method are

	A	B	C	D	E
1	PRODUCT CATEGORIES				
2	Level 1	Level 2	Level 3		Equivalent terms
3	Cable Modems & Gateways				
4		Hardened Cable Modem			
5		Optical Amplifiers			
6		Cable Modems			
7		Cable Modem Gateways			
8			Wireless Cable Modem Gateways		
9		Broadband Command Center eMTA Test Appliance			
10		Diagnostic Suite Software			
11	CMTS & Routers				
12		Routers			
13		Broadband Services Routers			
14		Embedded Multimedia Terminal Adaptor (eMTA) Test Appliance			
15		CMTS (Cable Modem Termination Systems)			
16		CMTS Modules			
17	Consumer Products				
18		Cordless Phones			
19			2.4 GHz Digital		
20			5.8 GHz Digital		
21			2.4 GHz Analog		
22			5.8 GHz Analog		
23		Digital Audio Players			
24		Home Entertainment			
25		Digital Audio Receivers			
26		Broadband Media Centers			
27		Remote Controls			
28			Digital Cable Set-Top		
29			Digital C-Band satellite receiver		
30		Home Monitoring & Control Systems			
31			Wireless Cameras		

Figure 5.1 Using Excel to create a three-level taxonomy

clear. If each top-level term has multiple narrower terms and each of these second-level terms has multiple narrower terms, then rather quickly it becomes difficult to visualize the complete hierarchy as higher-level terms become increasingly spaced apart. This cannot support polyhierarchies, though. There is only space for a single nonpreferred term unless you use separate worksheets for this purpose.

A larger, although still simple, taxonomy can be created in Excel if multiple worksheets and multiple Excel files (workbooks) are used. Rather than trying to portray a complete hierarchy on a single page, you can use each worksheet to indicate just a single pairing of terms, and thus a pair of levels, broader and narrower. You can then use one workbook file to represent two hierarchical levels, the first sheet for the top level and subsequent sheets for pairings of

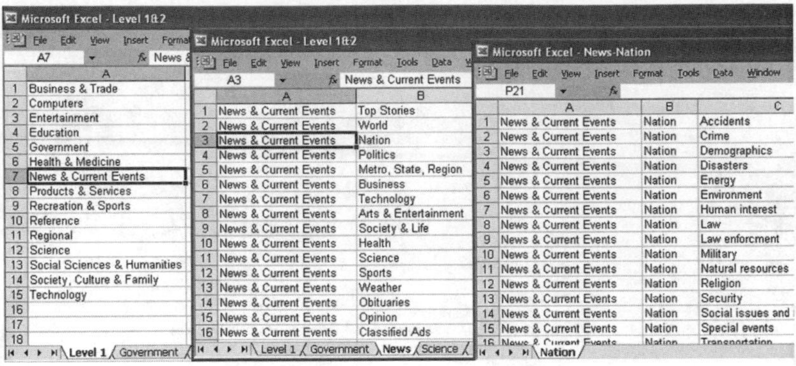

Figure 5.2 Using multiple Excel files to create a three-level taxonomy

the top- and second-level terms. A second, separate Excel work-book file pairs the second-level terms with third-level terms in its first sheet, and with third- and fourth-level terms in subsequent sheets. Figure 5.2 illustrates the usage of two workbook files, with two sheets in the first and one in the second, to represent a hierarchy that is three levels deep.

Utilizing this method, you can create a very simple taxonomy that is lacking nonpreferred terms, associative relationships, poly-hierarchies, scope notes, term attributes, etc. Either you accept that, or it is time to import your Excel-created CSV file into a taxonomy or thesaurus software program for further enhancements.

Mind Mapping, Concept Modeling, and Ontology Software

To capture more than just hierarchical relationships and include other relationships, categories, attributes, and so on, some taxonomists are now using mind mapping and other concept modeling software. A mind map is a diagram, used for brainstorming, visual thinking, or problem solving, that illustrates ideas, concepts, actions, and/or tasks and how they interrelate. Similar to mind maps and mind mapping software are concept maps and concept mapping software. There is not much distinction between the two, except that concepts maps are not necessarily as complex as mind maps. Concept maps are not as simple as flowcharts, however.

While hand-drawn mind maps have been in use for a long time, only recently have advanced graphics technologies enabled the development of mind mapping software. Now there are more than two dozen commercial and free and open source mind mapping software tools for Windows and Macintosh and a few for Linux [3] Mind mapping software that taxonomists have used includes free tools such as XMind (www.xmind.net), FreeMind from SourceForge (freemind.sourceforge.net/wiki/index.php/Main_Page), and Cmap from the Florida Institute for Human & Machine Cognition (cmap.ihmc.us) and commercial software TheBrain from TheBrain Technologies LP (www.thebrain.com), MindManager from Mindjet (www.mindjet.com), and VisiMap from Coco Systems Ltd. (www.visimap.com).[4] Depending on the tool, you can create polyhierarchical diagrams or different relationship types in mind maps, and usually you can easily move concepts and branches. It may or may not be possible to export the output. Figure 5.3 is a screenshot of a mind map in FreeMind.

Using mind mapping or other concept modeling software is not an efficient or practical way to develop or manage a large taxonomy. Mind maps can become unwieldy and get too large to print. Nevertheless, visually minded taxonomists might find them a desirable way to put down and organize their initial ideas for a taxonomy. Other practical applications of mind mapping software are brainstorming taxonomy structures in a group or team setting and presenting a proposed taxonomy to an audience, especially at the early point in its creation, to sell the idea of the taxonomy to stakeholders.

Ontology editing software, on the other hand, often both supports graphic representations of concept interrelationships and provides a means of managing a large number of concepts, along with their categories or attributes. Software for designing ontologies

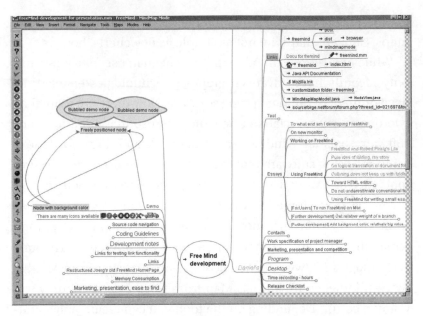

Figure 5.3 Mind map display in FreeMind (Source:
en.wikipedia.org/wiki/File:Freemind-0.9x_Screenshoot.png)

includes TopBraid Composer from TopQuadrant (www.top
quadrant.com) and the freeware Protégé (protege.stanford.edu).
Compared with mind mapping software, ontology editing software
has a steeper learning curve, as it can have rather complex capabilities. Also, you cannot as quickly and easily generate graphic
representations of taxonomies in ontology editors. If the goal is to
quickly get an initial graphic sketch of a budding taxonomy or to
have a nice graphic representation of the start of a taxonomy for a
presentation, then mind mapping software is more practical than
ontology editors. Ontology editors, on the other hand, are compli-
ant with standards for the semantic web, so they are a good option
for generating web-based ontologies.

Thesaurus Software

When it comes to building and managing a taxonomy, dedicated taxonomy/thesaurus management software should be the preferred choice. Whether what you are creating is called a taxonomy, a thesaurus, or a controlled vocabulary, and whether the emphasis is on design and creation or management, the same kind of software is generally used. We will refer to all such full-featured software simply as thesaurus software. If a taxonomy is purely hierarchical and does not utilize related-term relationships, then the related-term feature of the software is simply not used. One important characteristic to consider in choosing software for building classification systems is whether it supports established standards. Our interest here is in software that supports thesaurus standards (namely ANSI/NISO Z39.19 or ISO 2788), but there are other standards. For example, records management standards include the business activity classification schemes described in ISO 15489. While you could build a simple hierarchical taxonomy in almost any "classification" tool, a thesaurus tool that meets the criteria listed in the following paragraphs is a wiser choice to support future taxonomy enhancements or the importing, exporting, or merging of your taxonomy with others from other sources. The ANSI/NISO Z39.19 standard also provides detailed thesaurus software requirements in its final chapter, and anyone developing software for thesaurus management should consult the standards.

Thesaurus Software Characteristics

The basic requirement of thesaurus software is to maintain terms, their associated relationships, and other attributes. As we have seen, the relationships are reciprocal between pairs of terms. By using thesaurus software, you create or edit the relationship in only one place. If you decide to rename or delete a term, the change will be reflected in all of the relationships of the term. Features for adding optional scope notes and user-defined classification categories are also standard in thesaurus software. In addition to meeting these requirements, most thesaurus software includes the following features: merging and subsuming terms, designating candidate and approved terms, indicating term creation date and modification date, permitting multiple hierarchies (polyhierarchies), disallowing illegal relationships (e.g., circular relationships), generating reports in different displays, and exporting taxonomies in platform-neutral file formats (namely XML) for use in other systems. When one is building a taxonomy, speed and ease are important. Therefore, most software permits adding successive relationships of the same type (nonpreferred terms, narrower terms, or broader terms) simply by hitting the enter key. You should consider the following characteristics when comparing various thesaurus software packages.

Taxonomy Display

Just as there are various formats to display a taxonomy or thesaurus to end users (described in Chapter 9) or to indexers, there are different display options in the user interface for the taxonomist who is editing the taxonomy. Typically thesaurus software provides the option of both alphabetical and hierarchical display views that the taxonomist may switch between, such as by using tabs. The alphabetical display may also have the option to include or exclude nonpreferred terms.

Related to how the software displays the taxonomy is how the software organizes a complex taxonomy. Additional types of displays may be available in a reporting feature. Thesaurus software products also differ in whether they create single isolated thesaurus files or multiple named hierarchies that can be linked to each other.

Term Display and Editing

Each taxonomy term has relationships and other details that can be individually displayed and edited. The various thesaurus software products differ in how term details are displayed, how the editing is done, and what additional term attributes are present. The process of creating terms and their relationships may be performed through various means: main menu selections, context menu selections, shortcut key combinations, other keyboard commands, toolbar buttons, and mouse drag and drop. Features that may or may not be present include single-step merging/subsuming terms, single-step moving of a branch (a term and all its narrower terms), and drag-and-drop adding of relationships.

Rules Enforcement

A thesaurus should follow the guidelines spelled out in Chapter 4 on term relationships. While it takes human thought to create relationships correctly, certain rules in the software can help, for example, by not permitting the following:

- Terms that are related to themselves
- Pairs of terms that have more than one kind of relationship between them (both associative and hierarchical, both equivalence and hierarchical, or both equivalence and associative)
- Terms that have a broader term that is narrower to a narrower term of the first term (circular references)
- Terms that are duplicates within the same hierarchy or category

It should be possible to identify for further scrutiny terms that lack any hierarchical or associative relationships with other terms (orphan terms). Actually permitting orphan terms is up to the policy of the specific taxonomy. Software controls, though not necessarily "rules," may also be desired in additional areas, such as whether to allow multiple *use* references.

Taxonomy Searching

Taxonomy search and navigation are important, not only for the end user of the implemented taxonomy, but also for the creator of the taxonomy, who needs to know, for example, whether a given term already exists. You need the capability to search for terms in order to find appropriate terms with which to make relationships, to avoid inadvertently duplicating concepts, to make global changes on terms if a style policy changes, etc. Different software tools vary in their list of options for searching.

Customization of Relationships and Attributes

The ability to define and customize relationships, types of notes, and categories of terms is important in making a thesaurus software product versatile and extensible. Although standard thesaurus relationships are limited to broader/narrower term, related term, and use/used for, you might also wish to create specific user-defined relationships, as described in the final section of Chapter 4. Thesaurus software varies in the degree to which it supports customizing relationships based on the three basic relationships (hierarchical, associative, and equivalent).

One of the benefits of thesaurus software, with is based on database management software, is that additional information can be assigned and stored with each term as a database record. A scope note is the most typical kind of such additional information, but there could be other kinds of notes as well, such as standardized industry codes for industry terms or birth/death dates for person name terms. Categories are often used in taxonomies to classify terms for end use, by source, or for any other purpose that you may have. Categorizing terms makes it easier to batch edit them and to designate terms for certain end-use search interface characteristics. Categories are explained in greater detail in Chapter 8.

Importing, Exporting, and Reports

In addition to building a taxonomy from scratch (i.e., manually typing in each term), you may want to take advantage of external lists of terms to import and incorporate into the taxonomy. Most often, these might be lists of names, organizations, or places, but they could also be legacy taxonomies, along with their relationships, for incorporation into a new system. Thus, the ability to import or batch load data is an important feature of a thesaurus software package.

Exporting the taxonomy into formats that can then be imported into other systems is crucial for thesaurus software. A taxonomy is not just something to look at but is to be used in the indexing/tagging of files, documents, or webpages, and then by a final end user for search and retrieval of those documents and pages, often through one or more other software systems.

You will want software that can generate interim reports of various kinds to aid in the task of building the taxonomy. These could include lists of candidate terms, deleted terms, or orphan terms, in addition to taxonomy reports that include only certain specific data or relationships for each term. Occasionally a taxonomy is published for third-party use, in which case various outputs, including a printed document, might be desirable. These outputs are usually based on options in the report feature. Chapter 9 describes in detail the various kinds of taxonomy output displays.

Checklist for Comparing Features

The thesaurus software products mentioned in this chapter all have the characteristics just described, but they differ in some areas. Following is a list of variable features you may want to consider when comparing products:

- Interface design and ease of use
- Speed (limited mouse clicks) in adding repeated terms and relationships
- Single-step creation of new terms and relationships
- Single-step branch (term and narrower terms) moving
- Drag and drop relationship adding
- User-defined relationships of all three types
- Multiple taxonomy display options in the user interface
- User-defined term notes
- User-defined term attributes
- Spell checking
- Import of formats
- Export of formats
- Support for bilingual or multilingual taxonomies (equivalent preferred terms in more than one language; different character set displays)

Your specific user preferences and the nature of the taxonomy project will ultimately determine which software product you should choose.

Thesaurus Software Resources

No complete or authoritative list of thesaurus software products exists, for various reasons, including the blurred definitions of *taxonomy* and *thesaurus*, the integration of thesaurus management capabilities into software with wider applications, the presence of both general and vertical market software, and the regionalism of smaller vendors in Europe and other parts of the world. Most significantly, thesaurus software alone does not provide a solution to any information management and retrieval problem, since taxonomy creation skills and expertise are also required. Consequently, even though it is growing, the market for such specialized software is relatively limited. Thus, industry analysts do not see the need to follow the thesaurus software industry specifically as compared to more automated solutions, such as enterprise search and auto-categorization.

To complicate matters further, *taxonomy software* is a vague notion. Some auto-categorization or auto-classification software systems have gone further to develop technology for the automatic generation of simple taxonomies. Thus, taxonomy software today can include these automatic taxonomy creation systems and not just software to aid the human creation and editing of taxonomies. In fact, auto-categorization or auto-classification tools, whether they can actually generate taxonomies or merely make use of them, are now also included within the broader category of taxonomy software. The realm of taxonomy software may also extend to vendors of software that utilize text analytics or entity extraction to suggest terms. To further complicate matters, thesaurus software is not always called that. Some vendors prefer the name *business semantics management software.*[5] If the software supports customized relationships, then it might be called ontology software.

There is, however, some software vendor information maintained by individuals or on a voluntary basis. The independent consultant Leonard D. Will currently provides the most comprehensive list of thesaurus software on the website of his business Willpower Information (www.willpowerinfo.co.uk/thessoft.htm), which lists more than 30 tools, including freeware, single-user, and large-scale systems. The project was begun in the mid-1990s, and unfortunately at this writing, most information on the page was more than a year old. Although Will has added new information, older vendors that have gone out of business remain on the list. In addition, there are several European software vendors with websites not in English. The Taxonomy Community of Practice wiki also provides a listing of what it calls taxonomy software (taxocop. wikispaces.com/TaxoTools). This list includes both thesaurus software and auto-categorization tools. Some software offers both taxonomy-creation and content-indexing features. Another listing of taxonomy software is provided by TaxoTips (www.taxotips.com/ resources/tools), a voluntary information service site maintained by content management industry analyst Bob Doyle. This listing, however, includes any software somehow related to taxonomies, including text analytics, and is not limited to thesaurus software. It is also not kept up to date.

Single-User Desktop Thesaurus Software

Offerings in commercial single-user desktop thesaurus software are somewhat limited. However, because they are the most accessible and affordable type of software for creating taxonomies, they should be the first tools for consideration by accidental taxonomists. This section looks at the leading Windows tool MultiTes and the leading Macintosh tool Cognatrix. Other PC software that has been evaluated in previous literature,[6] WebChoir's TCS-10 and Term Tree, are no longer on the market. WebChoir Inc. appears to have gone out of business, and Term Tree's vendor Active Classification Solutions (www.acs121.com) is now promoting its "classification" software One-2-One instead. One-2-One has thesaurus-creation capabilities but does not have all the features of Term Tree. According to the vendor, however, the company is concentrating more on the records management market.[7] Additional products exist in other language markets in Europe and Latin America. Both MultiTes and Cognatrix meet the expected requirements described in the earlier section, Thesaurus Software Characteristics, and free trials of both are available, along with tutorials or manuals.

MultiTes Pro

MultiTes Pro (www.multites.com), which runs on Windows, is the primary product of Multisystems, based in Miami, Florida. It is the most popular single-user thesaurus software package, due to the fact that it has been around the longest (since 1983), is the least expensive, and is from the United States. The 2009 price was $295 for a single user (there are pricings for five and 10 users, and an enterprise deployment costs $3950).

In MultiTes, the taxonomy list takes up the entire window width, so viewing or editing a term's details involves clicking on the desired term and opening a pop-up window rather than using a screen pane/area (see Figure 5.4).

MultiTes's primary strength as a single-user tool is its full support for user-defined relationships, term notes, and term categories. Its

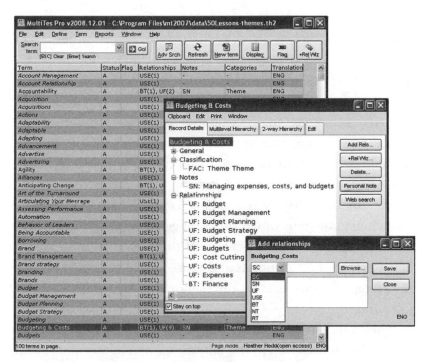

Figure 5.4 MultiTes taxonomy display with selected term details

major drawbacks are the need to generate a report in order to see a hierarchical view, the inability to subsume or merge terms in a single step, and the lack of spell-checker capability. MultiTes creates single taxonomy files, and you cannot create relationships across files.

MultiTes accepts imported data as text only, either in a text file or pasted to a clipboard. The data must follow a specific format and cannot use tags. Export formats are ANSI text, HTML, XML, and CSV delimited, or an output directly to the printer. Two add-on products for MultiTes facilitate web and enterprise deployment. MultiTes WDK (Web Deployment Kit) enables publishing of a live MultiTes taxonomy on the internet/intranet. MultiTes EDK (Enterprise Deployment Kit) consists of a set of tools for transferring and publishing thesaurus data onto corporate servers.

Cognatrix

Cognatrix (www.cognatrix.com), the primary product of LGOSystems Pty. Ltd. (Australia), appears to be the only dedicated Macintosh application for thesaurus construction. Cognatrix is priced at US$499 (as of 2009), or $199 for an "education" version limited to 500 terms. An importer tool and a search tool are available as free add-on applications. Cognatrix stores all information about thesaurus terms and their relationships in a property list in XML format, rather than in SQL databases.

The Cognatrix display is a split screen, showing a view of the taxonomy at the top (which can be toggled between hierarchical tree and alphabetical list views) and the individual term details below (Figure 5.5). Nonpreferred terms are interspersed among the preferred terms, even in the hierarchical view, with a *V* label (for *variant*).

When a term is selected and highlighted in the tree or list view, its details are displayed in the bottom portion of the split screen interface. Requiring that a pair of terms be selected first before a

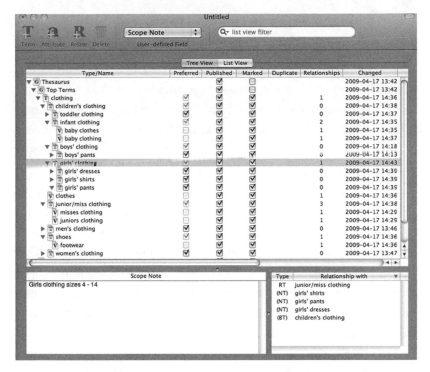

Figure 5.5 Cognatrix display of its tree view and term details

relationship is created ensures that only valid relationships are created. Cognatrix supports user-defined notes, categories, and groups, but not user-defined relationships, although it does provide more specific kinds of equivalence relationships.

Cognatrix supports importing from plain text with tab separations and, with the CognatrixImporter add-on, can import from various XML schemas: Cognatrix, MultiTes, Term Tree, and Zthes. Cognatrix supports exporting to XML and HTML formats. When exporting to XML, users have three options for XML schemas: Cognatrix, Zthes, and MultiTes. You can also print reports directly to a printer, with the option to restrict the number of hierarchical levels to be printed.

Large-Scale Thesaurus Systems

Commercially available enterprise-level thesaurus management systems have been around only since the late 1990s. These are either client-server systems or web-based systems, which allow simultaneous work by multiple users, any number of which can be remote. Thus, even if you do not purchase such software, if you work as a taxonomy consultant, you could end up using such software as a remote contractor. There are also various levels of access privilege, ranging from full administrator, taxonomy-level administrator, and taxonomy editor to read-only access. Certain configuration functions, such as customizing relationships, can be performed only in the administrative area or module. Companion software modules, add-ons, and custom integration allow these thesaurus management systems to be integrated with indexing systems and end-user search systems. These software systems are often supported with onsite custom integration and training services.

Free trials for most of these commercial systems require a prospective customer request rather than a simple download from the website. Pricing varies but can be in the thousands or tens of thousands of dollars and is based on the number of servers, numbers of users or seats, degree of support, installation and configuration services, etc. Therefore, before making a purchase, you must carefully evaluate how a software system and any additional modules might best suit your organization's needs.

Dedicated large-scale thesaurus management systems that are not limited to a vertical market include the following: Data Harmony, Synaptica, Wordmap, SchemaLogic Enterprise Suite, Smartlogic Semaphore, STAR/Thesaurus, SourtronTHESAURUS, Mondeca ITM T3, and TheMa. Each of these systems includes all the capabilities described in the earlier section, Thesaurus Software Characteristics, unless noted otherwise. The short descriptions that follow are not meant to be complete lists of features. Individual software tools may also share features that are highlighted in the description of other tools. Software in which thesaurus management is integrated within a product that has other nonthesaurus capabilities is addressed in a later section.

Data Harmony Thesaurus Master

Data Harmony Thesaurus Master (www.dataharmony.com) has been commercially available from Access Innovations (Albuquerque, New Mexico) since 1998. Prior to that, the software had been developed and used only in-house for the indexing and taxonomy services that the company has been providing since 1978. The software is multi-platform Java-based (used on Windows, Mac, Solaris, and Linux). Client software allows remote access, but a single-user desktop version is also available. Another Data Harmony product is M.A.I. (Machine Aided Indexer), a partner tool for categorization described in Chapter 7. Thesaurus Master and M.A.I. are available as an integrated product called MAIstro, and additional software extensions are also available.

Some of Thesaurus Master's additional features include support for all standard thesaurus display types as view options; support for "facet indicators" (node labels), user-defined notes fields, and additional user-defined relationships based on the equivalence and associative (but not hierarchical) relationship types; the option to make all sibling terms automatically related terms to each other; and a term rules editor for use with machine-aided indexing. The administrative module provides for password-governed security and nine levels of user access. Import formats include text, Word documents, XML, CSV, and MS Excel as tab delimited. Export formats include XML, HTML, OWL, SKOS, Zthes, MARC (concise or expanded), and tab delimited. Export options also allow for various display types, such as hierarchical, permuted, and alphabetical flat format. Thesaurus Master's output can be integrated with search systems for a navigable tree display linking to indexed content, and there are application programming interfaces (APIs) and ready-made connectors to several established software systems.

Synaptica

Synapse, the Knowledge Link Corp., based in Denver, Colorado, developed Synaptica (www.synaptica.com) and first made it commercially available in 1999. Dow Jones Factiva acquired the company in 2005 and later made the product part of the Client Solutions division of Dow Jones. In 2009, it was spun off as an independent company, Synaptica LLC, still in the Denver area. Synaptica is a web-services-enabled application accessible via a web browser. Licenses are available in annual or perpetual forms based on the number of users and number of vocabularies to be managed. Training services are usually an additional part of a customer package. A separate indexing module, IMS (Indexing Management System), is also available.

Synaptica features include a global term and relationships editor that can create a list of terms to edit; a side-by-side editing view; a drag-and-drop capability; a term subsume function; the ability to assign relationship weights (an added level of complexity more suited for ontologies than most taxonomies); custom category assignment; thesaurus replication/versioning; an independent search and browse utility for non-taxonomy editors; and up to 12 gradations of permission levels, and user-defined relationships at the administrative level. Import formats are CSV, text, Excel, XML (including schemas of Zthes, RDF, SKOS, and OWL). Export formats are CSV, HTML, Word, Excel, and XML (including schemas of Zthes, RDF, SKOS, and OWL). Synaptica also offers a SharePoint connector.

Wordmap

Wordmap (www.wordmap.com) was launched in 1998 by the U.K. company of the same name, and in 2007 the taxonomy consultancy Earley & Associates (Concord, Massachusetts) acquired

Wordmap Inc. as a wholly owned subsidiary. Wordmap now comprises a suite of products that can be purchased separately or integrated together. The enterprise taxonomy management system, Wordmap Designer (also known as Wordmap Taxonomy Management System), is the base product for creating, managing, and distributing taxonomies and thesauri. Add-on products include Wordmap Navigator (for end-user searching/browsing), Content Author (for manual indexing), and Intelligent Text Classifier (for automated indexing). Wordmap Designer is an Oracle application with a Java-based browser user interface. Since Wordmap Designer uses Oracle 10+ as its repository, a separate Oracle license is a prerequisite.

One of the unusual aspects of Wordmap is its nomenclature, which includes the following:

Wordset = node, object
Lead word = preferred term
Members = nonpreferred terms
Physical relationships = hierarchical (BT/NT) relationships
Nonphysical relationships = associative (RT) relationships

Wordmap Designer's features include the ability to display two taxonomies side by side with drag and drop, support for creating customized attributes and relationships (and the ability to turn on or off the relationship name display), and the ability to set user access/privileges at various levels, including the individual node level. Wordmap also has a feature for mapping different taxonomies to each other, which could be used, for example, in creating a unified enterprise taxonomy. Import/export formats include CSV, Excel, and XML, with the added import format of text. In addition, Wordmap offers connectors for third-party systems, for exporting taxonomies formatted for use with Endeca search software, and for integrating taxonomies with Microsoft SharePoint

Server. Finally, custom direct application access to Wordmap taxonomies is available through a Java API.

SchemaLogic Enterprise Suite

SchemaLogic (www.schemalogic.com) of Kirkland, Washington, calls itself a provider of "metadata management software" for otherwise unstructured content. Its main product, SchemaLogic Enterprise Suite (SES), in addition to supporting taxonomy management according to ANSI/NISO Z.39.19 guidelines, provides broader structural metadata support. Product literature refers to a collection of taxonomies and their categories as a "semantic standard." Taxonomy management in this software is based on objects, which include vocabularies, vocabulary views, content classes, terms, term relationships, and elements. Thus, term categories and term attributes are emphasized in this product. You can also create custom relationships between terms, based on the hierarchical, associative, and equivalence types. There are several permissions levels, and these permissions can be assigned to vocabularies, nodes in vocabularies, or individual terms. You can create terms manually one by one, bulk load new terms through the Term Manager feature, or import taxonomies in CSV or XML formats.

Through connectors, SES can be integrated with Microsoft SharePoint and EMC Documentum and with the search system FAST ESP. Included in SES is the SchemaLogic Classification Module, which provides support for various third-party automated indexing capabilities discussed in Chapter 7. According to taxonomy consultant Wendi Pohs, "SchemaLogic's differentiators are its built-in workflow functionality, the fact that you can easily build a content-rich taxonomy with its named relationship types, and its very robust API that developers can use for integration."[8]

Smartlogic Semaphore Ontology Manager

Semaphore is a suite of products from the London company Smartlogic Semaphore Ltd. (www.smartlogic.com). Ontology

Manager can be licensed and used separately or integrated with the rest of the suite. The public company Smartlogic has a varied and interesting history of different names, owners, predecessor companies, and acquisitions that were in the field of information service, not just software products. At one point, a predecessor company, MAID, was the owner of the online information service Dialog. Now Smartlogic is purely a software vendor, and the Semaphore suite is its only product. Semaphore can run on Windows and Linux and either in a client-server configuration or as a fully hosted solution, but it is currently not web-based.

The Ontology Manager (Figure 5.6), despite its name, is a full-featured thesaurus software. It supports the ISO 2788 thesaurus standard, the international version of ANSI/NISO Z39.19 (which is essentially the same), so it is completely appropriate for any

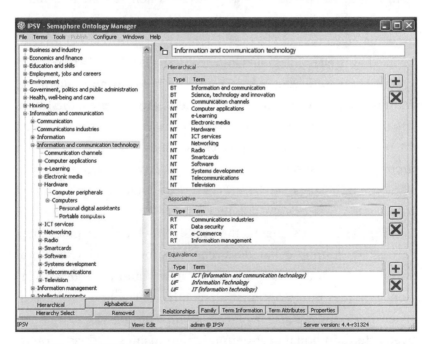

Figure 5.6 Semaphore Ontology Manager's split-screen display, with the browsable taxonomy in the left pane and selected editable term details (term record) in the right pane

taxonomy or thesaurus. Ontology Manager can import or export files in CSV, XML, Zthes, SQL databases, and MultiTes files.

Additional related products are the Classification Server, which uses rules generated by Ontology Manager to automatically classify information, and the Ontology Service, which provides a navigation system based on the semantic relationships created in Ontology Manager. In addition there are connectors available for Google Search Appliance, Microsoft SharePoint, and FAST ESP.

STAR/Thesaurus

Cuadra Associates, Inc. (www.cuadra.com), headquartered in Los Angeles, California, develops and sells a lesser known but comparable client-server thesaurus management system, STAR/Thesaurus. The company's STAR product family provides systems for archives management, collections management, knowledge management, digital asset management, and records management. STAR/Thesaurus can be used by itself or integrated into any of these other STAR software systems to provide vocabulary control for indexing and cataloging. Although the STAR product line has been around since the 1980s, the thesaurus software has been on the market only since the late 1990s. Cuadra's market emphasis has been libraries, museums, archives, associations and societies, government agencies, and database publishers, but STAR/Thesaurus could certainly be used in any enterprise or application.

STAR/Thesaurus meets the ANSI/NISO Z39.19 guidelines through its support of standard relationships and enforcement of various rules. It also supports *used for and* and *used for or* relationships and offers optional alternative designations of *See* in place of *use* and *See also* in place of *related term*. It does not, however, offer additional user-defined relationships. It does support unlimited user-defined notes and categories. STAR/Thesaurus can generate numerous kinds of output reports, including rotated display, hierarchical, and statistical reports. Import/export format options are ASCII text and CSV, but not XML.

SoutronTHESAURUS

Corporate library management software vendor Soutron Ltd. offers a thesaurus software product, SoutronTHESAURUS (www.soutron.com/soutronthesaurus.html), which is available in a stand-alone version or integrated with SoutronGLOBAL or SoutronSOLO library management systems. Like Synaptica, it is web-based and thus supports an unlimited number of remote users. A U.K. company, Soutron has entered the U.S. market through a partnership with Inmagic Inc., a vendor of social knowledge management and information management software. SoutronGlobal thus also integrates with Inmagic Presto.

SoutronTHESAURUS supports user-defined relationships (in addition to the standard relationship types), multilingual thesauri (including non-Western character sets), and the ability to merge terms. Multiple related taxonomies can be maintained within a single domain. Thesauri can be imported from XML and exported to XML or CSV.

Mondeca ITM T3

There are also thesaurus management products developed in non-English-speaking countries, some of which offer English-language versions and support. If you are interested in creating multilingual taxonomies while also utilizing different language interfaces in the languages supported, then these products might be worth considering. Since some of these are web-based, you could have taxonomists working on the same project in multiple countries.

Mondeca ITM T3 (www.mondeca.com), which stands for Intelligent Topic Manager: Thesaurus, Taxonomies, Terminologies, is a relatively new product, made available in 2008 by Mondeca S.A., located in Paris. The thesaurus software is based on Mondeca's existing Intelligent Topic Manager semantic software platform. Other Intelligent Topic Manager products are designed for knowledge management, semantic portals, and ecatalog publishing.

ITM T3 conforms to both SKOS vocabularies and OWL-standard ontologies (described in Chapter 10), so in addition to supporting the creation of taxonomies, it enables the creation of true ontologies. As a web-based collaborative application, it is priced on a per server basis. Features includes connectors to text mining tools, classification tools, and search engines; ability to import and export thesauri in XML, RDF, and SKOS; and the management of multilingual thesauri in Latin, Cyrillic, Arabic, and Chinese scripts.

TheMa

Thesaurus Manager, or TheMa for short (www.triga-services.de), from TRIGA IT-Systeme + Grafik GmbH of Germany, also has an English-language version and support. As the company name implies, the vendor was originally a graphics design company, founded in 1986, that moved into IT consulting. TheMa, a web-accessed Java-based system for Oracle, is its only product. In consulting, the company specializes in archiving and planning systems, which mostly are operated within customers' intranets. An additional custom edition of TheMa enables integration into a customer's system environment, such as a web content management system.

TheMa supports standard thesaurus relationships, with the addition of *instance*, *generic*, and *partitive* types of hierarchical relationships. Scope notes, term translations, and term information fields are also supported. Additional features include multiple user privileges, thesaurus search, statistics reporting, and importing/exporting as XML or native Oracle databases. The software interface is bilingual for English and German, but you can create term translations in additional languages.

Free and Open Source Software

There are several free and open source offerings of thesaurus software. In addition to being free, these applications tend to have the advantage of being able to run on multiple platforms, not just Windows, and can be used by a single user. While they may not have all the features of commercial software, they are worth considering for long-term experimentation (with no time limit as in commercial demo software) or for volunteer, nonprofit, or low-budget projects. The editing features tend to be a little less standard and thus less intuitive, and so it may take a little longer to get your thesaurus up and running.

One crucial basic feature that free software may lack is enforcement of valid relationships between terms, allowing, for example, circular and multiple simultaneous relationships. Freeware tools that, at the time of this writing, come up short in this area include Amicus Thesaurus (www.amicuscom.com/thesaurus.htm), web-based TemaTres (www.r020.com.ar/tematres/index.en.html), and ThManager (thmanager.sourceforge.net), so they are not included in the following descriptions.

TheW32 and TheW for Java

TheW is free thesaurus software that (despite its interface shortcomings) does enforce rules of relationships between terms. It is one of several freeware tools developed by Timothy Craven, professor of Information and Media Studies at the University of Western Ontario, Canada (publish.uwo.ca/~craven/freeware. htm). Craven originally developed his software tools in the areas of indexing and abstracting as academic research projects and then provided them to his students for instructional purposes. He has subsequently made all his software tools available to the public as freeware and as of 2009 was still making minor updates to them. TheW is available in two versions, TheW32 for 32-bit Windows and

TheW open source for Java, which can run on any platform that has the Java Runtime Environment.

TheW displays the thesaurus as an alphabetical list only, with nonpreferred terms included. Lacking graphical enhancements, the display does not distinguish nonpreferred terms in any way; for example, they are not italicized. Like most of the commercial products, TheW features a split screen, but it is reversed in comparison with all the others: The thesaurus list is the in the right-hand pane, and the term details are in the left-hand pane. Terms display in all caps only, which is a significant drawback. The method of creating terms and their relationships in TheW is not as efficient as in the commercial tools, but the software is functional. Features include user-defined relationships, summary statistics, and the ability to export to text, XML, or JavaScript.

TheW can be integrated with other software tools created by Tim Craven, including XRefHT, designed for manually indexing webpages to create a site A–Z index. A thesaurus created and stored in TheW can be accessed and used by XRefHT as a source of controlled index terms, along with their cross-references.

Protégé Ontology Editor

Protégé (protege.stanford.edu) is actually an open-source ontology editor, not a thesaurus management program, but it is mentioned here because it is sometimes used by taxonomists and is reasonably well known in the field. There are workshops, conferences, training, and several discussion groups supporting the Protégé user community. Protégé was developed by the Stanford Center for Biomedical Informatics Research at the Stanford University School of Medicine in the early 1990s and is most often used by scholars to create scientific ontologies. It is available for Windows, Mac OS X, IBM AIX, Sun Solaris, HP-UX, and any other UNIX or Java-enabled platforms.

In the Protégé-Frames editor, there is a hierarchical/faceted display in the left pane and editable term details in the right pane. Terms are called classes. The Protégé platform supports two main ways of modeling ontologies:

1. The Protégé-Frames editor, which enables users to build ontologies that are frame-based, in accordance with the Open Knowledge Base Connectivity protocol (OKBC)

2. The Protégé-OWL editor, which enables users to build ontologies for the semantic web in the W3C's Web Ontology Language (OWL)

As an ontology editor (not a thesaurus editor), one of the main drawbacks of Protégé is that it does not have a standard feature for the equivalence relationship. Some taxonomists have developed work-arounds, though, and thus have successfully implemented nonpreferred terms in Protégé-developed thesauri, but it takes extra effort to learn and implement such methods. Taxonomists have claimed Protégé to be powerful, but it use is not necessarily user-friendly or intuitive.[9] An SKOS editor plug-in for Protégé 4 (code.google.com/p/skoseditor), however, facilitates to the creation of standard thesauri.

Besides Protégé, other free ontology software includes SWOOP and Knoodl, but there is a relative lack of information available on their successful use in creating taxonomies

Other Software With Taxonomy Management Components

Since taxonomies are used in combination with certain other functions—indexing, document management, or search—software systems designed for these other purposes may also include a taxonomy management component or module. Taxonomy management is sometimes, but not always, a feature of the following:

- Metadata or cataloging software, especially for archives and libraries

- Content management and document management systems

- Records management software

- Automatic indexing and enterprise search and discovery software

The taxonomy management features of such systems, however, may not comply with the standards. So, the eventual usefulness of the taxonomy in a final application may be limited.

Library Management Software

Library management software may include thesaurus management components, although this is often not the case since libraries and archives typically utilize existing controlled vocabularies or taxonomies (such as Library of Congress Subject Headings, Library of Congress Thesaurus for Graphic Materials, or the Getty Thesauri). As mentioned previously, SoutronGLOBAL offers a product that integrates library management and thesaurus management capabilities. Adlib Information Systems (www.adlib soft.com) is another library systems vendor whose software contains a thesaurus feature. Each of its products, Adlib Archive, Adlib Library, and Adlib Museums, has the added feature for creating and editing thesauri, which the software can then use for cataloging archive documents, library materials, or museum objects. The thesaurus management feature of Adlib supports hierarchical, associative, and equivalence relationships and also scope notes.

Content Management Systems

Content management systems (CMS), a category that includes enterprise content management, web content management, and document/records management software, are a logical place for integrating taxonomies. Indeed, some CMS products do claim to have "taxonomy" features, but they may be rather rudimentary tagging systems. According to content management and taxonomy consultant Lynda Moulton, "It is not common for any content management systems to be tightly integrated with advanced thesaurus management capabilities. Exceptions would be solutions from two vendors that have strong roots in technology for corporate and special libraries, Access Innovations (Data Harmony) and Open Text, which acquired the BASIS TechLib system over 10 years ago."[10] Open Text Collections Server Webtop Thesaurus Manager (www.opentext.com) does in fact support ANSI/NISO Z39.19 relationships (hierarchical, associative, and equivalence), along with scope notes for terms.

As with library systems, though, it is more common to import taxonomies into a CMS than to create them within such systems. In general, a CMS should be thought of, not as a system for building and management taxonomies, but rather as an application in which a taxonomy can, and perhaps should, be implemented. Updating and managing an imported taxonomy within a CMS can become an issue, though.

Records Management Software

Electronic records management software, which can be considered a form of a CMS, is an area with more potential for thesaurus management features. Records managers, the users of such software, tend to have a library and information science background and thus may already have a familiarity with taxonomies. Furthermore, thesaurus capabilities are included in government-recommended guidelines for records management software. Records management is important not only in the financial and legal industries but also for government agencies. The National Archives and Records Administration has endorsed the 2002 and 2007 editions of the U.S. Department of Defense records management application (RMA) standard (DoD 5015.2 STD). Adherence to the standard is required for all defense agencies and strongly encouraged for all other federal agencies. Among the nonmandatory features, Section C6.2.9 Retrieval Assistance states, "RMAs should have additional search and retrieval features, such as full text search, to assist the user in locating records. The search utility should include the capability to create, modify, or import additional thesauri."[11] British and Australian national standards for records management software have similar specifications.

An example of records management software with significant thesaurus management capabilities (and which appears on lists of taxonomy software) is the product called a.k.a., which stands for "also known as," from Synercon Management Consulting (www. a-k-a.com.au) of Australia. The a.k.a. software package has two components: 1) records classification—for creating and managing classification schemes in accordance with both the business activity classifications standard of ISO 15489 and the thesaurus standard of ISO 2788, and 2) disposition management—for creating retention and disposal schedules in accordance with the DIRKS (Designing and Implementing Records Keeping System) methodology, also a part of ISO 15489. Yet even within the records classification component, the business activity classification features are more prominent than the standard thesauri features.

Another Australian vendor, Active Classification Solutions (www.acs121.com), sells One-2-One, which is essentially Windows-based thesaurus software with additional features to support records management. It includes disposal maintenance features and connectors to integrate with electronic documents and records management systems, including Trim Context, Objective, OpenText eDocs, and Termwise.

Automated Indexing and Search Software

Like content management systems, automatic indexing/auto-categorization/enterprise search software may or may not have taxonomy support. Even when it does, it rarely includes full-featured thesaurus management capabilities. As the emphasis in these systems is on automated information retrieval, their components for taxonomy creation and management also tend to be automated or minimally manual, although there are a few exceptions. Chapter 7 covers automated indexing software in more detail.

Integrated Systems Conclusions

With the exception of Data Harmony and SchemaLogic, the technology and features in the various integrated software systems discussed here are focused, not on taxonomy creation, but rather on one of the other areas of information management, search and discovery, automated indexing, records management, or web publishing. Thus the capabilities and ease of use of the taxonomy management features are generally inferior to those of dedicated thesaurus software and may vary greatly from one product to another since they are competing primarily in other areas. You should consider these other capabilities carefully with respect to your organization's requirements. Otherwise, you may be paying for features that you don't need or missing features that you do need or will need as your taxonomy and its application grow. Finally, unlike the sector of dedicated thesaurus software discussed in detail in this chapter, the industry of auto-categorization and content management software is less mature and more dynamic and therefore subject to more changes in vendors and product offerings.

Endnotes

1. Lynda Moulton, email to author, October 28, 2009.
2. Darin Stewart, *Building Enterprise Taxonomies* (Portland, OR: Mokita Press, 2008), 137.
3. "List of Mind Mapping Software," Wikipedia, en.wikipedia.org/wiki/Mind_mapping_software (accessed May 11, 2009), and dMoz,

www.dmoz.org/Reference/Knowledge_Management/Knowledge_
Creation/Mind_Mapping/Software (accessed May 11, 2009).

4. Postings to Taxonomy Community of Practice discussion group,
    "Subject: mind mapping software?" April 21–22 and July 10, 2009,
    finance.groups.yahoo.com/group/TaxoCoP, and the additional sug-
    gestion of TheBrain by Lynda Moulton, email to author, October 28,
    2009.

5. Theresa Regli, "Taxonomy management, or BSM? It's all semantics,"
    CMS Watch Trendwatch Blog, July 16, 2007, www.cmswatch.com/
    Trends/972-Taxonomy-management,-or-BSM?-It%E2%80%99s-all-
    semantics

6. This comparison of MultiTes, Term Tree, and TCS-10 first appeared
    in an article by the author, "Taxonomy Tool Roundup," *EContent* 31,
    no. 3 (April 2008): 40–44.

7. Alan Chate (director at Active Classification Solutions), email to
    author, January 9, 2009.

8. Wendi Pohs, email to author, July 23, 2009.

9. Postings to the Taxonomy Community of Practice discussion group,
    "subject "protégé," November 19–20, 2008, 20, 2008.finance.groups.
    yahoo.com/group/TaxoCoP

10. Lynda Moulton, email to author, May 29, 2009.

11. Department of Defense Directive 5015.02-STD: *Electronic Records
    Management Software Applications Design Criteria Standard* (April
    25, 2007), 114, jitc.fhu.disa.mil/recmgt/p50152stdapr07.pdf

Chapter 6

Taxonomies for Human Indexing

Taxonomies: Find what you really want.
                    —Mike Gardner

As explained in Chapter 1, support of indexing is one of the main purposes or applications of a taxonomy, with the other purposes being retrieval support and organization/navigation support. There are different methods of indexing, and you need to consider these differences when developing a taxonomy. The two fundamental kinds of indexing are human (or manual) and automated. This chapter will discuss issues pertaining to creating taxonomies for use by human indexers, and Chapter 7 will deal with particularities of taxonomies for automated indexing. Sometimes the same taxonomy will be used for both human and automated indexing, a situation that requires attention to many issues and possibly a few trade-offs.

What Is Human Indexing?

Before considering the issues involved in developing a taxonomy for human indexers, we need to have an understanding of who indexers are and what they do.

Tagging, Cataloging, Classifying, or Indexing

When we speak of human indexing with a taxonomy, we are referring to analyzing content and assigning appropriate descriptive terms selected from a taxonomy. Within a given organization, this process might not be called indexing but could be referred to as tagging, keywording, classifying, or cataloging. There are subtle differences in these designations.

Tagging, sometimes called *keywording*, by definition does not necessarily imply using a taxonomy (controlled vocabulary) but rather could involve creating new terms as desired with little or no authority control. However, since the designations of tagging and keywording are more familiar outside the library science profession, and the term *indexing* has its own ambiguities, there are organizations that choose to call the process of assigning controlled vocabulary terms tagging or keywording. What the process is called may also depend on who does it. While there are people with the job title "indexer," there are no "taggers" or "keyworders." Tagging or keywording, when described as such, is often done by people whose main job function is not indexing but rather something else, such as content creation or editing. The designations tagging and keywording imply a degree of simplicity, a task that can be done by someone without formal training in indexing. How simple it actually is depends on the content, the taxonomy, and the indexing policies.

Cataloging has a more specialized meaning and is generally restricted to the organization and description of library materials (both physical and digital), archive documents, and museum collections. Cataloging often involves assigning descriptive subject terms from a taxonomy (subject cataloging), but it also includes recording other metadata that may be bibliographic, may refer to source type and history, or may include a physical description (descriptive cataloging). Additionally, when cataloging physical materials, an important part of the task is classification, the assigning of a unique locator, such as a call number, to the material, because the material can have only one physical location (a shelf, file box, display case, room, etc.). Essentially there is overlap between cataloging and indexing. Cataloging often, but not always, includes subject indexing, but it also involves more. In any case, subject catalogers do utilize taxonomies, usually called authority files or thesauri.

Classification, which is not limited to physical library materials, means assigning an item to a class. Assigning organisms names in a biological taxonomy or naming scientific or technical concepts and grouping them is also called classification. Classification is actually different from indexing or tagging in that an item can only go into one class. In classifying, you ask "Where does this item go?" whereas in indexing, tagging, or subject cataloging, you ask "What terms describe this item?"

Indexing really means to create an index, a list of terms, each of which indicates or points to (the original meaning of *index*) where to find information/content on a desired subject. Traditionally an index appears as a browsable, alphabetical list that you can run your index finger through. Of course, in the online environment, the browsable index may not always be displayed to the end user, but the process of indexing—that is, assigning index terms to content—may be the same.

Indexing With a Taxonomy

Indexing content that is diverse, often from multiple sources, and also spread out over time requires the use of a taxonomy in order to maintain consistency. Indexers may not remember exactly which index terms they chose for similar topics in the past, but a taxonomy ensures that their choices will be consistent. The use of a taxonomy also enables consistent indexing by multiple indexers who are needed when there is a large quantity of content or time-sensitive content. Consistent indexing is necessary to enable comprehensive retrieval on a given search term.

For indexing with a taxonomy, the taxonomist completes the taxonomy (although it will of course be subject to revision) prior to any indexing other than test-indexing. Then the indexer (or indexers) uses the taxonomy by linking its pre-defined terms to the content. The indexing is usually performed using a software system that allows access to the taxonomy, through browsing or searching, validating the indexer's choice of terms while also connecting to the repository of content being indexed or at least to references (URLs, URIs, file paths, etc.) to the content items. The indexing software may or may not connect with the taxonomy management software. This kind of indexing is sometimes called database indexing because some form of database management system is used to correlate index terms with documents. Each indexable document or media file is treated as a distinct database record, which has index terms and other metadata in its various database record fields, and users query the database to obtain their search results.

This type of indexing typically deals with numerous documents, articles, files, or webpages, and each is usually indexed as a unit. Thus, index terms may be assigned to reflect the most important concepts or names in the document or file as a whole, rather than at a more granular paragraph or sentence level. A large document may be broken into defined sections. The indexer may be expected to index a certain number of documents or document-section records per hour.

The indexing of multiple documents with taxonomy terms results in a dynamically growing list of documents for each term. Typically, the end user is offered options for sorting the list of retrieved results, such as by date or relevancy. The option for relevancy opens the possibility that the indexer could "weight" the assigned index terms. When choosing a term from the taxonomy, the indexer may also be able to designate the term as *primary* or *secondary* (or *major* or *minor*) by means of a scroll menu or check box. Then, when an end user searches on a term from the taxonomy, the retrieved documents that were indexed with the term as *primary* will sort to the top of a relevancy-ranked list, above documents that were indexed with the term as *secondary*.

Database indexing, sometimes known as *open* indexing, differs in several ways from back-of-the-book indexing, which can be called *closed* indexing.[1] Book indexing is "closed" because the indexing comes to a close once all the pages have been analyzed and indexed. The index itself can be finalized and thus usually goes into print as part of the book. Closed indexing usually does not involve using a taxonomy/controlled vocabulary, and the indexer will try to come up with terms that reflect the language of the work. Open indexing, on the other hand, usually involves a taxonomy, and the indexer is challenged to translate from the author's choice of words to the preferred terms in the taxonomy. Book indexing also tends to be more granular, to the level of detail of paragraphs or even sentences, compared with open indexing, which takes place predominantly at the document level.

Who Are Indexers?

Indexers of open/database indexes, who are making use of taxonomies, vary in terms of their backgrounds, degree of training, and subject specialization. They could be taxonomists, information specialists, librarians (especially corporate librarians), or subject area specialists with an advanced degree in a specific field. Some organizations have taxonomist-indexers who take on a combination of taxonomy management and indexing tasks, while other organizations clearly split the roles. A large volume of indexing usually requires a number of dedicated indexers, however, and the largest commercial periodical database indexes have at times employed dozens of indexers. Since employers of full-time database indexers are few, they cannot expect their new-hire indexers to have previous indexing experience. Thus, these employers usually provide thorough on-the-job training for such indexers. Indexers might have a degree in the subject matter of the content being indexed or a general humanities or social sciences degree if they are indexing nonspecialized content. They may work in-house, or they may work remotely if the indexing system and taxonomy database support remote access.

If remote access is supported, then independent contractors may also be used. However, unlike closed indexing, which can involve a different indexer for each book, it is only practical to have open indexing done by freelancers if they are long-term, steady contractors. Indexing is less costly to the organization and more profitable to the indexer if speed and efficiency can be attained, which takes time and experience. There is a long learning curve, not only to become proficient in using an organization's unique indexing system, but, more important, to become familiar with the terms in the taxonomy. An indexer who knows the most commonly used terms in a taxonomy spends less time navigating to desired terms and will also index more correctly. This can be an obstacle to new freelance indexers. Freelance indexing is profitable to the indexer who can work quickly, because contract indexing rates tend to pay per record (document/file) indexed rather than hourly. The rate for database indexing is comparable to the book indexing rate.[2] A document may comprise multiple pages, but unless the article is unusually long or scholarly, the depth of indexing and number of index terms assigned to a periodical-type article are similar to those assigned to a single page in a book.

Finally, indexing is sometimes performed by people whose primary task is not indexing but rather some other content-related duty, such as writing, editing, or content management, especially if the quantity of indexing is not great enough to constitute a full-time job. Nevertheless, these people should be trained in the use of the organization's taxonomy, indexing techniques, and policies, with emphasis on the policies. Lack of training, which often happens with a supplemental task, will likely result in poor indexing.

When to Use Human Indexers

Automated indexing, described in Chapter 7, is becoming increasingly popular for large indexing projects. For most other situations, the greater accuracy provided by trained human indexers is more important than speed and volume. Humans can identify concepts, not just words or strings of words, and they can discern whether a concept is significant and worthy of being indexed. Obviously, they cannot index as quickly as automated systems, but if the volume of content is not overwhelming and indexing quality is of great importance, then human indexers are preferred. The following factors favor human indexers:

- A high emphasis on quality and accuracy in indexing and retrieval

- A manageable volume of documents

- The presence of nontext files for indexing (images, video, audio)

- Content that is varied in document types/formats and varied in subject areas (making it more difficult to "train" automated systems)

- A corporate culture that is more comfortable with hiring, training, and managing employees or contractors and/or developing its own human indexing software than with making a large financial investment in externally purchased technology

Scholarly, academic, scientific, medical, and sometimes legal documents are more likely to be indexed by human indexers as these are areas in which indexing accuracy takes precedence. Publishers, which are the creators of content, also tend to favor human indexing, since humans can easily index at the same time as they are editing or publishing a document. If the volume of content is relatively small, then human indexing is cost-effective for any subject area or industry. For indexing any nontext media, humans are needed to assign index terms, tags, or other metadata because automated indexing relies on text-based algorithms and analysis. As multimedia is an increasingly significant form of content, the role of human indexers will remain significant.

Terms, Relationships, and Notes for Indexers

When creating a taxonomy for use by human indexers, you need to pay attention to certain issues with respect to terms, relationships between terms, and notes for terms.

Preferred and Nonpreferred Terms for Indexers

Although you should create preferred terms that are appropriate for end users, nonpreferred terms can take into consideration the indexers as well. In the rare cases of a taxonomy that will be viewed by the indexers only and not by end users (because they are accessing it only by a search box), you can consider the indexers' expectations for preferred terms, too. In such cases, factors to consider include whether indexers are subject-matter experts, who expect certain concepts and preferred term names for them, or whether the indexers are generalists.

As for nonpreferred terms, certain kinds of terms are particularly helpful for human indexers. If the indexer will access an alphabetical list of terms that combines both nonpreferred and preferred terms (even if simply by means of truncated start-of-word searching), nonpreferred terms should begin with a word likely to be looked up alphabetically (i.e., a keyword). Consequently, inverted terms can be useful as nonpreferred terms, as in the following example:

libraries, public USE **public libraries**

If the indexer reads a document about public libraries, the first word that comes to the indexer's mind would likely be *libraries*. Therefore, the indexer types in *libraries*. Depending on the design of the indexing software, the indexer could retrieve the exact broader term of **libraries**, which could be expanded to reveal its narrower terms, a list of all terms with the word *libraries* within them, or a short list of terms that start with the word *libraries*. (The indexer may even have the option to choose the display type.) In such a case when the more specific nonpreferred term **libraries, public** appears and the indexer selects it, the corresponding preferred term is applied to the document. Accessing the preferred term via the nonpreferred term can be more efficient than first selecting the broader term **libraries**, then calling up its term details screen to see what its narrower terms are.

If the end user can see the nonpreferred terms (which is less often the case in the hypertext environment), then there may be nonpreferred terms that you want the indexer but not the end users to see. Examples include inverted terms or older names of terms (names that are no longer used but are still familiar to indexers). In any case, a different kind of equivalence relationship would be appropriate, such as USE-I and UF-I, as discussed in Chapter 4.

Another type of nonpreferred term that is useful specifically for indexers is what we might call a shortcut. It is an acronym, abbreviation, or code for a commonly used term that indexers understand within a term type, category, or facet but that is not suitable for end users or in automated indexing due to its potential ambiguity. A good example would be a two-letter state or country abbreviation limited to geographic terms; for outside the geographic context, two letters, such as *ma*, would be ambiguous. A shortcut could also be an internal custom abbreviation for industry types, if there is a short list of industries, or action types, or any term limited to a vocabulary type. The purpose of these shortcut types of nonpreferred terms is to save the indexer keystrokes and make the indexing go faster. For example, there could be a facet for business actions, limited to around 50 to 60 terms, and each could have a three-letter shortcut code, such as **ACQ** for **acquisitions, divestitures & mergers**, **FRE** for **financial results & earning**s, **NPS** for **new products/services,** and **ORD** for **orders & contracts**. The idea is that the shortcuts should be easy to memorize by virtue of being logical and limited in number.

Term Relationship for Indexers

Relationships between terms, even if not as efficient as nonpreferred terms in directing the indexer to the best preferred term, are also very helpful for navigating a taxonomy. In addition to guiding indexers to the desired term, the set of relationships for a given term also provides the indexer with a better understanding of the intended meaning and scope of the term.

It is often the policy in indexing to use the most specific terms appropriate, and hierarchical relationships can guide the indexer to the most specific term. Only by means of hierarchical relationships or a hierarchical display can an indexer be certain which is the most specific term available. Additional broader terms may or may not be suitable for indexing the given content, but if they are, the indexer can also benefit from seeing these relationships.

Associative relationships are also highly useful to indexers, who otherwise might overlook the existence of an additional appropriate term—or perhaps what turns out to be a more appropriate term than the one first selected. This could be the case with related terms such as a process and an agent, an action and a product, or a discipline and an object. For example, for a document about programming software, the indexer initially selects the product-type term **software** but then sees the related action term **programming** and realizes that indeed programming is the focus of the article so decides to select that term instead. Similarly, for an article about weather predictions, the indexer initially selects the object term **weather** but then sees the related discipline term of **meteorology** and recognizes it as the more appropriate term. For the benefit of indexers, associative relationships should be as comprehensive as practical. Chapter 4 discusses how many associative relationships to make.

Term Notes

As mentioned in Chapter 3, taxonomy terms may have short descriptive notes attached to them. Whether they are scope notes aimed at both end-use searchers and indexers, or indexer notes visible only to the indexers, these notes are very useful to the indexers. Even if end users do not bother to look at scope notes, indexers who work daily with the taxonomy know where and how to view a term's notes. Thus, even though scope notes may be for dual audiences, the primary readers of scope notes tend to be the indexers.

Indexer notes, which are aimed only at indexers and thus displayed only to indexers, may be similar to scope notes in their content and style, or they may explain more. Often indexer notes focus on usage, with instructions from the taxonomist to the indexer on when or how to use the term in indexing. A typical usage note for indexers might be "Use a more specific term if possible" for a relatively broad term. Here is a specific example of an indexer note in a thesaurus that also uses scope notes, from the Cengage Learning (formerly Gale) controlled vocabulary:

> **African American churches**
> Indexer Notes: Use this term primarily for articles related to the church as an organization. For African American church buildings, please use this term and Church buildings.[3]

Although this explanation could certainly serve as a scope note, it may have been decided that such instructions were unnecessarily complex for the end-user searchers of this particular resource.

Indexer notes can also give brief explanatory information for a specific term that is not about scope or usage. This is particularly the case for a name of an organization or a technical or scholarly concept that is not widely known and therefore not likely familiar to an indexer but that would be the term chosen by the searcher who wanted to look up this topic. This information is certainly helpful, if not necessary, for the indexer, who cannot be expected to be thoroughly knowledgeable on all the topics to index, especially if the content is broad in scope.

In conclusion, when creating taxonomy terms for human indexers, it is best to have 1) supportive nonpreferred terms, including phrase inversions and shortcuts; 2) extensive relationships between terms; and 3) indexer-focused term notes for clarification.

Taxonomy Structure and Indexing Interface

If human indexers will use a taxonomy, then the broader taxonomy structure and display may include features of which human indexers can take advantage. Maintaining distinct vocabulary or authority files can make access to and usage of the vocabularies more logical to the indexers. Although not common, secondary-level subdivision terms, which allow more precise precoordination of concepts, could be supported. Additionally, how the taxonomy is displayed and how the indexer accesses it are matters of concern.

Distinct Vocabularies and Authority Files

The organization of terms into distinct sub-vocabularies, facets, or authority files can be helpful for indexers, especially in ensuring thoroughness of indexing. If the end-user interface breaks the taxonomy out into more than one vocabulary or facet (such as topics, organization names, industries, locations, and actions), then the indexer's view of the taxonomy should similarly be broken out into the same vocabularies or facets for a consistent perspective with that of end users. Even if the end user sees only a simple search box, there still should be term-type distinctions for the indexer. The segmentation of multiple different vocabularies makes it easier for the indexer to look up terms, especially in alphabetical browse lists and when named entities are involved.

Distinct vocabularies also aid in enforcing indexing policy to support consistent indexing. For example, an editorial policy might call for indexing individual names of people, places, companies, and organizations, but with a limit of four each per document, and might also require at least two topic terms, but no more than five, per document. Maintaining separate vocabulary files for each of these types makes it easier to meet the indexing criteria. Furthermore, customization of the indexing software could enforce the editorial policy.

Finally, by maintaining distinct vocabularies or authority files, you can also support distinct policies for maintaining each vocabulary and manage indexer involvement in that maintenance. For topical terms, for example, indexers may be required to use only the terms provided, but for named entities they might be permitted to enter new candidate terms and use them immediately for indexing prior to taxonomist approval. Some files in your taxonomy might permit this kind of overriding, while others would not.

If you have human indexers and separate facets or vocabularies, you could conceivably support having more than one term with the same name, each in a distinct facet or vocabulary type. Examples are the term **French** in a language facet and **French** in a people or nationality facet, **churches** in a places or structures facet and **churches** in an organizations facet, or **mergers** in a topics facet and **mergers** in an events/business activities facet. Automated indexing would not necessarily make the correct distinction, but human indexers can.

Structured Indexing and Subdivisions

Some commercial periodical index databases, such as InfoTrac and the Readers' Guide to Periodical Literature, support what is called structured indexing or second-level indexing, which is a form of precoordination. Structured indexing makes use of a secondary controlled vocabulary set of what are called subdivisions, which serve to narrow or qualify the main term for more refined retrieval results. An example is:

Alzheimer's Disease—Diagnosis

The first term in the sequence, in this case **Alzheimer's Disease**, is called the heading, and the next term, **Diagnosis**, is the subdivision, because the content indexed with the heading is further "subdivided" based on various subdivision terms, which may include **treatment, demographics**, **genetic aspects**, **case studies**, and others. This is *not* the same as a broader term and a narrower term; **diagnosis** is *not* a narrower term for **Alzheimer's Disease**. Rather, a subdivision acts as a kind of modifier. Indexing policy may require that the indexer always use subdivisions for certain headings, unless the content is a general discussion of the topic, so that main headings will display multiple subdivisions in the index. Subdivisions function in a similar manner to subentries in a back-of-the-book index, allowing the user to narrow a search result with prescribed taxonomy terms. Some systems support the use of third- and even fourth-level subdivisions, assuming there is sufficient material indexed at the second level. An example is:

Massachusetts—History—Local

Subdivision terms, which in the two preceding examples are **Diagnosis**, **History**, and **Local**, are typically controlled vocabulary terms themselves, maintained in their own vocabulary lists. Thus, as a taxonomist, you might maintain a controlled vocabulary file of standard subdivisions. Typically, subdivisions are classified and certain headings use certain subdivisions. For example, the subdivision **Diagnosis** is used only with headings that are types of diseases, but **History** could be used with places or any topics (including diseases).

Structured indexing can yield more precise retrieval results, but to be accurate, structured indexing requires human indexers. Thus, if you are making use of human indexers, you might consider implementing structured indexing. However, the indexing software and the end-user search interface need to be designed and developed to support structured indexing. A generic database management system with simple index term fields would not be adequate for structured indexing.

Taxonomy Display and Access

How a taxonomy is displayed and how it can be searched are also important considerations for indexers, enabling them to find the terms they need quickly. Since the indexing interface may be designed even before there are any indexers, the taxonomist may be the one to provide input into the indexing interface design. Desired display features would include the following:

- A searchable alphabetical list of terms, displaying the section of the alphabet starting with a truncated search. It may have a toggle option to display both nonpreferred and preferred terms or to display preferred terms only.

- The option to browse the hierarchical display of the taxonomy.

- Hyperlinks leading from nonpreferred terms to their corresponding preferred terms

- Details of a selected preferred term (also called the term record), including all its relationships (BT, NT, RT) and notes, to display in a new window or pane.

Indexers benefit from being able to browse terms alphabetically. A hierarchical display alone, which can guide a user to a more specific term of interest, may be less appropriate for indexers than it is for end-use searchers. End users might need guidance in coming up with concepts, whereas skilled indexers usually can identify the concepts to describe the content that they are indexing but often need references to the appropriate preferred terms. If the taxonomy is very small, however, and the entire hierarchy can fit on one browsable page/screen, then there is no need to have an alphabetical display in addition to the hierarchical display.

Efficient methods of searching for terms in the taxonomy should be made available to the indexer, including options for truncated or start-of-word searching and word within a term phrase searching. The indexing software interface should also be optimized for ease, speed, and accuracy in indexing. For example, common operations should have keyboard shortcuts and not always require the use of a mouse. If indexers have memorized certain index terms, they should be able to enter these into the index fields with validation, rather than being required to browse the taxonomy every time to pick a term. Of course, what methods are "efficient" varies with the individual. Different indexers may prefer different approaches, depending on their experience or cognitive style.

The term record, or the standard thesaurus display for details of a term, and the relationship abbreviations in particular may not make much sense for an end user, but for an indexer they provide clear and useful information. The display to the indexer may be quite similar to that displayed to the taxonomist. Following is an example of a term with its "details" that are useful for an indexer.

> **Water supply**
> > SN **The supply of public potable water**
> > UF **Water utilities**
> > UF **Water works**
> > BT **Utilities**
> > NT **Reservoirs**
> > NT **Water mains**
> > NT **Water towers**

When indexers are certain they have found the correct term, they add it to the record without further consideration, but if they are unsure of a term's appropriateness, they will check the term's details to see any nonpreferred, broader, narrower, and related terms, and check for any scope notes or indexer notes.

Taxonomy Updates and Quality Control

A taxonomy used by human indexers presents particular concerns with respect to two interrelated issues: updating the taxonomy and maintaining indexing consistency and quality.

Communication and Updates

Maintaining and updating a taxonomy used by human indexers requires communication in both directions: from the taxonomist(s) to the indexers and from the indexers to the taxonomist(s). As the taxonomist who is continually updating the taxonomy, you need to inform the indexers of newly added terms, term changes, merging of terms, or splitting of terms. Meanwhile, the indexers need a method of informing you, the taxonomist, that there is a need for a new term, based on a new concept appearing in the content, or a need for additional nonpreferred terms or term relationships, because an existing term is difficult to find.

The taxonomist does not necessarily have to inform the indexer of every new term, especially not every new named entity term (person names, company names, etc.). New topical subjects, along with changes in such terms, however, are more significant, and the taxonomist should mention their availability. In addition to new and changed terms, other information regularly communicated to indexers might be suggested combinations or sets of terms for indexing certain new or recurring subjects or issues, whether current events or new topics from a newly acquired set of content. This communication can be in any form that is practical for the organization, such as an email distribution list, bulletins posted in an intranet, or collaboration workspace.

Communication in the other direction, from the indexers to the taxonomist(s), is also necessary. Indexers are often the first to notice new concepts appearing in the content, so they should have a method to suggest new terms. While this could be by email or through an intranet/collaboration bulletin, even more effective for gaining indexer input is to have a method for suggesting or nominating terms right within the indexing software interface. Sometimes, rather than suggesting a new concept/term, an indexer may want to suggest a new term name for an existing concept, to be considered either as a change or merely as a nonpreferred term. Although less likely, indexers might even suggest additional term relationships, based on their understanding of term usage from the texts being indexed. These more complex suggestions from indexers could be communicated either through a notes/messaging field in the indexing software or through email or collaboration bulletins.

Maintaining Indexing Quality

Human indexers need comprehensive indexing policy guidelines and training in order to perform consistent, accurate indexing.

Editorial Policy for Indexers

Usually the taxonomists who create the taxonomy are also those who write the policy on how to use it. At the very least, in writing indexing policy, taxonomists work closely with technical writers who document how to use the indexing software. Indexing policy would include the following:

- Criteria for determining whether a subject or name is sufficiently relevant for indexing

- The level of detail for indexing: how much information needs to be present on a given topic to make it worthy of being indexed

- The number of terms to assign to any given document and whether terms of certain types or facets must always be assigned

- The permissibility of combinations of certain terms

- The permissibility of using both a term and its broader term

- A threshold number of sibling narrower terms, at which point the broader term should be used instead (e.g., **apples**, **oranges**, **bananas**, **grapes**, or use instead the broader term **fruit**)

- Editorial style conventions (forms of entry) for taxonomy terms, to aid the indexer in looking up terms and in creating candidate terms

- If a weighting system is used for assigned index terms, the criteria for choosing primary versus secondary weights and whether the majority of assigned terms are expected to be at the primary or secondary level

The editorial policy for indexers should be comprehensive enough so it is clear what constitutes correct versus incorrect indexing. Indexing is somewhat subjective, and two well-trained indexers will not index everything identically, but they should be close. A clear indexing policy is necessary, both to identify indexing errors and to prevent them from recurring.

Training for Indexers

An indexing supervisor or senior indexers typically train new indexers, but the trainer could be a taxonomist. If the indexing operation is completely new or there is just one indexer, then the responsibility for indexer training is most likely to fall on the taxonomist. An important part of training is instruction in the indexing policy, but if the new indexers are inexperienced, then training will also involve basic instruction in indexing principles, such as the goal to capture the "aboutness" of a document rather than matching words in the text to taxonomy terms. Another important part of training is reviewing sample indexing and providing feedback. Initial indexing can be on sample documents (which must be carefully chosen for their representative nature) and then, when performance is satisfactory, on live documents. Even live indexing requires monitoring and checking for a period of time, as the diversity of documents that require indexing might bring up questions not covered in the sample indexing.

Taxonomy Improvements

If policy and training are sufficient, continued inaccuracies in indexing can indicate a need for improvements in the taxonomy. The work of all indexers, even experienced indexers, should be periodically reviewed, not so much for the purpose of providing individual feedback but for overall quality control. Indexing results can be spot-checked, but statistics on term usage in indexing would also be useful. Incomplete or inconsistent indexing could point to the need for improvements in the taxonomy:

- If certain index terms are not used as much as they ought to be, this indicates the need for additional nonpreferred terms and perhaps also additional relationships to other terms.

- In a small taxonomy with no nonpreferred terms, the overlooking of a particular term might indicate that it needs rewording or even relocation to somewhere else in the taxonomy.

- If a term is overused, than perhaps the concept should be divided into two or more new terms.

- If two terms are frequently used in combination, this may indicate a concept in need of a single, precoordinated term.

- If a certain index term is misused, then perhaps you should reword the preferred term, create more nonpre-ferred terms, and/or add a scope note.

Levels of Vocabulary Management

Human indexers obviously can make good use of taxonomies, but they can also be permitted to use terms that are not in a taxonomy, that is, to create their own terms, either as candidate terms for the taxonomy or simply as keywords. Whether they do so, and to what extent, depends on an organization's editorial policy and the capabilities of the indexing software. Permitting indexers to propose new terms has its benefits, since they are the first to see new concepts and names in incoming documents. There are a number of possibilities for managing term suggestions from indexers, listed here from the most controlled to the least controlled:

1. The indexer uses terms only from the taxonomy. The indexer may suggest terms (candidate terms), but such terms must be reviewed and approved by the taxonomist first and thus cannot be used immediately for indexing the document at hand (unless the document is put on hold).

2. The indexer primarily uses terms from the taxonomy but is also permitted to suggest and immediately use additional candidate terms as "unapproved" terms, which the taxonomist will review later. (If the taxonomist subsequently changes an unapproved term name, the system still keeps track of the term the indexer entered, so that the taxonomist can add it as a nonpreferred term to enable retrieval of the previously indexed document.)

   a. Unapproved terms are restricted to named entities, and the indexer cannot create subject terms.

   b. Unapproved terms may be created for any kind of term, whether named entities or subjects.

3. The indexer uses a combination of terms from the taxonomy and indexer-created terms (keywords) of all types. The indexer-created keywords, like author keywords, are *not* formally suggested to the taxonomy as candidate terms, and they may or may not be reviewed by a taxonomist.

   a. Taxonomy terms are in the majority, and keywords are supplemental.

   b. Taxonomy terms are used only for a few basic categories, and more of the indexing/tagging is done with keywords.

   Each of these options involves some trade-offs affecting the simplicity of the indexing system, the ability to index new concepts not yet in the taxonomy, and the consistency of indexing. Option 1, requiring taxonomist approval of new terms, is relatively simple to implement with respect to technology, but since it cannot support new names and emerging concepts, it works well only for a small taxonomy and a limited scope of content that does not deal with current events. Option 2, allowing unapproved or candidate terms in indexing but with the option for the taxonomist to "fix" them, is a good compromise that allows indexers to capture new concepts as needed while also ensuring vocabulary control. However, it is more complex to implement, so it is preferable for a relatively large indexing operation with multiple trained indexers. Option 3, permitting a dual system of a taxonomy and uncontrolled keywords, is relatively simple to implement but would present a more complicated set of three options to the end user: taxonomy terms, indexed keyword terms, and free text search strings.

Managing Folksonomies

Following the continuum of decreasing levels of control over a taxonomy described in the previous section, one might expect a fourth option whereby the indexer creates keywords, and these keywords immediately become available for repeated future use by this and other indexers, without a taxonomist's reviewing and approving them. This scenario actually takes place in what we call a *folksonomy*, except that the creation and use of a folksonomy does not involve people who work as indexers. It is the authors and/or the users of the content—in other words, common "folk"—who create folksonomy terms or tags. The folksonomy approach has become easy to implement with the rise of commercial software for that purpose. Let us first consider the background of folksonomies.

While the uncontrolled terms in folksonomies might seem beyond the scope of a taxonomist's responsibilities, such uncontrolled terms can in fact reflect emerging concepts and are actually prime candidates for future taxonomy terms. Therefore, if relevant folksonomies are available, the taxonomist should pay close attention to them. At some point, a taxonomist may review and edit the folksonomy and convert some or all of it into a taxonomy.

Social Tagging and Folksonomy

New technologies that enable interactive use of the web, commonly referred to as the semantic web or Web 3.0, allow users to assign keyword tags of their choice to all kinds of web content. These tags can be used by the individual tagger for later retrieval, but other people may also view and use these tags. This type of uncontrolled indexing or tagging is called *social tagging* because anyone in an online community or society can tag any content, see the tags of others, and search on the accumulated tags. Furthermore, new social communities can be built around shared sets of popular content or popular tags. This phenomenon, which began around 2004, is also known as social bookmarking, collaborative tagging, social classification, social indexing, or ethnoclassification.

Social tagging can be done by the content creators (authors, photographers, etc.), the content viewers (readers or consumers), or both. The same content can be tagged repeatedly over time, rather than having a page or document indexed and then closed to future indexing, so social tagging is very dynamic. Even if the content remains static, the tagging can change over time, but usually the content is changing or growing as well.

The term *folksonomy* was coined by Thomas Vander Wal in July 2004 on the discussion group of the Information Architecture Institute (then called the Asilomar Institute for Information Architecture) in response to a question about what to call the new informal social classification comprising user-defined tags on information-sharing websites. Following up on Eric Scheid's suggestion of a "folk classification," Vander Wal responded: "So the user-created bottom-up categorical structure development with an emergent thesaurus would become a Folksonomy?"[4] A folkson-omy should not be confused with a folk taxonomy. The latter is a concept that has been around much longer, a term in anthropol-ogy that refers to the unscientific naming and classifying of things by lay people within a given culture.

Websites or services that make use of social tagging include social bookmarking management sites Delicious (delicious.com), Connotea (www.connotea.org), and Diigo (www.diigo.com), and the site for uploading and tagging images, Flickr (www.flickr.com).

Social tagging has its strengths and weaknesses. Its advantages over taxonomies include the following:

- It reflects trends, is up-to-date, and can monitor change and popularity.

- It is cheaper and quicker than building and maintaining a taxonomy.

- It is responsive to user needs.

- It facilitates democracy (as in votes for popular content and popular tags), the distribution of tasks, and the building of virtual communities of shared interest and knowledge.

There are also drawbacks to social tagging, which include the following:

- The tagging is inherently inconsistent, so there are serious deficiencies in precision and recall for content retrieval.

- The tagging is inevitably biased. Users may disagree with prior tagging.

- Social tagging does not scale well to a large volume of content.

- For social tagging to be effective, it requires a critical mass of user involvement, which is not always possible.

A folksonomy differs from a taxonomy, not merely in terms of who creates it and the lack of authority control, but also in the approach to its creation. A folksonomy represents a bottom-up creation of a vocabulary, as opposed to the top-down nature of a taxonomy. Actually, a folksonomy generally has no hierarchical structure, so it is probably incorrect to speak of bottom-up when there is no "up." Relationships between terms can be explicit, if the tagging software permits users to create such relationships, or implicit, by displaying tags that commonly co-occur. Users create relationships between terms based on their personal perceptions and biases, and they usually make no distinctions between hierarchical and associative relationships.

Folksonomies in the Enterprise

The phenomenon of social tagging has recently spread from public websites to inside enterprises. The success of social tagging within an organization, however, depends on the number of people involved. An organization may not have a critical mass of employees, and even if there is a potentially large number, the level of participation may not be sufficient. People tend to engage in social tagging because they enjoy it, not because it is part of their job.

If a folksonomy is used within an organization, there is an opportunity to manage it or leverage it. Vocabulary for social tagging, although user created, can be semi-controlled. A taxonomist may periodically intervene to "clean up" tags by merging multiple synonymous terms, choosing a preferred term, and designating the others as nonpreferred terms. Taggers would then no longer use terms designated as nonpreferred, but they could still create new equivalent terms for the same concept. Even when a folksonomy comes under greater control, inconsistent and biased tagging will still occur as long as taggers can invent their own terms and need not follow an editorial policy. Commercial enterprise social bookmarking software may not support folksonomy editing, so internal development may be necessary.

Social tagging is most suitable for collaboration and for following trends in rapidly growing and changing content. Therefore, for organizations that want to support creativity and innovation, social tagging might be a good idea. It is not so appropriate for critical research, which requires retrieval of all the relevant documents on a topic. Marketing and customer relations departments may also implement social tagging, encouraging customers and potential customers to engage in tagging for the purposes of stimulating and gauging market interest. Thus, for differing purposes, an enterprise can have both a controlled vocabulary and a social tagging area. In addition to periodically cleaning up folksonomy terms, a taxonomist might evaluate, edit, and promote popular folksonomy terms into a taxonomy that is used for other search purposes. A folksonomy, thus, is not an alternative to a taxonomy but rather is supplemental. Each has its own place and purpose.

Endnotes

1. Susan Klement, "Open-System Versus Closed-System Indexing: A Vital Distinction." *The Indexer* 23, no.1 (April 2002): 23–31.
2. American Society for Indexing, *American Society for Indexing 2009 Professional Activities and Salary Survey* (Wheat Ridge, CO: American Society of Indexers, 2010), 12. The average range reported was $2 to $4/page, 70 cents/entry, or $31 to $35/hour.
3. From the subject authority file of Cengage Learning, Inc., accessed via taxonomy management system, June 2, 2009.
4. Thomas Vander Wal, "Folksonomy Coinage and Definition" (February 2, 2007), www.vanderwal.net/folksonomy.html

Chapter 7

Taxonomies for Automated Indexing

What's taxonomy got to do with IT!
—David Riecks

As we all know too well, the volume of electronic content is growing at an increasingly rapid rate, and at the same time, the need to find meaningful information is becoming more critical in our competitive, interconnected, global world. The task of indexing content to make it retrievable has become too great for human indexers in many contexts. Meanwhile, technologies for automated indexing have been improving. Although under certain conditions human indexing is still preferred, many organizations are turning to automated indexing to serve their needs.

Automated Indexing, Search, and Taxonomies

Automated indexing is a very broad notion that encompasses various technologies and techniques, some of which involve taxonomies and some of which do not. Automated tagging, auto-classification, and auto-categorization refer to automated indexing technologies that utilize taxonomies in some way or another. Simpler search engines perform a form of automated indexing without using taxonomies, but more recently, some search systems have incorporated taxonomies.

When to Use Automated Indexing

Automated indexing is, of course, more practical than human indexing when there is vast volume of content to index in a short period, although there is a trade-off in the form of lower levels of accuracy. Rapidly changing content (such as news), government intelligence, content of a very large enterprise, or other high-volume flows of data all benefit from automated indexing. Although accuracy is never as high as with skilled human indexing, if the volume of content is great, then near perfect accuracy may not be needed to find desired information or discern trends. The following factors favor choosing automated over human indexing:

- A very large number of documents, which would require multiple human indexers and would be costly to index.

- Content that changes quickly and perhaps unpredictably

- A need for speed in indexing, such as for time-critical information, current awareness, or news

- Relatively common document types or formats or pre-tagged (structured) content types

- Content related to a relatively uniform subject area or a single industry (so there is less ambiguity of terms)

- Text content only (although a few technologies can identify digital video and audio data)

- A corporate culture that is more comfortable with investing in externally purchased technology than in hiring, training, and managing human indexers

Consumer-oriented content (such as product/service directories), news and information publishers and aggregators, and large intranets are all areas in which indexing speed and volume are of greater concern than the improved accuracy yet higher cost of human indexers. This is not to say that automated indexing systems are cheap. They can be quite expensive, too, but over an extended period they will most likely pay for themselves. Automated indexing systems also vary greatly in capability.

Structured content (such as database records) or unstructured content that already has structured metadata assigned to it is much easier to auto-index than is totally unstructured content. Thus, the original users of auto-categorization systems were large publishers or vendors of structured content. The trend toward creating more structured content within organizations, such as in technical documentation and reports, has resulted in more enterprise content that is suitable for automatic indexing. (That is not to say that the proportion of unstructured content has decreased.) At the same time, automated indexing technologies are improving with regard to unstructured content. So, for both these reasons, automated indexing is becoming more popular within organizations to make large volumes of internal content retrievable. The same automated indexing system may work on both structured and unstructured content.

Although automated indexing saves the expense of human indexers, it still requires human involvement to be effective. People need to create and maintain the taxonomies, of course, and human intellectual work is needed either to "train" the system on the taxonomy terms or to write rules for individual terms, as this chapter will explain in more detail.

Taxonomies and Search Software

Although search engines, whether for the entire web or for large websites or intranets, create what are called indexes, they do not usually make use of taxonomies. Search engines retrieve webpages by sorting words according to their location and retrieve the locations by matching search queries to the words or phrases listed in the search engine's inverted index of words. Algorithms and rules can increase the sophistication of matching search terms with words in webpages, but a taxonomy is not necessarily involved. Building and updating a comprehensive taxonomy to support searching the entire World Wide Web would be nearly an impossible task. The closest that web search engines come to implementing any sort of controlled vocabulary is by including word lists of common misspellings or "fuzzy" matches, but such lists are certainly not taxonomies and not even synonym rings.

However, search software for a single site, such as an enterprise's intranet or content management system, or software for searching across a corpus of online documents, may incorporate taxonomies. The scope of the subject matter, while still vast, is at least restricted to the interests of an organization, and the content may be more structured in its formatting and metadata. Site or enterprise search software, which is a growing niche industry, may or may not make use of taxonomies, however. Such software was originally based on web search engine technology and thus did not incorporate taxonomies. But as enterprise search software becomes more sophisticated and tailored to the enterprise's needs, and as users come to appreciate the benefits of taxonomies, the incorporation of taxonomies in enterprise search is becoming more common.

A basic search engine matches user-entered query words with words or phrases found within the documents' metadata field (such as title) or anywhere in the text and returns those documents that are sufficiently relevant based on the position and frequency of those words, among other considerations. Relevance ranking takes into consideration many factors and may determine the display order of results. The deficiencies of free-text search are obvious. If the user enters a word in the search box, but the text uses a synonym for that word and not the same word, the search engine misses the document. In other cases, the word entered by the user may occur in the text but not in the same context; it may have a different meaning or use, or it may occur in the text only because it is negated. In any of these cases, the search may retrieve an irrelevant document.

Search engines have become more sophisticated over the years. It is now common to match singular and plural forms of the same word. More specialized search engines also employ grammatical stemming so that words with the same root, such as **writers** and **writing**, will also match, perhaps with a lower relevance ranking than for an exact word match. More sophisticated search engines incorporate text analytics technologies to take grammar and inter-word relationships into consideration, relationships that can help determine whether a given word occurring in a text has the meaning intended by the words in the search query. Nevertheless, it remains difficult to discern concepts, and not merely words, without first establishing some kind of controlled vocabulary and a way to link text words to the taxonomy term.

Controlled vocabularies or taxonomies support search in two different ways: 1) through nonpreferred terms or synonym rings, or 2) as browsable taxonomies. Synonym rings for each concept in a controlled vocabulary include terms likely to be searched and terms likely to appear in the content. This facilitates the matching of user-entered search strings with words or phrases in the content texts, as in the example illustrated in Figure 7.1. Despite the name, the terms in a synonym ring need not be exact synonyms but should in fact be nonpreferred terms in accordance with the guidelines described in Chapter 4. A synonym ring typically does not display terms in the user interface, whereas when the taxonomy makes a distinction between preferred and nonpreferred terms, the preferred terms are usually displayed.

In actual practice, the mere presence of a taxonomy with non-preferred terms does not guarantee that its nonpreferred terms will function as desired. Unless specifically set up to do so, in many cases search engines will ignore the relationships of nonpreferred

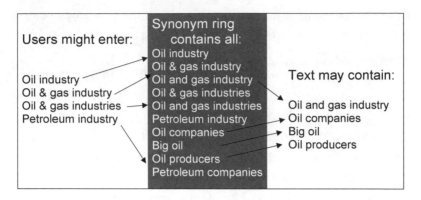

Figure 7.1 Example of how a synonym ring supports search for a concept

terms to the preferred terms and will treat them as any other keywords.[1] As the taxonomist, you need to ensure that whoever con-
figures the search engine takes into account the intended role of
the nonpreferred terms.

   The arrangement and display of terms for end-user browsing is
another way in which taxonomies support search for automated
indexing, just as they do for human-indexed concepts. In a hierarchical taxonomy, when the terms are visible and therefore browsable, users can browse and locate more specific subjects of interest,
they find out what is included in the taxonomy and what is not, and
they may find related subjects of interest. Users who are not entirely
sure what they are looking for generally prefer a browsable hierarchical taxonomy to a blank search box. If a taxonomy or a set of categories is displayed to the user, then the software involved is more
likely called auto-categorization or auto-classification software,
rather than search software, because the interface includes categories. Faceted taxonomy displays, described in more detail in
Chapter 8, also support search, but the indexing (or metadata tagging, as it may be called) requires a degree of human involvement,
so it is not a completely automatic method.

Automated Indexing Technologies

Just as there are different kinds of human indexing, there are also different forms of automated indexing and retrieval. Although there are multiple technologies involved, basically there are two different technology approaches that concern the taxonomist: 1) rules-based methods, involving spelled-out conditions, and 2) statistical methods, most often involving indexing by example or machine learning. Each method has its benefits and drawbacks. Some automated indexing products now combine the two techniques in order to achieve better results.

Independent of these different technology methods, there are two different basic approaches to automated indexing and retrieval: information extraction and auto-categorization. They differ from each other both in technology and in purpose. Information extraction, which involves pulling information from text, focuses on identifying which key names, concepts, and data in a text are sufficiently significant in comparison with those with a mere passing mention. Auto-categorization, on the other hand, seeks to categorize each document based on what it is fundamentally "about." Information extraction is similar to back-of-the-book indexing in that it seeks to identify significant names and concepts within a chunk of text, whereas auto-categorization is more like article database indexing in that it assigns one or more taxonomy terms to describe the subject matter of the document as a whole. Consequently, results may differ between the two approaches. Information extraction is more suitable for disparate unstructured content, such as all the different documents a company might generate, including email, whereas auto-categorization is better for retrieval of traditional information, such as articles and related documents. Finally, information extraction does not necessarily use a taxonomy, and when it does, it is usually a simple synonym ring. (Certain information extraction systems, though, can put named entities, such as geographic places and organizations, into a hierarchy.) Auto-categorization, on the other hand, usually involves a taxonomy, specifically a hierarchical taxonomy. As our interest is in taxonomies, this chapter will focus primarily on auto-categorization, after a brief look at information extraction and its most common form, entity extraction.

Information Extraction and Text Analytics

Information extraction, in some contexts called data extraction, and the overlapping fields of text analytics and text mining are technologies within the broader field of natural language processing that aim to extract useful information from varied unstructured content (that which lacks any metadata). These technologies, based on computational linguistics and pattern recognition, have been under development since the 1980s, building on natural language processing research begun as early as the 1960s, and have produced commercial products since the 1990s. A newer, even broader field of content extraction has also emerged that encompasses technologies to extract information from any kind of content including images, audio, and video, not just text. There are various technology approaches used in information extraction, including both statistics and rules-based techniques. A basic system might comprise components for the following tasks: dividing text into segments, sequencing text sentences, filtering out irrelevant sentences, detecting the basic parts of speech within sentences, parsing lexical fragments to produce a tree structure, semantically interpreting the parse tree, etc. On top of these tasks, either rules or machine learning might be added.

Entity Extraction

Entity extraction, also called entity recognition or entity identification, is the most common form of information extraction and comprises technologies to identify named entities in text documents. Named entities include people's names, company or organization names, locations, products, and sometimes named events or time designations. Proper nouns are, of course, easier to identify than other concepts, so entity extraction has a higher rate of reliability than concept-based information extraction. Therefore, some of the earliest automated indexing software was of this type. One of the first major commercial entity extraction tools was NetOwl, which SRA International (www.sra.com/netowl) has been offering since 1996. Organizations utilizing NetOwl include several large publishers of online content, including LexisNexis, Gale (part of Cengage Learning), KnightRidder, and Edgar Online.

There is a lot more involved, though, than just identifying words with capital letters that are not at the start of a sentence. Grammar-based linguistic rules and statistical models, as in topical auto-categorization, are required to develop an effective entity extraction system. Entity extraction thus does not necessarily involve a significantly different technology than the auto-categorization method previously described, but there are nuanced differences, requiring distinct software coding and rules. Thus, software products might be differentiated as either auto-categorizers or entity extractors. A single software product might also combine both, sometimes with the technology for one or the other feature developed by a third-party partner or vendor.

Entity extraction, along with its broader field of information extraction, does not presuppose an existing named term in a taxonomy, although in many cases it will make use of such terms. A controlled vocabulary will reconcile the variant forms of a name through its nonpreferred terms, but a new named term can also be extracted or indexed even if it is not included in a taxonomy. This may in fact be desirable to identify new names, especially of newly prominent people, companies, and products.

In addition to NetOwl, other entity extraction software products include the Inxight ThingFinder (www.inxightfedsys.com/

products/sdks/tf), Rosette Entity Extractor from Basis Technology (www.basistech.com/entity-extraction), and Data Harmony Metadata Extractor (www.dataharmony.com/products/meta dataextractor.html). There are also many others products that include entity extraction as a component rather than as a stand-alone product, such as SAS Enterprise Content Categorization, described later in this chapter.

Auto-Categorization

Automatic categorization, or auto-categorization for short, refers to automatically associating appropriate taxonomy terms, in this case called *categories*, with a document, based on one or more different technologies that automatically analyze the text and compare it with data stored with the taxonomy terms and possibly other data as well. In addition to assigning documents to one or more categories, some auto-categorization systems, especially those that are called auto-classifiers, might also assign some other metadata values.[2]

Referring to categories rather than terms in such a taxonomy is not merely a matter of simplicity. The designation *category* implies something broader than the designation *term*. Auto-categorization does better at the broader category level than with subtly different specific terms, which call for the discernment of human indexers. The categories involved in auto-categorization might have some hierarchy to them, but in general they do not get as specific as the terms found in a thesaurus used for human indexing. Thus, auto-categorization may be best used with taxonomies that are not too large.

As with automated indexing software in general, there are two different fundamental approaches to auto-categorization that uses an already developed taxonomy: rules-based systems and statistical systems, the latter usually based on machine learning. A third method, called statistical clustering, does not necessarily require a pre-existing taxonomy, as it can automatically generate taxonomy terms. Therefore, as far as taxonomists are concerned, there are just the two methods, rules-based and machine learning, to consider.

Rules-Based Auto-Categorization

Rules-based auto-categorization puts more emphasis on matching text patterns than on statistical analysis. Software that is entirely rules-based is not quite as common as machine learning-based auto-categorization, simply because greater human intervention is required, and the customers for auto-categorization tools tend to seek the most "automated" method. However, tools that combine rules-based and machine learning-based auto-categorization are becoming more common. For rules-based auto-categorization, humans, often taxonomists, write rules for taxonomy terms. These rules are conditional statements that often involve Boolean logic and may use operators that look at word order, word proximity, and content structure to identify patterns in the text and apply taxonomy terms accordingly. The collection of rules is sometimes called a *rule set* or a *knowledge base*. Auto-categorization systems may automatically generate basic rules for every term, and the taxonomist then only needs to write additional conditional statements for the terms that are more ambiguous.

Sometimes a word found in the text matches a term in the taxonomy as a true synonym, in which case no conditional rules are required. However, when a term in the taxonomy has multiple meanings, rules are needed for clarification. Nonpreferred terms also require qualification through rules in order to serve as unambiguous matches. For example, the term **earthquakes** has a number of possible nonpreferred terms, but these all have other meanings: **quake**, **tremors**, **trembler**, and **aftershocks**. These all could be used as nonpreferred terms, provided there are rules restricting these terms to texts that also include certain other words or phrases, such as **Richter scale**, **disaster**, or **structural damage**.

Both topical concepts and named entities may utilize rules. Rules are especially useful for distinguishing individuals with common surnames (Smith, Brown, Johnson); names that could apply to individuals, organizations, or places (Washington, Columbus, Madison, Jackson); or names that are also common words (Bush, Rice, Gates).

Rules can refer to many different conditions regarding the word or phrase of text to match. These include:

- Truncation of the word

- The mention of other words in the text

- Proximity to other words in the text

- Relation to other words in the text, based on Boolean AND, OR, and NOT operators

- Initial capitalization or full-word capitalization

- Text placement within a sentence (a rule usually used in combination with capitalization)

Software tools vary in how they require the rules to be formatted, but a common construction involves IF, IF ELSE, or more complex variations. The following example, in which terms following the statement USE are in the taxonomy, comes from the Data Harmony Machine Aided Indexer User's Guide.[3]

> *Text to Match:* **norwegian**
>
> **IF (MENTIONS "language")**
>   USE **Norwegian language**
> **ELSE IF (MENTIONS "country")**
>   USE **Norway**
> **ENDIF**
> **ENDIF**

Some rules-based systems also utilize regular expressions (*regex* for short), which are special text strings for describing complex search patterns. Writing regular expressions, usually done by someone called a knowledge engineer rather than a taxonomist, involves following numerous coding rules. It is like creating filter rules for incoming emails to automatically go into a spam folder or other folders, but without a dropdown list of options and with countless more possible rules.

Machine Learning-Based Auto-Categorization

Auto-categorization that is based on machine learning involves initially having the auto-categorization software "ingest" numerous sample documents that are already correctly indexed according to the taxonomy. This method is also called *catalog by example*. The system then uses algorithms and statistical analysis to "learn" patterns of text content to determine what kind of text is typically indexed with which taxonomy terms. The statistical analysis is based on various techniques, including:

- Bayesian computations: Methods of probability and statistics named after the 18th-century mathematician Thomas Bayes

- Support vector machines: Classification performed initially by the construction of a hyperplane that separates the data into two categories

- Neural networks: Statistical analysis procedure based on models of the nervous system (less common than the other two techniques)

All these methods can "learn" from a collection of examples to discover patterns and trends and to determine what is useful and what is statistically rare.

In machine learning, feeding numerous sample pre-indexed documents is required for what is called *training the system*, and the documents are called *training documents*. The minimum number of training documents required and the degree of auto-mated indexing accuracy achievable after training depends on various factors:

- The statistical method used

- The algorithms used

- The word count of the training documents

- The quality and content of the training documents

- The nature, meaning, and clarity (lack of ambiguity) of the individual taxonomy term

Depending on these circumstances, tens of documents or hundreds of documents could be required to train a particular term. Some documents provide very clear examples of a taxonomy concept, while others express it less concisely, directly, and clearly. It is possible that less than ten training documents might suffice under ideal circumstances, including a perfectly clear and unambiguous term and clear, simple training documents, but this is not always the case.

If an existing indexing business or operation is migrating from human indexers to automated indexing, then there should be no difficulty in coming up with the desired number of pre-indexed training documents for a given term, except perhaps for some rarely used terms. This is because there already exists a large published collection of human-indexed content to tap for training documents.

If you are starting up an indexing operation from scratch, however, without an existing corpus of indexed documents, then coming up with training documents demands a lot more work.

Someone, most likely the taxonomist, must either test-index a large number of documents or find training documents indexed by someone else for each term. Test indexing of documents is useful only to a limited degree. While it is a realistic method to determine what combinations of terms are often needed for typical documents, the documents used might not include some of the taxonomy terms. The other approach, taking each taxonomy term and finding suitable training documents, ensures that all terms are covered. However, finding ideal documents for training is not always easy and requires good online searching skills. It can also take a lot of time.

In some machine-learning systems, the training documents then yield additional automatically generated "keywords" from the multiple texts that are associated with the taxonomy term being trained. The statistical analysis assigns a percentage relevancy or weighting for each automatically generated keyword, but the taxonomist (or perhaps *machine-aided indexing analyst*) can manually change individual keyword relevancies if the automatically assigned relevancy seems too high or low (usually too high).

Whether starting with a corpus of pre-indexed content, test-indexing individual documents, or searching for new documents for each term, machine-learning automated indexing requires the additional step of quality testing. You will need to check samples of automatically indexed documents matched for each term to determine whether they are sufficiently acceptable (minimal inappropriate documents retrieved) and then make appropriate changes to the collection of training documents. This process involves removing training documents whose content is skewing the results and perhaps adding more appropriate documents or making refinements to the given term by adding or deleting non-preferred terms. Depending on the nature and source of the training documents, you may even be able to edit the documents in order to provide more ideal content. All these adjustments are part of what is called *tuning* in the machine-learning process, and it can be a time-consuming task, even a full-time job. If the taxonomy is large, it may not be possible to check and tune every term, so only the high-usage terms get tuned.

Comparison of Auto-Categorization Methods

Whether auto-categorization is based on rules for each term or on machine-learning and training documents, it still requires human involvement, and that human is often the taxonomist who created the taxonomy and continues to maintain it. The tasks and skills required in ensuring that the auto-categorization system properly matches text with taxonomy terms are very different for each method, though.

Writing the rules for rules-based auto-categorization requires intimate familiarity with each taxonomy term and its appropriate usage, so usually the taxonomist who creates the taxonomy also writes the rules. In addition, high-level analytical and problem-solving abilities are needed. Skills in traditional command-line online searching are helpful, although not necessary, for constructing Boolean and nested search expressions, which may remind long-time librarians of command-line Dialog searching.

If regular expressions are also required, then the work is a little more like scripting or coding. You do not need to be a software programmer, but you do need to have a certain comfort level with coding, such as HTML or XML. Some information professionals get into this, and some do not.

The tuning of machine learning, on the other hand, requires the kinds of skills used by a periodical/database-type of indexer or an online searcher to come up with and/or evaluate sample training documents. Thus, former periodical indexers are well qualified for this task. In fact, taxonomist-level skills are not necessary, although one does need to be familiar with the taxonomy. A single taxonomist might have several other people who are not taxonomists aid in the task of identifying, assigning, and managing training documents to terms.

The degree of human involvement in auto-categorization systems has a direct impact on the indexing accuracy and retrieval success rate. This includes additional human effort to refine and improve a term's nonpreferred terms, training documents, or rules. In evaluating the success rates of different auto categorization methods, vendors will claim that their system is better, but there are in fact too many variables for any accurate comparison of the methods. Machine-learning systems may have a 60–70 percent retrieval success rate without tuning,[4] but tuning can achieve a rate of more than 80 percent correct retrievals for certain unambiguous terms. With enough effort in the rules writing, rules-based auto-categorization may achieve a 90 percent success rate.[5] Rules-based auto-categorization tends to have a higher success rate than machine learning on average, simply because a high level of tuning is not a requirement to run a machine-learning system, and if sufficient training documents are lacking, there is not much that can be done. Writing rules for each term, however, is a necessity for rules-based auto-categorization to function at all, and whoever writes the rules has greater control over the end results than does the person who gathers training documents for a machine-learning system. In other words, because rules-based auto-categorization involves greater taxonomist involvement, it tends to have higher success rates.

Automated Taxonomy Generation
Both rules-based and machine-learning-based auto-categorization methods rely on pre-built taxonomies (built by taxonomists) and match the terms in these taxonomies to the documents being indexed. Some auto-categorization vendors, however, have taken the notion of "automated" one step further by implementing technology to automatically generate what they call taxonomies along

with the auto-categorization of content. The method usually used is statistical clustering, which involves the grouping together of documents that share words with the same meanings, as determined by a text analytics component that parses the text and then assigns these clustered documents to a category. Not only do these systems automatically create something like a taxonomy, but the categorization is also fully automated, requiring no humans to assign training documents or to write rules for each taxonomy term. Although more rudimentary than human-created taxonomies, these automatically generated "taxonomies" may even have a hierarchy. In such cases, though, a taxonomist usually creates the top-level categories. For example, many entity extraction systems can populate predefined entity categories or facets with appropriate name terms upon search execution.

These automatically generated "taxonomies" are far from meeting the standards described in the ANSI/NISO Z39.19 guidelines. They also tend to include redundant concepts and mixed degrees of specificity (granularity).[6] However, such systems should not be dismissed merely as inadequate substitutes for human-crafted taxonomies but should instead be viewed as good sources for suggested terms that the taxonomist can edit into a proper taxonomy. Vendors of automatic taxonomy generation software include Autonomy (www.autonomy.com) and iQuest Analytics (www.iquestglobal.com).

Software for Auto-Categorization

Compared with the field of thesaurus management software, the field of auto-categorization and other automated indexing software, such as for entity extraction and text analytics, is a less mature industry segment, with companies appearing, disappearing, and being acquired at a relatively high rate. In the first few years of the 2000s, there were perhaps 50 automated indexing software vendors, but this number has since gone down by about half.[7]

Commercial auto-categorization systems that utilize taxonomies handle these taxonomies in different ways. The software may:

- Come with preinstalled taxonomies that cannot be edited

- Come with preinstalled taxonomies that the user may edit and extend through the user interface

- Automatically generate a taxonomy that can be edited

- Support the import of taxonomies but not the editing of those taxonomies

- Support both the import of taxonomies and the editing of those taxonomies

There are also combinations of the aforementioned capabilities. For example, the systems that come with preinstalled taxonomies often also support the import of additional taxonomies. Finally, even auto-categorization software without a feature for taxonomies can often integrate with taxonomy management software through APIs (application programming interfaces), connectors, or custom programming. Vendor partnerships are widespread in this industry.

Auto-categorization software that can import taxonomies but that lacks user-interface features to edit those taxonomies is quite common and includes products of Microsoft SharePoint, IBM Classification Module, Fast, Endeca, Temis, Vivisimo, Mindbreeze, Exalead, and PerfectSearch. Many of these companies collaborate with others that develop taxonomies or have taxonomy editing capabilities. Automated indexing/search software that allows importing of taxonomies varies, however, with regard to the degree of complexity it can support in the imported taxonomies. For example, the auto-categorization software may not support associative relationships, only hierarchical, and it may be limited to a certain number of hierarchy levels. Features that support the building and editing of taxonomies exist in only the minority of auto-categorization systems, but more vendors are taking an interest in taxonomy management capabilities. Their taxonomy management features may be weak, however, especially from the perspective of skilled taxonomists. Therefore, it may still be more efficient to build and edit a taxonomy in an external thesaurus management program and then import it into the auto-categorization system, keeping in mind any import limitations.

The auto-categorization software that comes with preinstalled taxonomies, which may or may not be editable, tends to cover specific vertical markets such as pharmaceuticals, insurance, or law enforcement, and to include named entities such as company names and geographic places. Product or industry types are also common as pre-built taxonomies. From vendors in the U.K., a typical preinstalled taxonomy is the Integrated Public Sector Vocabulary (IPSV), the standard vocabulary for use by local public sector agencies. Pre-built taxonomies with auto-categorization systems are usually simple hierarchical taxonomies, not thesauri, and in addition to lacking associative term relationships, they may even lack nonpreferred terms. Chapter 1 mentions additional sources of pre-built taxonomies.

Combined Auto-Categorization/Taxonomy Management Software

A number of software systems combine auto-categorization with varying degrees of taxonomy development and management capabilities. Software products typically have strengths in one area or the other but not both, so those that are more robust in auto-categorization may be weaker in taxonomy management features, and those that are superior in taxonomy management tend to be inferior in auto-categorization.

Software that focuses on auto-categorization or text analytics while providing at least some degree of internal taxonomy management includes Inxight SmartDiscovery Analysis Server (www. inxightfedsys.com), Autonomy Collaborative Classifier (www. autonomy.com), Autonomy Interwoven MetaTagger (www.inter woven.com), and Lexalytics Classifier (www.lexalytics.com), among others. These systems compete on the basis of their auto matic indexing capabilities, and less attention is paid to taxonomy management features. Additionally, since search/retrieval remains the primary goals of these tools, with taxonomy development only a supporting task, the vendors' literature on such software tends to focus on the needs of the content manager rather than the needs of the taxonomist. So it is difficult to discern the extent of the taxonomy management capabilities of these tools without trying them out. Evaluating auto-categorization software with taxonomy management is not a simple software evaluation, however, but ideally involves a proof-of-concept procedure.

Software that fully supports thesaurus management (as described in Chapter 5) while also including some degree of auto-categorization are the automated indexing programs probably of the greatest interest to the taxonomist. These include offerings from Data Harmony, Smartlogic, SAS, Wordmap, and Nstein. Software from the young company conceptSearching is not quite as full-featured in its taxonomy management as the others are, but the company puts a lot of emphasis on taxonomy, so it is also described in this section. Additionally, the taxonomy and metadata tool SchemaLogic, while not incorporating auto-categorization technology itself, supports tight integration with third-party auto-categorization systems through its classification module, connectors, and APIs. The products described in the following paragraphs are not being endorsed, and industry analysts would likely present potential customers with a different list of products, but the products are mentioned here because the taxonomist might encounter or use them.

Data Harmony MAIstro

As mentioned in Chapter 5, Access Innovations sells a large-scale taxonomy management system called Data Harmony Thesaurus Master (www.dataharmony.com). An additional product from Access Innovations is its Machine Aided Indexer (M.A.I.), which enables categorization through the rules-based method. M.A.I actually serves two functions: 1) machine-aided indexing, whereby the system suggests terms based on rules for individual documents, which the indexer can then accept or reject (the indexer can also add missing terms), and 2) fully automated indexing of documents in batch mode, typically used only after sufficient fine-tuning of the rules so that the top returns on the list are reliably accurate. According to Access Innovations Chief Taxonomist Alice Redmond-Neal, most of the company's clients utilize M.A.I. for machine-aided indexing rather than for fully automated indexing and find it increases indexing speed up to 6.7 times that of completely manual indexing.[8]

While Thesaurus Master and M.A.I. are each available as separate products, an integrated system is also available, called Data Harmony MAIstro. In MAIstro, there are three tabs for the three window displays: Thesaurus Master, M.A.I. Rule Builder, and Test MAI. Thesaurus Master is the same as the stand-alone product for creating thesauri, the MAI Rule Builder is used to edit existing rules and also create new rules (basic rules are included programmatically), and Test MAI allows you to paste text from a document to test how well your rule works in assigning taxonomy terms to it. Although you can use the stand-alone M.A.I. by itself on any term list, in MAIstro the M.A.I. component automatically creates a basic rule for every term and nonpreferred term in the Thesaurus Master's thesaurus, and the terms and rules stay synchronized. An additional feature is an internal statistics module that tracks the editor's term choices and compares them with M.A.I. term suggestions, sorting them as hits, misses, and noise to guide and prioritize the editor's fine-tuning of rules. MAIstro has connectors to link to search engines and content management systems, including SharePoint.

Smartlogic Semaphore Classification Server

Smartlogic (www.smartlogic.com), whose Semaphore Ontology Manager is described in Chapter 5, also offers a rules-based classification engine called Semaphore Classification Server. The Classification Server has three components: Automatic Rules Creator, Rule Template Editor, and Semantic Processor. Utilizing taxonomies created in the Ontology Manager, the Classification Server has the capability to automatically generate rules based on the relationships of the terms in the taxonomy. The user can then edit those rules, create new manual rules that take precedence, and test those rules in the Rule Template Editor. The system supports 20 different kinds of rules and various kinds of wildcards. In addition, a text miner tool accelerates taxonomy and ontology development by suggesting additional terms. The vocabulary and the relationships in the ontology are used when creating the rule bases.

Smartlogic also offers editions of its Ontology Manager that connect to enterprise search engines FAST ESP and Google Search Appliance for additional means of integrating taxonomy with automated searching.

SAS Enterprise Content Categorization

SAS, a company that has been providing business analytics software since the 1970s, offers a suite of automated indexing and taxonomy products called SAS Text Analytics (www.sas.com/text-analytics). The SAS Text Analytics suite is based on the products of Teragram that SAS acquired in 2008 and includes the following components: Enterprise Content Categorization, Ontology Management, Sentiment Analysis, and Text Mining.

Enterprise Content Categorization (ECC), formerly Teragram TK240 Taxonomy Manager, is an auto-classification tool that includes the capability for building, maintaining, and testing taxonomies, whether built from scratch by the taxonomist, auto-generated and then edited, or preinstalled by SAS. ECC has both auto-categorization and entity/concept extraction capabilities. For its rules-based auto-categorization, ECC supports the writing of rules with a graphical tree view of Boolean operators and commands for selection. It also supports entity extraction rules and regular expression. The user can define weighting of terms for a more statistical approach to auto-categorization

Because ECC also comes with prebuilt taxonomies, nontaxonomists often use it, and thus less emphasis is put on the manual taxonomy creation features. Although ECC does support creating the basic kinds of term relationships (equivalent, hierarchical, and associative), taxonomists may choose to use the other SAS product, Ontology Manager, to build more complex thesauri and ontologies, which support custom relationships and term attributes. These ontologies can easily be exported into ECC for auto-categorization use.

Wordmap Designer and Intelligent Text Classifier

Wordmap (www.wordmap.com), also described in Chapter 5, sells a suite of products for taxonomy creation, indexing, and navigation/search, which can be purchased separately or integrated together. Wordmap Designer is the taxonomy management base package, and Wordmap Intelligent Text Classifier is the auto-classification tool. The auto-categorization technology employed is a statistical method based on Support Vector Machine algorithms and machine learning with training documents. The Intelligent Text Classifier is prepackaged with statistical algorithms based on a generic taxonomy, the U.K.'s IPSV, for which hundreds of terms have already been "trained" with representative documents. Wordmap also offers Taxonomy Connectors for taxonomy-driven tagging and search within Microsoft SharePoint Server and Endeca. This is another way in which a taxonomy created in Wordmap might be used for automated indexing.

Nstein Text Mining Engine

Nstein (www.nstein.com) is a Montreal-based company that provides content management, digital asset management, image management, and automated indexing especially to large periodical and database publishers. (In early 2010, Nstein was acquired by Open Text Corp.) It offers a combination of taxonomy management and automated indexing/search in its Text Mining Engine (TME), a product suite comprising several modules. Some TME modules can be purchased separately, whereas others need to be purchased in combination. Modules include the Nconcept Extractor for concept extraction, Nfinder for entity extraction, Ncategorizer for auto-categorization, Nsummarizer for automated abstract creation, Nsentiment for sentiment analysis, and NLikeThis for finding similar documents. TME and any of its individual modules include Nstein's Taxonomy Manager tool, which is not sold separately.

The Taxonomy Manager component of TME is a full-featured thesaurus management tool that supports hierarchical, associative, and equivalence relationships in accordance with ANSI/NISO Z39.19 standards and other library group standards. There is also the option to maintain named entities separately in TME's Authority File Manager. With Taxonomy Manager, you can build taxonomies from scratch or import them via XML, CSV, text, or other formats. TME also ships with prebuilt taxonomies: the International Press Telecommunications Council taxonomy, the Industry Classification Benchmark database of companies and securities from Dow Jones, and the Library of Congress Thesaurus for Graphic Materials. Nstein's auto-categorization technology combines the concept extraction technology of Nconcept Extractor with the use of training documents for each taxonomy term. You provide training documents for your own taxonomies, but all of the preinstalled taxonomies come already trained.

conceptSearching

The conceptSearching software is a web-based auto-classification and search product from Concept Searching Ltd. (www.concept searching. com), a company founded in 2002 in the U.K. The conceptSearching product uses a statistical method for search, not with the usual machine learning and training documents but rather a different technology called Compound Term Processing, which conceptSearching introduced in 2003. Compound Term Processing, based on Shannon Information Theory, computes the incremental value of compound terms (i.e., multi-word terms) over their component parts. The process uses algorithms, which adapt to each customer's content. In addition to this search technology, conceptSearching includes a rules-based auto-categorization module. A separate version of the product is for indexing/classifying specifically SharePoint content.

The integrated conceptSearching suite includes a simple taxonomy management tool, Taxonomy Manager, which allows the user to define both hierarchical and nonhierarchical relationships. While the underlying SQL tables allow for naming the relationships, the user interface does not yet provide a way to view or edit the relationship names.[9] There are various taxonomy import formats, with XML, including OWL, being the easiest to import. Through the Taxonomy Manager, the user can manage and adjust the weights of the keywords, or "clues," that the software automatically generates from the content.

The conceptSearching product also offers a choice of various general industry taxonomies for sale from its taxonomy library, intended more as a means to accelerate a customer's taxonomy development process than to replace it. In fact, its literature says these taxonomies offer the benefit of the "ability to modify the taxonomy to meet specific organizational requirements."[10]

Creating Taxonomies for Automated Indexing

Taxonomies for automated indexing, whether by information extraction or auto-categorization, are not fundamentally different from those for human indexing. After all, the end users and the search/retrieval interface may be the same, regardless of the indexing method. Taxonomists should try to follow the best practices suggested in the ANSI/NISO Z39.19 guidelines with respect to term format and relationships, no matter how the taxonomy is used. Nevertheless, automated indexing calls for certain considerations with respect to taxonomies.

Terms for Automated Indexing

Despite the increasing sophistication of automated indexing, no automated system can achieve the level of interpretation of subtle ideas that humans can. Therefore, a taxonomy used in automated indexing cannot support as great a number of concepts. This is particularly the case for statistical methods of auto-categorization. For example, in a taxonomy used by human indexers, you could maintain distinct concepts/terms for each of **insurance companies, insurance agents**, **insurance brokers**, and **insurance underwriters**, but automated indexing would not be able to distinguish the subtle differences among these terms. You should also avoid creating terms for both an action and a topic within the same taxonomy, especially if they share the same root, such as **investing** and **investments** or **contracting** and **contracts**, although in separate facets this might be acceptable. While the usage of one term or the other is clear to the trained indexer, it is difficult for an automated system to discern.

Precoordination works better for automated indexing, whether rules-based or statistical, than leaving simple terms for postcoordination. Examples of precoordinated terms, explained in more detail in Chapter 3, include **software training**, **federal aid to education**, and **materials handling equipment industry**. Such phrase terms will more likely match phrases in the texts and what users may enter in the search box. As described earlier, leaving terms for postcoordination (such as **software** AND **training**) is more subject to ambiguity in search and retrieval. Meanwhile, subdivisions for structured indexing, sometimes used for human indexing, as mentioned in Chapter 6, are too complex for automated indexing.

Although with automated indexing there are no human indexers to read term notes, such notes are still helpful for the end user, so taxonomies for automated indexing often have scope notes or other forms of expanded explanations.

Nonpreferred Terms for Automated Indexing

Nonpreferred terms are especially important in taxonomies used for automatic indexing since a crucial part of the process is creating automatic matches between taxonomy terms and words in the content texts. In general, you will want more nonpreferred terms for automated indexing than for human indexing. While a human indexer will search and browse for different possible terms, the automated system must make exact matches, subject only to possible grammatical stemming and any filtering conditions in rules. On the other hand, for automated indexing you do not need phrase inverted nonpreferred terms (such as **photography, digital**) that are useful to the human indexer who is searching for terms alphabetically. The following example compares possible nonpreferred terms for the term **presidential candidates** for human and automated indexing:

Nonpreferred terms for human indexing of **presidential candidates:**
   candidates, presidential

Nonpreferred terms for automated indexing of **presidential candidates:**

campaigning for president	**presidential candidate**
candidacy for president	**presidential hopeful**
candidate for president	**presidential nominee**
presidential candidacy	**running for president**

As shown in the preceding example, nonpreferred terms for automated indexing may include verbal phrases that do not conform to standard formats for terms. In fact, when it comes to proposing text string matches, there may be a blurred distinction between taxonomy nonpreferred terms and the suggested matches in a rules-based auto-categorization system. Where you put these suggested variant matches depends on the software system you are using.

For automated indexing, you might also want to distinguish between different types of nonpreferred terms, such as those that are auto-generated and those that are human-created. Acronyms can be ambiguous, especially in automated indexing. Thus, designating acronyms as acronyms and not just generic nonpreferred terms may help.

Term Relationships for Automated Indexing

Hierarchical relationships are the same whether a taxonomy is used for human or automated indexing, and polyhierarchies are useful in either application. Automated indexing tends to make use of hierarchical taxonomies, while thesauri are more common in human indexing.

Associative relationships may occur in taxonomies used in automated indexing, but they are not quite as common as in taxonomies used in human indexing. Associative relationships are highly useful for the human indexer, and they are also useful for the end-user searcher to suggest possible related concepts of interest. If there are no human indexers and no browsable display of a taxonomy to end users, then it is simpler to omit associative relationships, despite their potential usefulness. Furthermore, auto-categorization systems that make use of auto-generated keywords from content may automatically suggest related terms on the fly, based on shared keywords among the preferred terms.

Summary of Taxonomy Creation Differences

In creating taxonomies for human or automated indexing, there are different areas of emphasis. Taxonomies for human indexing should have:

- Extensive relationships, hierarchical and associative, between terms
- Term notes for clarification
- Additional common-use shortcuts and phrase inversions as nonpreferred terms

Taxonomies for automated indexing should have:

- No subtle differences between terms
- Precoordinated terms, but no structured subdivisions
- Many varied nonpreferred terms, including non-noun phrases

In addition, automated indexing is more suitable for applying weighting or relevance ranking to assigned index terms, whether as primary or secondary, or by even further gradations measured in percentages. In human indexing, this process requires an additional step and decision for the indexer, but in automated indexing, especially that which is based on statistical methods, it is easy to implement.

The same taxonomy may be used for both human indexing and automated indexing. Within an organization, autocategorization may be applied to some content while humans still index other content. There are also hybrid strategies of machine-aided indexing, which provide automated assistance to human indexers. The humans' skill and analysis are combined with software to raise productivity and speed, while still allowing indexer-editors to make final choices to ensure indexing accuracy. If a taxonomy is to be used for both human and automated indexing, whether separately or combined in machine-aided indexing, there are not necessarily any conflicts. You will need to put additional work into the taxonomy, though, so that it serves both methods of indexing well. Thus, it is important to know from the beginning how the taxonomy will be used.

Endnotes

1. Lynda Moulton, speaking at the Boston KM Forum, Waltham, Massachusetts, June 18, 2009.
2. Bernard Chester, "Auto-Categorization and Records Management," *AIIM E-Doc Magazine* 18, no. 2 (March 2004): 16.
3. *Data Harmony Version 3.3 User's Guide–M.A.I. (Machine Aided Indexer)* (Albuquerque, NM: Access Innovations, 2006), 53.
4. Bonnie Burwell, "Auto-Categorization Tools," *Intranet Professional* (Mar/Apr 2002), www.intranetstoday.com/Articles/Default2.aspx?ArticleID=5058&AuthorID=96
5. Tom Reamy, email to author, June 23, 2009.
6. Louis Rosenfeld and Peter Morville, *Information architecture for the World Wide Web*, 2nd ed. (Cambridge, MA: O'Reilly, 2002), 325.
7. Tom Reamy, email to author, June 23, 2009, in follow-up to the article Tom Reamy, "Auto-Categorization: Coming to a Library or Intranet Near You!" *EContent* (November 2002): 18.

8.   Alice Redmond-Neal (Chief Taxonomist, Access Innovations, Inc.), email to author, July 20, 2009, and Margie Hlava (President of Access Innovations, Inc.), email to author, July 21, 2009.

9.   John Challis (CEO/CTO of Concept Searching Ltd.), email to author, July 26, 2009.

10. Jumpstart Taxonomy Development, www.conceptsearching.com/Web/Userfiles/File/Concept Searching Taxonomy Library.pdf

Chapter 8

Taxonomy Structures

Taxonomies: find, organise, discover.
—Patrick Lambe

We have discussed the importance of well-designed terms and relationships, as well as considerations in human and automated indexing, but a taxonomy usually involves structure as well. After all, the technical designation for a taxonomy or controlled vocabulary is *knowledge organization system*. If taxonomies are to organize knowledge, then they must be organized themselves. This chapter looks at structure via hierarchies, facets, and categories. These different methods of organizing and structuring a taxonomy are not mutually exclusive and may overlap. Chapter 9 addresses the impact of taxonomy structure on the display of the taxonomy.

Hierarchies

Hierarchies, also known as tree structures, are the extension of broader term/narrower term relationships to include every term within a controlled vocabulary. They are the defining feature of hierarchical taxonomies. The emphasis of a hierarchy is on categorization, classification, or sorting. They are created—and used—largely from the top down.

Hierarchies were originally developed to classify things—plants, animals, tools, products, books, or other creative works—but are increasingly used now to organize concepts or topics as well. Examples of hierarchies for classifying things include the following:

- Linnaean taxonomy for classification of living organisms
- Dewey Decimal Classification for books
- SIC or NAICS codes for businesses and industries
- Yahoo! directory (dir.yahoo.com) and Open Directory Project (www.dmoz.org) for websites

When classifying physical things, which can go into only one place, such as books on a shelf or an object in a museum, each taxonomy term can have only one broader term. However, most modern taxonomies exist in electronic form, and so do the items to which they refer, such as websites or digital media. Therefore, a concept can virtually exist in more than one place in the hierarchy. In other words, a term can have more than one broader term; this is called a polyhierarchy. However, even if a taxonomy supports polyhierarchies, they should be created with discretion. There still needs to be an overarching general structure that is logical and easy to use; too many polyhierarchies could become confusing. Designing a clear hierarchical structure takes more than just knowledge of the subject area, as there is often more than one way to create a hierarchy.

Certain subject areas lend themselves more easily to hierarchies than others. Those areas that already have a natural, intuitive, or standard classification scheme are good candidates for hierarchical arrangements of terms. Examples include geographic places, organizational or governmental department structures, industries/ products, academic disciplines, scientific/natural objects, and chemicals. Subject areas that are more challenging to arrange into tree-type hierarchies include methods and activities, current events, and any broad area of knowledge.

Arrangements of Hierarchies

Even a "logical" hierarchy may not be as easy to create as first anticipated. When alternatives for classification exist, you first face the decision of how to design a categorization structure. Industries, for example, can be organized by a standard classification system, such as SIC or NAICS codes, or alternatively by vertical market sector, such as information technology (hardware, software, and services), healthcare, transportation, and media. A similar decision would be whether to organize products by material and manufacturing technology (metal products, glass products, plastic products, etc.) or by end use (office products, kitchen products, giftware, toys, etc.) In other areas, terms for organizations can be grouped differently, such as by their objectives (charitable work, political action, educational outreach) or by political or religious affiliation. Government agencies can be categorized by type or by state/country affiliation. Finally, places, which initially may seem perfectly simple to classify, can be organized either by geospatial location on the globe or by type of place (country, city, body of water, etc.). Figure 8.1 illustrates these two different ways to classify places.

Factors to Consider

In determining the arrangement of the hierarchy for your taxonomy, you need to consider user requirements and expectations.

Geo-spatial hierarchy:

Geographies
- North America   - South   - Europe   -Asia   - Africa   - Oceania
-- United States   America
--- New England
---- Massachusetts
----- Boston
------ North End
------- Old North Church

Term-type hierarchy:

Geographies
- Cities   - U.S. States   - Countries   - Continents   - Landmarks
-- Amsterdam   -- Alabama   -- Afghanistan   -- Africa   -- Abu Simbel
-- Athens   -- Alaska   -- Albania   -- Asia   -- Angkor Wat
    etc.   etc.   etc.   etc.   etc.

Figure 8.1 Two possible arrangements for a geographic hierarchy

Ask yourself this: Based on their background and perspective, how would the majority of the users most likely classify the subject matter? For products, classification by end use makes most sense for users who are consumers, whereas classification by material type is more appropriate for wholesalers. For organizing national and international government agencies, a U.S.-centric taxonomy structure would be appropriate for U.S. federal employees but not for international users. For scientific or technical subject areas, while a "correct" hierarchy may exist, if users are not knowledgeable about the subject, then they will not know under which broader term to find desired narrower terms. For example, a classification of world languages based on language families (Indo-European languages, Ural-Altaic languages, etc.) makes sense if your users are scholars, but for the general public or younger students, classification by world region (European languages, Asian languages, etc.) might make more sense. User testing, if you have access to it, is ideal for supporting this kind of decision making. Having users participate in card sorting exercises, described further in Chapter 10, can reveal valuable information about how your users prefer to categorize concepts.

In designing hierarchies, additional factors to consider include:

- Support of polyhierarchies: If policy prohibits polyhierarchies, then input from stakeholders and user studies are even more critical in helping you decide how to arrange the hierarchies.

- Permissibility of node labels: If node labels (category designations, not linked to content, described later) are allowed, you will have greater flexibility to design truly accurate hierarchies.

- Retrieval inclusive of all narrower terms (also called recursive): If searching can automatically retrieve all content linked to a term's narrower terms, you should be extra careful that the hierarchies function as expected.

Named Entities in Hierarchies

A more specific issue in designing hierarchies is deciding at what level to relate corresponding named entity terms, if at all. A hierarchical taxonomy comprises primarily generic-specific hierarchical relationships, but instance relationships could be included within it. Sometimes named entities are in a completely separate list, an authority file (as discussed later in the section Multiple Vocabularies and Categories). Even if named entities are maintained separately, there still could be hierarchical relationships created between these entities and their corresponding generic terms. You then need to decide at what level within the generic hierarchy to create the relationships to the entity instances. Creating relationships from the most specific (lowest hierarchy level) generic term to named entity instances may seem to be the most logical policy, but it is not always best from the end-user perspective. Users might not know or expect to have to go so deep into the hierarchy to find named entities. Furthermore, entity relationships could change over time, requiring greater attention to maintenance.

In the following example, a generic-specific hierarchy of political occupations has instance relationship to named entities of individual people. As the taxonomist, you may choose to create the entity instance relationships to the most specific terms of **presidents** and **prime ministers**, or you may choose to relate all these named entities at one level higher to **heads of state & government**.

> **Heads of state & government** ← names of all kinds of
> heads of state linked here,
> *or*

— Presidents   ← names of presidents
                                  linked here, *and*
— Prime ministers   ← names of prime ministers
                                  linked here

The reason to consider relating the names of individuals to the slightly broader **heads of state & government** instead of to one or the other of its narrower terms is that users might not know whether the head of state in a particular country is a president or a prime minister. It would be more convenient for these users to have a single alphabetical list for all. On the other hand, if the hierarchy belongs to the library of an educational institution, there may be an added objective to educate the student users as to the most complete and correct information. Another issue to consider is whether there are entities that do not neatly fall into a most specific generic term category (in this example Vladimir Putin, whose title has switched between president and prime minister), in which case moving the entities up a level would be better.

Depth and Breadth of Hierarchies

Related to the issue of how to design the classification structure are decisions regarding the depth and breadth of each hierarchical level. For a taxonomy on a website, a popular rule of thumb is to go only three levels deep and have only six to eight concepts per level. These numbers are based on user experience tests, which have shown that users have the patience to click down only to a third level and can scan only six to eight term entries at once. This rule makes sense for a small taxonomy integrated into a website navigation menu, where the space is confined to a strip along the top or a margin along the side. In reality, though, a taxonomy may have hundreds or thousands of preferred terms. Therefore, for a hierarchical taxonomy, you often need to consider how best to balance the number of levels (depth) and number of terms per level (breadth).

There are no hard rules on how to structure hierarchies. The following pair of examples shows how industry names could be placed in a deep hierarchy of many levels, which is what is done with SIC and NAICS industry codes, or in a relatively flat level category, which in this case comes from the job search site Monster.com.

NAICS (deep hierarchy)	Monster.com (flat hierarchy)
Industries	**Industries**
- Transportation services	**- Accounting & Auditing Services**
-- Air transportation	**- Advertising & PR Services**
--- Scheduled air transportation services	**- Aerospace & Defense**
---- Scheduled air freight transportation services	**- Agriculture, Forestry, & Fishing**
	etc.

Factors to Consider

Factors that may influence your decisions on the depth and breadth of a hierarchy include user expectations, the need to maintain consistency, and user interface design. The first consideration is the nature of the content and the users' needs and expectations. If the content for the taxonomy is scholarly or scientific or if the users are researchers or students, the users will expect many levels. A consumer or news-oriented service, on the other hand, accessed by the public, would likely have fewer levels but a greater number of top-level terms and terms at each level. Areas that users understand as naturally hierarchical, such as industries/product types and geographic places, can support more levels of depth than subjects that are less intuitively hierarchical, such as business management topics.

Another issue to keep in mind is that, inevitably, the greater the number of levels, the less consistency there will be across levels.

This may or may not be important. If users are experts in the subject area or are using the taxonomy frequently, providing accurate terms is more important than providing a uniform-looking hierarchy. If, on the other hand, users are from the general public and are likely to be new to the taxonomy, then a logically organized taxonomy with a relatively consistent number of levels and consistent degree of specificity at each level would be desirable.

The user interface display, with its vertical or horizontal space limitations, also has an impact on hierarchy design decisions. Therefore, it is advantageous to know in advance what the interface will look like. If each level will display in a separate webpage, then as many terms as can fit onto one page in two or three columns without scrolling could work nicely. Such long lists of terms at the same level, however, may be difficult for the user to skim quickly and are more appropriate for alphabetized lists of proper nouns. If the taxonomy will display as an expandable tree in which sublevels appear, such as by clicking on a plus sign, then more than three levels is fine, but the number of terms per level ought not extend beyond a single page length in a single column, because the position in the hierarchy cannot be seen. Finally, if the taxonomy will be implemented in facets (described later), then deep hierarchies are less likely to be needed or desirable. From the taxonomist's perspective, ideally the taxonomy design should dictate the user interface design, not vice versa. Often, however, a product development team designs the user interface without giving consideration to content and prior to creation of the taxonomy, and the taxonomist needs to adapt.

All, General, and Other

In certain areas, thesauri and full hierarchical taxonomies, by their nature, affect indexing and searching differently. One such area is the indexing and retrieval of *all*, *general*, and *other* topics pertaining to a taxonomy term that also has narrower terms.

All Uses of a Broader Term

Because a hierarchical taxonomy categorizes everything, users often expect to retrieve everything within a category at the broader level. This is sometimes called *recursive retrieval*. (The word *recursive* also has other usages in information science.) When the user selects a term, everything indexed to that term *and* everything that is indexed to all of its narrower terms are retrieved in a single large result set. Whether the indexing is done by humans or is automatic, recursive retrieval can be implemented automatically. In taxonomies or thesauri that do not consist merely of one single hierarchy or a few large hierarchies, recursive searching is not so common or at least is not the default. Instead, a broader term is indexed to its broader/general treatment of the subject only. The following example, using the term **crafts**, compares recursive retrieval in a hierarchical taxonomy with nonrecursive retrieval in a less hierarchical taxonomy or thesaurus (remember, capitalization of terms is more common in hierarchical taxonomies):

Recursive retrieval:

Crafts	← retrieves content on all crafts, including beadwork, embroidery, etc.
> **Beadwork**	← retrieves content on beadwork
> **Embroidery**	← retrieves content on embroidery

Nonrecursive retrieval:

crafts	← retrieves content on crafts in general only
NT: **beadwork**	← retrieves content on beadwork
NT: **embroidery**	← retrieves content on embroidery

General Usage of a Broader Term

If recursive indexing and retrieval is the default in a hierarchical taxonomy, and if the user does not have the option to change it, then there needs to be an additional way to index and retrieve only the content that truly is of a general nature as it corresponds to a broader term's meaning. Typically, to achieve this, the taxonomist creates a category under the broader term that has the word *general* in it, as in the following example for **crafts**:

Crafts   ← retrieves content on all crafts, including narrower terms and **crafts** in general

> Crafts in general   ← retrieves content on **crafts** in general only

> Beadwork

> Embroidery

You could also name the term **General crafts** instead of **Crafts in general**. On the indexing side, there may or may not actually be a term labeled *general*, as such an additional indexing term is not needed. Indexing of general content could still be to the broader term name, in this case **Crafts**, but the display of such indexing would be associated with the *general* term; and the results attached to the broader term name, **Crafts**, are the total recursive results. The need for a *general* term arises only in hierarchical taxonomies, and specifically in those hierarchical taxonomies that default to recursive retrieval.

Sometimes the end user has the option to select either general or all/recursive retrieval, using a radio button or a check box. Indexing/retrieval systems in which terms correspond with numeric codes may also allow this flexibility, whereby truncating the numeric code retrieves *all* narrower concepts and adding the trailing zeros matches the broader term only for *general*. In the following example, based on Predicasts[1] industry codes, a search on **6300** is for insurance in general, whereas **63** would be for all insurance, including life and health insurance.

6300	**Insurance**
6310	**Life Insurance**
6320	**Accident & Health Insurance**
6322	**Health Insurance**

Allowing such end-user control is more likely to be an option in a system aimed at relatively expert users.

Other Usage of a Broader Term

Parallel with the idea of *general* terms is the idea of *other* or *miscellaneous*. If a specific topic arises in the content being indexed and there is no matching term in the taxonomy (yet), then the content item should be indexed with the next broader term. This is standard indexing practice, whether or not the concept is an explicit narrower term.

However, in the case of a hierarchical taxonomy in which broader terms are *not* used as index terms but only for recursive retrieval results, and the broad concept itself is indexed with a *general,* a dilemma arises. The new narrow concept should *not* be indexed to a term used for *general*. The solution is to introduce yet another narrower concept called *other* or a variation thereof. Situations that call for such an *other* term are rare, and generally creating an *other* or *miscellaneous* term should be avoided, but sometimes it is a practical solution. Following is an example with **crafts.**

Crafts
> Crafts in general
> Beadwork

> Embroidery

etc.

> Other crafts

An example in practice is the SIC and NAICS industry codes/ terms, which have several industry classification types "for other establishments not elsewhere classified." The following are examples of NAICS codes/terms:

1129 Other Animal Production
3329 Other Fabricated Metal Product Manufacturing
51119 Other Publishers

The distinction between *general* and *other/miscellaneous* may be too subtle for automated indexing to discern, so this structure works better with human indexing. If you are using automated indexing that is only questionably reliable in this area, it might be best to avoid creating *other* and *general* categories altogether. The broader term would simply be used for all of these (*all*, *general*, and *other*), and the distinctions would be sacrificed. Another possibility would be to combine *general* and *other*, since they are difficult to distinguish, as the example in Figure 8.2 illustrates for subcategories of editorial jobs provided by the *New York Times*, where *all* is clearly made as separate option.

Node Labels

Another way to create a more detailed hierarchical structure in a taxonomy is by including what are called node labels. A node label can be considered a dummy term: a label to help organize the hierarchy, but not a real term used in indexing, hence the designation *label* rather than *term*. If implemented, node labels should be designated somehow (enclosed in brackets, or set in a different color, font, or style) so it is clear that they are labels and not index terms.

Editorial / Writing Jobs

DIGITAL CONTENT DEVELOPMENT (90)	New York City (31)
	Long Island (6)
DOCUMENTATION / TECHNICAL WRITING (335)	Northern New Jersey (14)
	Southern Connecticut (7)
EDITING & PROOFREADING (210)	Mid-Atlantic States (142)
JOURNALISM (280)	Midwestern States (91)
GENERAL / OTHER: EDITORIAL / WRITING (596)	New England (65)
	Pacific Northwest (29)
TRANSLATION / INTERPRETATION (217)	Plains States (13)
	Rocky Mountain States (18)
	Southern States (121)
	Southwestern States (42)
	Western States (77)
	View All »

View All Jobs in Editorial / Writing »

Figure 8.2 Example of hierarchical categories of job listings from the *New York Times,* where *all* is distinct from *general* and *other* and the latter two are combined (Source: jobmarket.nytimes.com)

Node labels can appear anywhere in a taxonomy, but the most common are of two kinds:

1. Broad categories: as top terms or at intermediate to high levels in the taxonomy

2. Facet indicators: for the most specific terms

You may find that the designations *facet indicator* and *node label* are used interchangeably, but technically a facet indicator is a kind of node label.

In a hierarchical taxonomy, it is typical to have named hierarchies, which are named for their top term, such as **Politics &**

Government, Business & Finance, Buildings & Facilities, or **Occupations**, yet not have these top terms actually used in indexing, since they are too broad to be practical. These terms would then be designated as node labels that display to the users but cannot be linked to content. Even the human indexers see the node labels, which helps structure the taxonomy, but the indexing software does not support the use of the node labels in indexing. In some hierarchical taxonomies, not merely the top terms but even second-level concepts might be designated as node labels only, and only the lowest level(s) are actual indexing terms.

A particular kind of node label, called a facet indicator, is used to subcategorize a relatively large number of narrower terms, all at the same hierarchical level, by type or facet. This is the original application of the idea of facets in controlled vocabularies and is not exactly the same as top-level facets used to indicate complete separate taxonomies or vocabularies, which are discussed in more detail in the next section. When facet indicators are used, terms in a controlled vocabulary are first classified by subject area and then more narrowly by their facet aspect. Figure 8.3 is an example of the taxonomy term for **automobiles** and its narrower terms; the facet indicators appear in italics.

Use of brackets, angle or square, is another way to indicate facet indicators. Facet indicators tend to occur in thesauri used by human indexers, if they are implemented at all. They have become less common now that top-level facets have become more popular, but they remain useful for a thesaurus that is both broad in scope and detailed in coverage.

Facets

Facets are categorical groupings of terms within a taxonomy. They are used to support what is called faceted classification or faceted search. Facets serve to describe content from multiple angles,

Automobiles
  by body type
    Coupes
    Sedans
    Station wagons
    Minivans
    Sport-utility vehicles
  by engine type
    Gasoline engine automobiles
    Diesel engine automobiles
    Electric automobiles
    Natural gas engine automobiles
    Alcohol engine automobiles
  by transmission type
    Automatic transmission automobiles
    Manual transmission automobiles

Figure 8.3 Facet indicators for types of automobiles

perspectives, or attributes. Top-level facets have some similarities with the previously described concept of facet indicators but are implemented somewhat differently. In the case of top-level facets, terms are generally classified first by facet, and then within each facet there might be a subject hierarchy. This is the opposite of how facet indicators work, whereby terms are classified first by subject and then by facet (such as by a subject **automobiles** and then by a facet indicator *by body type*). Facets in faceted classification each represent their own distinct hierarchy and are mutually exclusive. The facet values could be a flat list or, if numerous, organized into a hierarchy. The objective of facets is to allow for searching on multiple terms in combination (postcoordination), with one term from each facet. Whereas facet indicators in a hierarchical taxonomy are precoordinated, the facets in faceted search serve postcoordinated searching. In this sense, a facet is not merely a grouping of concepts but also a "dimension" of a query. In fact, the word *facet* comes from *face*, or side of something.

Types and Examples of Facets

The idea of faceted classification was first developed by the Indian mathematician and librarian S.R. Ranganathan in the late 1920s as an alternative to the Dewey Decimal Classification system for books, which he felt was inadequate because it permits only a single classification number for what are often multifaceted books. He called his system Colon Classification, as his call number notation display made use of colons and other forms of punctuation to separate the various facet terms associated with the title being cataloged. Ranganathan developed a set of five broad facets:

- Personality: topic or orientation
- Matter: things or materials
- Energy: actions
- Space: places or locations
- Time: times or time periods

The colon classification did not catch on, largely because it was too complicated for the average user. Today, with the use of computers and database management software, colon-type coding schemes are not needed to implement faceted classification, and searching by facets has become easy to implement and use. Each content item is a database record, and each field of that record is described by a facet. Thus, faceted search is sometimes called *fielded* search.

Modern designations of generic facets include those suggested for enterprise taxonomies by Patrick Lambe in his book *Organising Knowledge* (2007):[2]

- People and organizations

- Things and parts of things
- Activity cycles
- Locations

Louis Rosenfeld and Peter Morville, in *Information Architecture for the World Wide Web* (2nd edition, 2002), suggest the following facets for commercial websites:[3]

- Topic
- Product
- Document type
- Audience
- Geography
- Price

While it may be helpful to refer back to these generic facets, the nature of your content should be the primary determining factor in how you design your facets, if you choose to go this route. Faceted taxonomies and faceted search work best for content that is structured into records that all have at least some characteristics in common. Following are examples of more specific facets:

For job postings on the Monster job board site (jobsearch.monster.com/Browse.aspx):

- State (U.S.)
- Industry
- Category (of occupation)
- Posting date (range)
- Career level

- Years experience (range)

- Education level

- Job type (full-time, part-time, etc.)

For recipes on MyRecipes.com (www.myrecipes.com):
- Main ingredients

- Exclude (e.g., dairy, shellfish, etc.)

- Courses

- Occasions

- Cuisines

- Conveniences

- Cooking methods

- Dietary considerations

- Publications

- Sponsors

For the Kelley Blue Book site's Perfect Car Finder (www.kbb.com/kbb/PerfectCarFinder):
- Price range

- Vehicle type (new/used)

- Category

- Manufacturer

- Maximum seating capacity

- Miles per gallon (range)

- Size of vehicle

For museum art objects:

- Object type

- Artist/creator

- Country/culture

- Medium/materials

- Date made

- Collection/department

Implementing Facets

Facets work best with content that is of a somewhat consistent type. This way the same facets may be used across all the content. These could be collections comprising just news articles, technical reports, instructional materials, product data, or image files—but not a miscellaneous collection of all of these. Most of the content should be described by most of the facets, but it is not necessary that each facet apply to every content record. The more similar the content is, the greater the number of facets that can be supported. Thus, from the preceding examples, we see how job descriptions, which are quite uniform and structured, might be supported by up to eight facets, while other types of content would support fewer facets. For a diverse collection of articles, you might have as few as two facets—place and subject—and the subjects could comprise a large thesaurus or hierarchical taxonomy. This latter, more limited implementation of facets is actually quite common, though this type of taxonomy is not necessarily referred to as faceted.

The facets within a single taxonomy and content set can vary greatly. Some facets are relatively large, and some are very small. You could have a large hierarchical facet for over a hundred product types, and another facet that contains only three or four values for types of users/customers. Facets also permit you to have taxonomy terms that are mere adjectives, since facets tend to describe the attributes of things. These could be qualities, colors, sizes, etc. In general, though, faceted taxonomies are not as large as purely hierarchical taxonomies or thesauri. Figure 8.4 provides an example screenshot from the Land's End retail website, where, after the user initially selects a top category of Men, Women, Outerwear, and so forth, the facets displayed include one for types of clothing and then several smaller facets for size, style, fabric, and others. These latter facets vary slightly depending on the top category selected.

Developing facets also involves a slightly different analysis of the content than does developing regular term hierarchies. You look at the content to see the similar patterns and then determine all the different aspects and variables for searching. It is a top-down approach, coming up with facets first and populating them with terms afterward. Although usually it is clear which facet a given term belongs to, there are occasions when it is not so obvious. For example, it is common to have a location or place facet, which comprises geographic places. However, questions then arise regarding man-made structures and institutions. Institutions (schools, hospitals, museums, libraries, churches, etc.) are really organizations but sometimes are considered places as well. While in general they should not be included in a location facet, specific campuses and buildings could be. As another example, it is also common to have a facet for actions, activities, or events. This is often the case in a taxonomy for business information, which might include such concepts as **product introductions**, **orders/sales deals**, **partner contracts**, and **acquisitions and mergers**. Yet there may also be a general subject facet, which includes business-related topics such as **management, finance**, and **human resources**. In this case, it might be difficult to decide whether certain topics, such as **sales, contracts**, or **joint ventures**, belong in the actions or in the subjects facet. User search behavior, content, and indexing (manual or automatic) all need to be carefully considered in making such decisions.

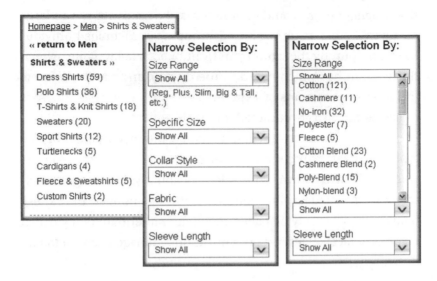

Figure 8.4 Facets for men's shirts on the Land's End retail
website; the dropdown (up) menu selection for one facet,
Fabrics, opened with its terms displayed (Source: www.landsend.com)

Top-level facets are sometimes confused with hierarchies or
categories. Categories, described in the next section, are not as
strictly defined as facets and may refer to any grouping of terms.
Hierarchies differ from facets in two ways. First, terms in hierarchies, unlike facets, are not limited to *aspects* of a search and thus
are not necessarily set up for postcoordination, as in the case of
one term from each of multiple facets. Terms may be selected from
multiple hierarchies to simply describe several topics (not aspects)
about a content resource. Second, while you cannot have polyhierarchies across different facets, because facets are distinct and
mutually exclusive, hierarchies are not always strictly separated,
and polyhierarchies may transcend them. As mentioned previously, the terms within a single facet may be arranged hierarchically, such as for facets of product types or geographic places. In
taxonomies in which each facet contains a multilevel hierarchy,

the designations *facet* and *hierarchy* may be used interchangeably. To test whether your proposed groupings are indeed valid as facets, try putting the word *by* in front of each facet name, even if this will not be implemented in the display, and see if the facets make sense as a means of searching.

Facets can also cover metadata that is not limited to topical taxonomies. This information could include author, content type, file type, language, source, audience, etc., but each of these facets would still have its own controlled vocabulary. If managed separately by a metadata librarian and not a taxonomist, then these fields will more likely be called metadata rather than being called taxonomy facets. Different organizations manage such metadata differently.

Multiple Vocabularies and Categories

Hierarchies and facets are ways of organizing taxonomy terms that have a direct impact on how the end user browses and makes use of the taxonomy. There are additional ways to organize a taxonomy or set of taxonomies that are more administrative and may or may not impact the end-user display. These include having separate vocabulary files and having categories or classes in the taxonomy.

Separate Taxonomy/Vocabulary Files

A given body of content with its own indexing system and its own search/browse/retrieval interface, or what together might be called a single taxonomy "project," may have a single taxonomy or a set of taxonomies, depending on how you define and organize your taxonomies. There is no standard to define what constitutes a single taxonomy as opposed to multiple taxonomies, since originally this word was not even used in the plural. Although all terms in a hierarchical taxonomy must belong to a single hierarchy, this does not necessarily mean that each hierarchy is its own taxonomy.

Sometimes taxonomies are defined this way, but not always. Additionally, if the controlled vocabulary is not hierarchical, it may be even less obvious how to distinguish one vocabulary from another.

Whether hierarchical or not, it is often useful to break out a large controlled vocabulary into multiple vocabulary files, lists, or databases, both for administrative purposes and to support certain user interface features. Separate vocabularies can support the following:

- Continued distinctions between preinstalled, user-created, and user-imported taxonomies

- Different sets of descriptive attributes for terms (such as location for organization, NAICS codes for companies, birth/death dates for people, etc.)

- Different access privileges by different taxonomists and taxonomy-editing subject matter experts

- Different administrative policies, such as indexer rights to add and approve new terms

- Systematic enforcement of different editorial policies for term format, such as title capitalization for named entities but not for topical terms

- Special features for different types of terms, such as subfields for last name and first name and modifiers for products or works.

- Indexing policies that require a minimum and/or maximum number of terms of certain types

- Use of auto-categorization or entity extraction with some vocabularies and not others

- Separate and more efficient searching and browsing by taxonomists, indexers, and end users, such as alphabetically for named entities

- Implementation of features such as filtering in the end-user interface

One of the most common ways to break out controlled vocabularies is between named entities and topical subjects, due to a number of differences between these two types of controlled vocabularies. Separate vocabulary files may also be maintained for different kinds of named entities, such as for people, places, and organizations. You might choose to call your sets of topical subjects *thesauri* or *taxonomies*, while calling your named entities *authority files*, and manage them somewhat separately, perhaps by different taxonomists and perhaps even with different titles.

Distinct vocabulary files may still permit relationships between terms across these different vocabularies, but the databases need to be deliberately designed to do so. As long as the vocabularies are maintained in a kind of relational database management system, then it is possible to set up a kind of table for each vocabulary, with a standard set of fields, and have records within each table relate to records in other tables. Thus, for example, named entities in one vocabulary file can still be linked to their respective broader term (instance-type) terms in another vocabulary file, such as linking **Mississippi River** to **rivers**. Leading taxonomy management systems support these cross-file relationships (such as Synaptica, which calls them objects), but simpler tools, such as MultiTes, do not necessarily include this feature.

Categories

Categories, also called classes, constitute an additional means of classifying and organizing terms in a taxonomy or set of taxonomies. Nearly all commercial taxonomy management software supports the use of such categories, often as defined within an administrative feature. Categories transcend hierarchies, facets, and vocabulary files and are applied to individual terms. Usually, though, terms within the same hierarchy belong to the same category, and we describe a narrower term as "inheriting" the category and other properties of its broader term. The taxonomist creates a set of category designations and applies them to taxonomy terms, in much the same way as an indexer applies terms to content. Categories are not types of terms, but rather part of the metadata of taxonomy terms. Categories can also be added to sets of terms in a batch method. The same taxonomy term may belong to more than one category. Depending on the purpose of the categories, the end-user searchers may not be aware of the presence of the categories, though.

Categories have unlimited uses, but a common purpose is to designate an intended end-use implementation of a set of taxonomy terms that are all in one master taxonomy. This could involve segmenting the taxonomies to serve any of the following:

- Different organizational uses, such as external website, extranet, intranet, product database, etc.

- Different group or department uses of internal enterprise taxonomies, such as human resources, finance, engineering, customer service, etc.

- Different industry markets or database products of published content taxonomies, such as healthcare, financial services, high-tech, government, etc.

There are no rules or standards regarding how you define or word your categories. They simply reflect their purpose. Thus, the category names **human resources**, **finance**, **engineering**, and **customer service** could be used for designating department use; or the category names **healthcare**, **financial services**, **high-tech**, and **government** could designate industry markets.

If your taxonomy management software does not support relationships between terms that are within separate vocabulary files, then you could also utilize categories as a means of breaking a single master taxonomy into differently administered sub-taxonomies.

Thus, categories could be used for many of the same purposes as separate vocabulary files, such a designating taxonomy types such as topics, named people, organizations, places, etc. As with separate vocabulary files, categories could also be implemented as a means for the end user to filter the taxonomy so as to contain only certain subsets of terms when performing a search in the user interface.

Finally, categories can be used to provide a little more structure to an otherwise nonhierarchical thesaurus. If, for example, a hierarchical display is desired for a nonhierarchical thesaurus, then category names could be treated as top terms. Although this would not be an ideal hierarchy and the number of second-level terms might be very great, it could prove adequate as long as the thesaurus is not too large.

Endnotes

1. Gale Group, *The Gale Group Guide to Predicasts Codes* (Foster City, CA: Gale Group, 1999).
2. Patrick Lambe, *Organising Knowledge: Taxonomies, Knowledge and Organisational Effectiveness* (Oxford: Chandos Publishing, 2007), 34.
3. Louis Rosenfeld and Peter Morville, *Information Architecture for the World Wide Web*, 2nd ed. (Sebastopol, CA: O'Reilly, 2002), 205.

Chapter 9

Taxonomy Displays

So many taxonomies, so little time.
—Seth Earley

A taxonomy has different kinds of users, and hence the same taxonomy may be implemented with different user interfaces or displays. Taxonomy users may include:

1. Taxonomists, searching and browsing the taxonomy in order to update and maintain it

2. Human indexers or taggers, using the taxonomy to index or tag content

3. Subject area researchers, using the taxonomy to better understand a subject area, without seeking linked content

4. End-user searchers, using the taxonomy to find specific content or discover information

All taxonomies are used at least by a taxonomist and by end users, but not all taxonomies display fully to the end users. Additionally, human indexers and possibly also subject area researchers use some taxonomies. These taxonomies are fully displayed, usually with more than one format option. Taxonomies that are made available to third-party subject area researchers (which may include other taxonomists) are usually also used by human indexers, but not all taxonomies used by human indexers are provided in a displayable format to other parties.

The first section of this chapter discusses various standard displays of the type of taxonomy called a thesaurus, as used by taxonomists, human indexers, subject area researchers, and occasionally end-user searchers. The following sections look specifically at end-user displays of different kinds of taxonomies, not just thesauri. Options for taxonomy end-user displays are largely determined by the taxonomy organization and structure, which could be any of the following:

- A thesaurus of terms, with no dominating hierarchies
- A hierarchical taxonomy or taxonomies
- A set of facets or categories

Unlike the taxonomy itself, the design of the end-user display is often a decision involving more people than just the taxonomist. Nevertheless, the taxonomist usually contributes to the design of the end-user display at least to some degree.

Thesaurus Displays

A thesaurus, in contrast to a simple hierarchical taxonomy, is often the most suitable kind of knowledge organization system when there is a relatively large controlled vocabulary, and human indexers are involved. A thesaurus differs from a hierarchical taxonomy not only in its focus on the individual term and its relationships, both hierarchical and associative, but also in its flexibility with regard to different displays. Although you could sort a hierarchical taxonomy into a single alphabetical list of terms, if the taxonomy lacks nonpreferred terms then an alphabetical list is not very useful. It would be like a book index without *See* references or double posts. A single thesaurus, by contrast, can display its terms hierarchically or alphabetically, as we have already seen in the user interfaces of thesaurus management software described in Chapter 5.

Not only are there different display options in the interface used by
the taxonomist, but the indexers, thesaurus researchers (not
searching for content), and possibly even end-user searchers may
also have the ability to choose different display or access options.
Printed thesauri will typically have at least two sections, one for an
alphabetical presentation of the thesaurus and one for the same
thesaurus in a hierarchical presentation. In addition to the choice
between hierarchical or alphabetical, there may be further variations on each of these formats. The various display formats are
typically available also as output or report options in full-featured
thesaurus management software.

Types of thesaurus displays include:

- Alphabetical simple list: Terms listed alphabetically without any details displayed

- Alphabetical flat format: Terms with all their immediate
  relationships (UF, BT, NT, RT) and notes if any (also
  known as a term record), and often the default alphabetical display for a thesaurus

- Full term hierarchy: Terms with multiple relationship
  levels displayed (such as BT1, BT2, etc.; NT1, NT2, etc.)

- Top term hierarchy: A listing of only the broadest terms,
  each one including a display of its hierarchy of narrower
  terms underneath

- Permuted/rotated index: Terms listed by their component
  words (i.e., an alphabetic list of words within terms); variations known as KWIC (keyword in context) and KWOC
  (keyword out of context)

Alphabetical Simple List

An alphabetical display of a thesaurus allows users to browse any
section of the thesaurus for a term they have in mind. Users have an
idea what concept they want but are not sure of the exact phrasing

of the term, so they look up the start of the first word. What makes an alphabetical display especially useful is that often nonpreferred terms are interspersed, usually in a different typeface. Users may have an option to show or hide nonpreferred terms in any of the alphabetical display formats. An example of a simple list alphabetical display is shown in Figure 9.1.

The simple list type of alphabetical display permits the quickest browsing. This option is usually made available to taxonomists or human indexers who are already somewhat familiar with the thesaurus and do not need to read all the details of a term to know which term they want. Hiding nonpreferred terms supports even more efficient browsing, but only if the user has a pretty good idea of the wording of the desired term. Simple lists are less common in

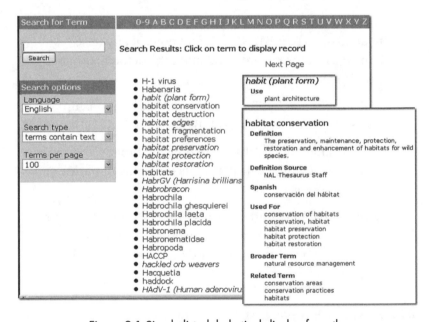

Figure 9.1 Simple list alphabetical display from the
National Agriculture Library Thesaurus: "Browse A–Z view,"
with additional screenshot of selected nonpreferred term and
selected preferred term details overlaid (Source: agclass.nal.usda.gov)

end-user searcher displays. In any case, if an alphabetical list is available, in an online environment it is typical to have terms in a simple list hyperlinked to their full-detail display, such as in the example shown in Figure 9.1.

Alphabetical Flat Format

The flat format is an alphabetical list of terms (usually both pre-ferred and nonpreferred) with each preferred term having all of its nonpreferred terms, broader terms, narrower terms, related terms, and any scope note listed under it. This is often the default "alpha-betical" output of thesaurus management software, and it is the commonly expected display of a thesaurus kind of controlled vocabulary. A subject area researcher interested in term details rather than linked content would also most likely seek out this dis-play. An example excerpt of a flat format alphabetical list of terms from the European Training Thesaurus is shown in Figure 9.2.[1]

The alphabetic flat format is common in printed thesauri, because all the term details are present, but there is no repetitive inclusion of terms, as is the case with full term hierarchy display (which would take up more space). In the online medium, it has become less common to see a complete alphabetical listing with the flat format display of terms. Instead, there might be a simple list, with the flat format term details appearing in a separate win-dow, as is the example in the second window in Figure 9.1.

The information provided for each term in flat format display typically includes the following: nonpreferred terms (UF), broader term(s) (BT), narrower terms (NT), related terms (RT), and scope note. The broader terms and narrower terms displayed are those that are in immediate relationships, just one level up or one level down. In a bilingual thesaurus, a term's foreign language transla-tion is also included. Less common but sometimes included is the term's ultimate broadest term, or top term, abbreviated as TT. In the following example of a multiterm hierarchy:

products > software > business software > spreadsheet
software

the broader term and top term of **spreadsheet software** are indicated as follows:

spreadsheet software
BT **business software**
TT **products**

```
A level
FD      Learning (3)
FR      baccalauréat
SN      Certificate of Education Advanced Level
        (A Level) is normally awarded at the end
        of 2 years of post-compulsory general
        education to pupils who meet the required
        standards. It is a qualification for entry to
        higher education (Eurydice).
UF      school leaving certificate
BT      certificate

ability
USE     aptitude

Abruzzi
FD      Countries and regions (14)
FR      Abruzzes
BT      Italy

absenteeism
FD      Enterprise (7)
FR      absentéisme
BT      work attitude

academic degree
FD      Learning (3)
FR      diplôme universitaire
UF      college degree
        university degree
BT      certificate
RT      higher education graduate
        university studies
```

Figure 9.2 Flat format alphabetical arrangement of terms
from the European Training Thesaurus (FD = field; FR = French)

Full Term Hierarchy

A full term hierarchy display is a variation on the flat format,
whereby not only are the immediate broader and narrower terms

displayed at each term but also further broader and narrower terms of those terms, all the way out to the ends of the hierarchy. The number of hierarchical levels may vary among terms within the same taxonomy.

There are two kinds of full term hierarchy displays: multilevel and two-way hierarchy. A multilevel display lists the relationships under the preferred term, with successive levels of hierarchy typically indicated by numerals following, or by greater-than/less-than signs (angle brackets) preceding BT or NT, such as BT1, BT2, or >BT, >>BT. Additional relationships (UF, RT, Scope Note) may or may not be included. A two-way hierarchy is a more graphical representation of a term's placement in a hierarchy, displaying its broader terms above it and its narrower terms below it and making use of indentations, carats, periods, colons, or other punctuation. A typical display might use successive periods (ellipses) preceding each narrower term and colons preceding each broader term. Figure 9.3 contrasts a multilevel hierarchy and a two-way hierarchy for the same term.

If using greater-than/less-than signs, then the full term hierarchy for *recreation facilities* would include the following terms and notation:

<< Facilities & Infrastructure

< Public buildings & facilities

Recreation facilities

> Amusement parks

>> Athletic facilities

Top Term Hierarchy

A top term display is the main hierarchical display of a thesaurus (or any taxonomy for that matter). Unlike the full term hierarchy display, the top term display does not involve any repeated inclusion of terms except in the case of polyhierarchies. It is an alphabetical list

```
Multilevel Hierarchy                              Two-Way Hierarchy

Recreation facilities                             : : Facilities & infrastructure
  UF: Recreation centers                          : Public buildings & facilities
  UF: Recreational facilities                     Recreation facilities
     NT1: Amusement parks                         . Amusement parks
     NT1: Athletic facilities                     . Athletic facilities
        NT2: Fitness centers & gyms               . . Fitness centers & gyms
        NT2: Skating rinks                        . . Skating rinks
        NT2: Swimming pools                       . . Swimming pools
        NT2: Tennis courts                        . . Tennis courts
     NT1: Bowling alleys                          . Bowling alleys
     NT1: Golf courses                            . Golf courses
     NT1: Skiing facilities                       . Skiing facilities
     NT1: Stadiums & arenas                       . Stadiums & arenas
  BT1: Public buildings & facilities
     BT2: Facilities & Infrastructure
```

Figure 9.3 Full term hierarchy displays,
both multilevel and two-way

of preferred terms that have no broader terms, and under each is the full hierarchy of narrower terms for each, usually arranged with indents or series of periods. Nonpreferred terms, related terms, and notes are not included. Relatively flat taxonomies will have a high number of top terms, whereas more structured hierarchical taxonomies will have a limited number of top terms. Figure 9.4 presents two different thesaurus top term display excerpts, one more hierarchical than the other.

A top term report is a useful way for a taxonomist to check the hierarchical balance of a thesaurus. For end users, a top term display is desirable for a more hierarchically structured taxonomy or thesaurus. For a taxonomy that has little hierarchy (is relatively "flat"), though, this display has less value for end users.

Permuted (Rotated) Index

A permuted or rotated index (two different names for the same display) takes each word within a term (most of which are multiword phrases anyway), sorts these words alphabetically, and displays all the terms with the given word (keyword) in it, grouped together by the keyword. Each taxonomy phrase-term thus appears more than

Top term display excerpt showing a single top term in a hierarchical thesaurus

Politics & Government
. Domestic policy & programs
.. Agricultural policy
.. Economic policy
... Monetary policy
... Fiscal policy
.. Energy policy
.. Health policy & programs
Social policy
. Foreign policy
.. Appeasement
.. Bilateralism
.. Foreign assistance
... Foreign military assistance
.. Foreign intervention
.. Unilateralism

Top term display excerpt showing three top terms in a relatively flat thesaurus

Political actions
. Campaigning
. Lobbying
. Political protests

Political ideologies
. Conservatism
. Environmentalism
. Liberalism
.. Socialism

Politicians
. Political office holders
. Political candidates

Figure 9.4 Top term hierarchy display excerpts:
one more hierarchical and one less hierarchical

once in the display, under each of its constituent keywords. This display is called an index because it is indeed an alphabetical index of words within terms. There are two variations on the display, as illustrated in Figure 9.5:

1. KWIC, whereby the terms tend to be indented in such a way that the keywords vertically align, whether they appear at the beginning, middle, or end of a term. The keywords are "in context" because they are displayed only within the full term phrases, rather than appearing in isolation, out of the context of the full term phrase.

2. KWOC, whereby the keyword is shown on its own (as an index heading), followed by the full terms.

An alphabetical display of a KWIC or KWOC index can provide a useful way to search for terms in a printed list. In the online environment, however, such an alphabetical display is unnecessary, so the permuted (rotated) index display has become less common. However, a user interface, whether for indexers or end-user

KWIC display	KWOC display
Agricultural **economics**	**Economics**
American **Economics** Association	Agricultural economics
Classical **economics**	American Economics Association
Comparative **economics**	Classical economics
Economics	Comparative economics
Economics historians	Economics
Economics literature	Economics historians
Economics theorists	Economics literature
Environmental **economics**	Economics theorists
Home **economics**	Environmental economics
Industrial **economics**	Home economics
Keynesian **economics**	Industrial economics
	Keynesian economics

Figure 9.5 Permuted (rotated) index example of a
single term entry showing both KWIC and KWOC

searchers, may offer the option of searching for words *within* terms and then return a list of matching taxonomy terms. This type of search essentially achieves the same objective as a permuted (rotated) display.

Thesaurus Displays for End-User Searchers

The various thesaurus displays described in the preceding section are typically an option reserved for the taxonomist and human indexers and sometimes for subject area researchers if the thesaurus is publicly available. However, end-user searchers do not usually have the option to select from such varied thesaurus displays for several reasons:

- Search product designers have enough other features to worry about, as they need to support search, discovery, alerts, reports, saving and sharing search results, etc.

- Having different ways to view a thesaurus may provide more information than is needed by the untrained searcher

- End-user searchers generally do not have as great an understanding of thesaurus principles, so they would not readily know what is meant by the relationship codes (BT, NT, RT, UF, TT) or the display type designations (flat, multilevel, two-way hierarchy, permuted, rotated, KWIC, KWOC).

- The thesaurus in electronic format can be searched anyway, so numerous types of browsable displays may not be needed. A single hierarchical browse display may be offered as an option in addition to the search box, but additional, alphabetical displays may be deemed unnecessary if there is also a search option. While a subject researcher may on occasion still browse a printed or PDF thesaurus or taxonomy, end-user searchers today view and use taxonomies in electronic format only, usually via the web.

If an alphabetical browse interface is available, then it may be divided into sections for each letter of the alphabet, as shown in Figure 9.6 for ERIC Thesaurus.

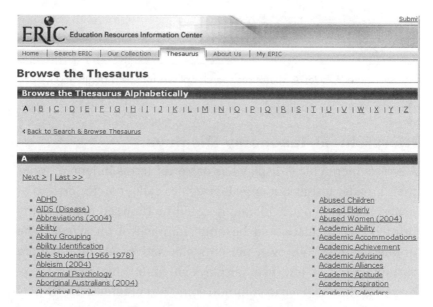

Figure 9.6 ERIC Thesaurus A–Z Browse display (Source: eric.ed.gov)

If the thesaurus is extremely large, then such alphabetical browsing may not be practical. In this case, users might have just two ways to access terms in the thesaurus, via a hierarchical view or a search box. The search feature, though, should ideally permit the option of searching for both:

- Terms beginning with a word or string

- Terms containing a word or string

The user then retrieves a limited alphabetical list of thesaurus terms. Figure 9.7 shows an example of a search box that presents both search options.

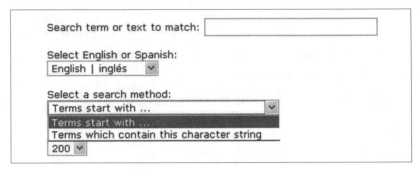

Figure 9.7 USDA Thesaurus search options for terms beginning with or containing text (Source: agclass.nal.usda.gov)

Hierarchical Taxonomy Displays

A typical hierarchical display has narrower terms indented under their broader terms, but large hierarchies can go on for dozens of pages. While a lengthy hierarchy could be browsed across many printed pages, this would be quite impractical on screen. The online medium, however, presents alternatives. While there are various kinds of end-user displays of online hierarchical tax-onomies, they all have in common some sort of interactive display that permits the user to navigate down from the top terms to terms that are more specific.

Although the presentation of a hierarchical taxonomy is similar to a top term hierarchical display of a thesaurus, there are stylistic differences. A hierarchical taxonomy does not necessarily use the designation NT or series of periods preceding narrower terms, but usually relies simply on indentation and perhaps a different type-face. Sometimes there are also graphical representations for the hierarchy. Additionally, to reflect their heading/category nature terms usually have initial capitalization, unlike terms in a the-saurus. Finally, terms in a hierarchical taxonomy are often called *categories* or *subjects*, rather than *terms*, to reflect the categorical nature of the hierarchy.

Hierarchical Display Types

There are two common online formats for displaying hierarchical taxonomies to the end user:

- One level per screen view, with terms hyperlinked to the next level of their narrower terms

- Expandable trees of terms, in which clicking on a term reveals its narrower terms beneath

One Level Per Screen

Using a separate screen to display each level of a hierarchical tax-onomy is the more traditional method as it requires less time and bandwidth to load as a webpage than the graphical expandable trees do. Each term is hyperlinked to a new page that displays all its narrower terms. Figure 9.8 is an example of this with three suc-cessive screenshots from the ThomasNet business directory (www.thomasnet.com).

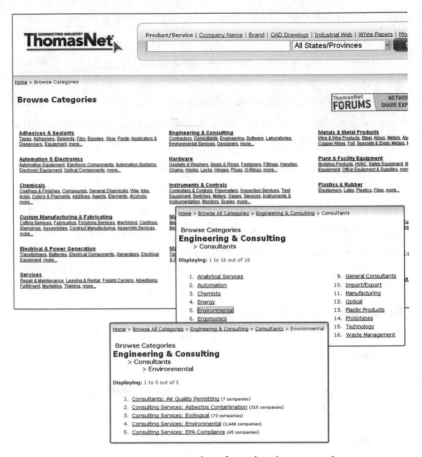

Figure 9.8 Successive screenshots from the ThomasNet business directory hierarchy, in which each lower level of narrower terms is on its own new webpage, with content (company information) linked at the lowest level only (Source: www.thomasnet.com)

This method has several advantages:

- There can be a large number of terms at any given level, so it works with a relatively large taxonomy.

- It works well with polyhierarchies.

- It is technically easy to implement.

Disadvantages to this method are:

- The display often takes up the entire screen and does not permit space for search results.

- Users can only see one level in one hierarchy at a time.

- It is less suitable when the taxonomy has varied levels or a narrower level consisting of just one or a few terms.

- There is often no prior indication whether the next level will have additional narrower terms or will finally link to the content.

This type of user interface typically displays the navigation path near the top of the window, so even when at a deeper level the user still can keep track of the higher levels/broader terms, such as the following example from ThomasNet:

> **Browse All Categories** > **Engineering & Consulting** > **Consultants** > Environmental

The terms in the path are hyperlinked to the page where they are the broader term, so that the user can easily go back to any previous broader level. This is sometimes referred to as a *breadcrumb trail* because it shows where you have come from and how to get back, a metaphor based on the story of Hansel and Gretel, who dropped breadcrumbs as they walked through the woods in order to find their way back home.

Expandable Tree Hierarchy
The other method for displaying a hierarchical taxonomy, an expandable tree hierarchy, is more graphical and interactive. It permits the user to click on a term or a plus sign next to it to display its narrower terms, usually indented underneath it or possibly in a new column to its right. Unlike the display with one level per

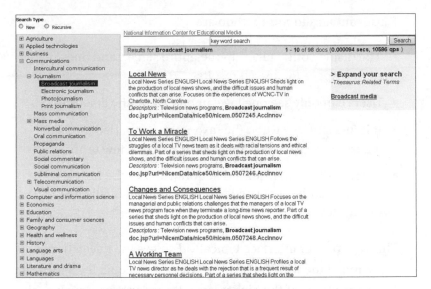

Figure 9.9 Example of the Search Harmony Presentation layer
from Access Innovations and PerfectSearch, covering content
of the National Information Center for Educational Media (Source:
www.accessinn.com:8081/PerfectSearch/navtree/index.html)

screen, in an expandable tree the entire higher levels of terms continue to display, even as each narrower level is displayed. Figure 9.9 presents an example from Access Innovations, in which the expandable taxonomy tree is in the margin to the left and the matching documents of the selected term are presented in the main area to the right.

This method has the following advantages:

- The hierarchical nature is made obvious to the user, and the format is familiar to users of Windows Explorer (analogous to folders on the desktop).

- It allows the user to visualize the taxonomy and supports a more interactive exploration of the hierarchy.

- The presence or absence of a plus sign next to a term makes it clear whether there is lower level under the term.

- Inconsistent numbers of levels and terms per level are easily accommodated.

- The display takes up only part of the screen, one-quarter or one-third, allowing for the display of other content in the remainder of the window, such as content tagged with the term.

Disadvantages to this method include:

- They are not suitable for displaying a large taxonomy or a large number of narrower terms at a given level, because when terms are expanded, the higher levels get pushed out of view. (Scrolling to see all the terms causes their broader term to scroll out of view.)

- They cannot accommodate polyhierarchies very well, due to the limited space of the display window, and they may even be confusing to the user if polyhierarchies are included.

- They may take longer to load and display, due to the graphic features.

- Implementing the display requires greater expertise in webpage development.

Choice of Display Type

A large taxonomy is best suited for display on one level per screen, whereas as small taxonomies can be accommodated with the expandable graphical tree display. Broad hierarchies, with many terms per level, are better displayed with one level per screen, whereas deep hierarchies work better in expandable trees. The expandable tree has become more popular with web designers regardless of taxonomy size and structure, however, because it is more attractive and interactive. Meanwhile, the demands in technology and bandwidth necessary for the interactive graphical displays have become less of an issue. In practice, the design of an attractive display often takes precedence over suitability for a given taxonomy. Thus you, as the taxonomist, might simply be instructed to create a taxonomy for an expandable tree rather than being asked for your input on interface design.

With either kind of display, it can be difficult to navigate too many levels, just as with term hierarchies in a thesaurus. If the interface displays one level per screen, then a maximum of three levels is generally considered user-friendly. With an expandable tree, perhaps up to four levels is acceptable. Studies show that users of a public website typically do not have patience for more, especially if they are visiting the site for the first time. They are eager to find information quickly, and they will move on to a different website if they do not find it soon enough. Taxonomies for content for a more restricted audience (such as on an intranet for employees, a specialized subject area, or some kind of reference information source) may have more levels, and indeed their users will expect more levels. Each taxonomy is unique, though, so you should not try to adhere to any strict rules on numbers of levels.

Sort Order Options

With hierarchical displays, the user may have various options for sorting terms within the same hierarchical level (sharing the same broader term). The default sorting in any system is alphabetical, and while this is usually fine, sometimes a different order is more suitable. Any set of terms having to do with time, events, sequence, or procedures could be arranged chronologically or sequentially instead. Other orderings of concepts might be based on well-known categorizations, such as industries arranged in the order of SIC codes (first agriculture, then mining, manufacturing, wholesale, retail, and lastly services). Variations in sort order can be applied to any level, including the top-level terms. If you have usage studies on what the most popular terms are, then popularity could even be used as a basis for sort order. An example of somewhat sequential ordering of six narrower terms is the following:

> **Personnel management**
>> **Recruiting**
>> **Hiring**
>> **Training**
>> **Promotions**
>> **Letting go of employees**

In general, the shorter the list, the less important alphabetical sorting is. If you have 20 to 30 terms or more at the same level displayed together, alphabetical is probably best, but with fewer than 10 terms, you should consider other, more "logical" sort orders. In addition, for predictability the sort order method should be consistent throughout the taxonomy. If you choose alphabetic, then use it throughout. If you choose nonalphabetical "logical," then use that throughout, although you can vary the actual logical basis by grouping.

Another issue in sort order, regardless of number of terms at a level, is that whenever there is any *general* or *other/miscellaneous* category, it should *not* sort alphabetically. *General* should appear first in the list, not under *G*, and *other/miscellaneous* should be at the end, not under *O* or *M*. The previous examples—ThomasNet (Figure 9.8) and the National Information Center for Educational Media (Figure 9.9)—present their terms alphabetically. However, in the middle screenshot in Figure 9.8, the term **General Consultants** is filed alphabetically in the middle (ninth out of 16 terms) of the list under **Consultants**, rather than being in the logical location as first in the list.

Term Display Names in Context

For hierarchically displayed taxonomies, the taxonomist has the option of creating short, simple term names whose meanings will be understood within the context of the broader term. *General* and *other* are examples, but you could use simple contextual term names for any concept. The following pairs of examples illustrate the difference between short, simple term names, whose meaning is known in context, and their corresponding unambiguous longer term names:

> Simple terms, understood in context: Full, unambiguous terms:
>
> **Personnel management**   **Personnel management**
>   **Recruiting**   **Employee recruiting**
>   **Training**   **Employee training**

The display with term names that are understood in context is thus similar in a way to subdivisions of main entries in a back-of-the-book index, in which the subdivision names might be of a rather general nature. The function in hierarchies is to label narrower terms, however, not precoordinated main entry/subentry combinations. Thus, if the same narrower term names are applicable with different broader terms in different hierarchies, then they should be treated as different terms, with different administrative identifiers and different names displayed to a human indexer. **Display name** can then be one of the equivalent variants of a term.

Node Label Usage

In a hierarchical presentation, it is not unusual for all broader terms to function as node labels, with only the narrowest terms ("leaf" nodes) linked to content. This structure contrasts with a thesaurus, in which all terms at all levels are expected to be linked to content, unless they are specifically designated as a node label, which is relatively rare. The use of node label broader terms is especially common in hierarchical taxonomies displaying one level of terms per page. After selecting a term, the next page would display either a list of content results for that term or a list of narrower terms for that term, but usually not a combination of both narrower terms and content results. In Figure 9.8, content is linked only to the lowest level of the taxonomy, so all the terms at the first three levels (in this example **Engineering & Consulting**, **Consultants**, and **Environmental**) are node labels.

In other hierarchical taxonomies, the terms at the top/first level and perhaps also the second level are node labels, whereas terms at lower levels are linked to content while still having even narrower terms beneath them. This structure requires a little more creativity in the display in order to show both content results and narrower terms. The Open Directory Project (www.dmoz.org) uses its top and most second level terms as node labels, but at lower levels the terms link to content and at the same time serve as broader terms to still narrower terms. A horizontal line separates narrower terms near the top of the page from a list of linked sites at the bottom of the page, as shown in Figure 9.10.

In an expandable tree display, broader terms also may or may not be node labels, although they are less frequently node labels than in the one-level-per-page display because there is usually space on the screen adjacent to the tree to display retrieval results.

Recursive Retrieval

In a hierarchical taxonomy, even if linked content is available for a selected broader term, that content might not actually be indexed to that term for its "general" usage. Instead, that linked content could be exclusively the result of recursive retrieval. Recursive retrieval returns inclusive results for all of a broader term's narrower terms. Typically, when there is space in the window to the right of the hierarchy (as in an expandable tree display), search

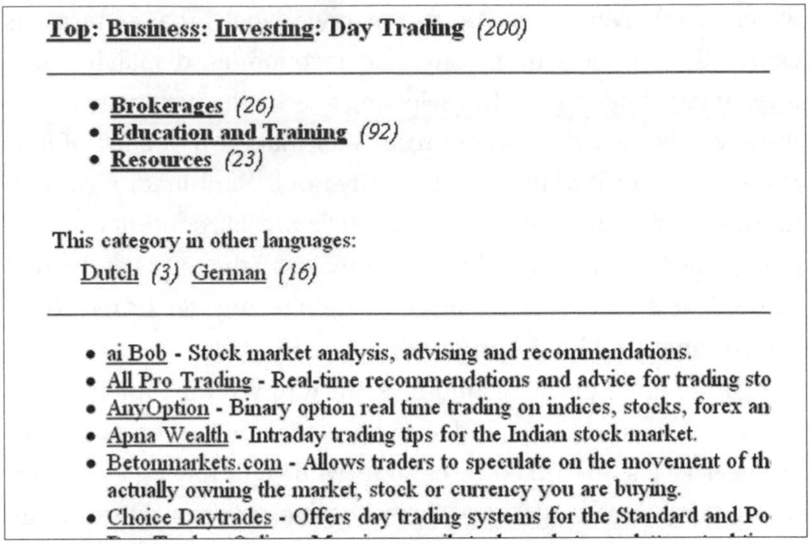

Top: **Business**: **Investing**: Day Trading *(200)*

- **Brokerages** *(26)*
- **Education and Training** *(92)*
- **Resources** *(23)*

This category in other languages:
  Dutch *(3)* German *(16)*

- ai Bob - Stock market analysis, advising and recommendations.
- All Pro Trading - Real-time recommendations and advice for trading sto
- AnyOption - Binary option real time trading on indices, stocks, forex an
- Apna Wealth - Intraday trading tips for the Indian stock market.
- Betonmarkets.com - Allows traders to speculate on the movement of th
  actually owning the market, stock or currency you are buying.
- Choice Daytrades - Offers day trading systems for the Standard and Po

Figure 9.10 Example of a hierarchical taxonomy from
the Open Directory Project, whereby the term *Day Trading*
is *not* a node label, as it is linked to website content while
also serving as the broader term to three narrower terms

results are displayed for terms at any level in the hierarchy, except perhaps for the top terms. The default *all* is more common, however, than *general* in a hierarchical taxonomy display result, especially if less sophisticated automatic indexing is involved. Thus, the broader term that provides only recursive retrieval serves as a node label on the indexing side but operates as an *all* index term on the retrieval/end-user display side. Some end-user displays provide the total count of matched records per term (often as a numeral in parentheses following the term). If the number next to a broader term is very high, it indicates to the user that the broader term is providing recursive results.

Figure 9.11 is an example showing recursive retrieval along with a number of other issues discussed previously—sort order, term names in context, node labels, recursive retrieval, and a breadcrumb trail—in four successive window screenshots from the hierarchical

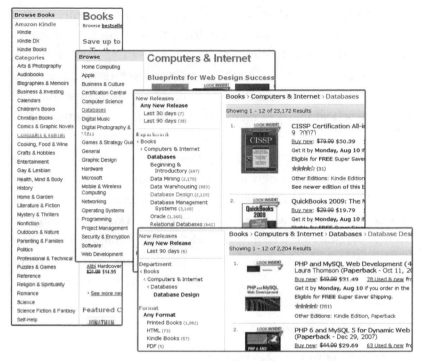

Figure 9.11 Example of the hierarchy of book categories on Amazon.com, which shows one level per page with alphabetic sort order, term names in context, node labels, recursive retrieval, and a breadcrumb trail

taxonomy of books on Amazon.com. Although the display type is one level per page, the number of terms per level is small enough to fit in a single column in the left margin, so the space to the right can be used to display search results or other content. Categories (terms) within the same level are arranged alphabetically, and at both the first and second level (window) they function as node labels, as they are not linked to any content. Space to the left of the taxonomy is used for select promotions. The second window, with the category heading **Computers & Internet**, shows a **General** category within the list of terms, although it does not sort to the top, as would be the preferred arrangement. Examples of term display names that are understood in the context of their broader terms include **Business & Culture** under **Computers & Internet** on the second screen, and **Beginning & Introductory** under **Databases** on the third screen. The third screen, for the category **Databases,** shows search results in addition to narrower terms. The high number of results at the third screen, 23,172, indicates that the retrieval at **Database** is recursive, comprising the sum total of books of all of its narrower categories. The fourth level and window, which is for **Database Design**, shows no narrower terms, so we know this is the lowest level, even though the result set is still large. At the top of this display, we see the breadcrumb trail of **Books > Computers & Internet > Databases > Database Design**. A shorter version of the path is available at the top of the preceding screen. By the way, Amazon.com allows the additional refinement of results by facet, a feature that is omitted from these screenshots for the sake of simplicity.

Fielded Search Displays

The third main kind of access to a taxonomy and end-user display is fielded search. A fielded search display presents a means for the user to select or enter a vocabulary term for each of several search values or fields. These fields can be facets or merely vocabulary files or categories, as described in Chapter 8. The user may enter terms in search boxes that clearly depict fields, or each "field" may merely be a display of a short hierarchical list, from which the user selects a term. The end users may or may not be able to actually see and browse the taxonomy in a fielded search interface, but preferably they can, if it is not too large.

Faceted Search Displays

A powerful application of fielded search is its use with facets, even if blank "fields" are not always used in faceted search. A fielded search display of a faceted taxonomy presents the user with all the facets and the option to choose a term (usually just one) from each facet and execute a search on them in combination, either after making all selections or in a step-by-step fashion. If step-by-step, then search results are displayed on a selection from the first facet and then are narrowed on selections of terms from subsequent facets, with the search set becoming smaller at each step. The order in which the user makes selections from the facets ought not to matter. Allowing the user to refine the search step by step has the advantage that if a step returns zero results, it is clear which condition (which facet) could not be met. A breadcrumb trail may also be used in faceted search results, even though the path is not always in the same sequence, as the user may select from facets in any order.

Figure 9.12, from the product review site Buzzillions (www.buzzillions.com), presents an example of a faceted display that involves step-by-step narrowing. Although "fields" are not apparent, each column/category represents a facet for selection. After using a traditional hierarchical taxonomy to arrive at the category for printers, the user sees the facet options in the top screen of the pair displayed in the illustration. After making a series of selections, one from each facet (**Photo Printers** from **By Category**, **HP** from **By Brand**, **$50-$200** for **By Price**, and **Casual User** from **By Use**), the original set of 1142 product reviews is narrowed down to six, and the facets available to further refine the result have also changed dynamically.

As discussed in Chapter 8, facets enable powerful searching and refinement by users. But facets only work with structured, unified types of content (such as all products, all people, all images) that share common facets and are not suitable for varied, unstructured content, across an enterprise. Peter Morville has gathered a nice collection of screenshots of faceted navigation user interfaces under his Search Patterns collection on Flickr (www.flickr.com/photos/morville/collections, with the faceted

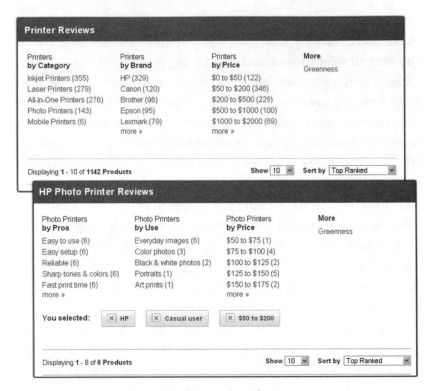

Figure 9.12 Facets for searching for printer reviews
on the Buzzillions website (Source: www.buzzillions.com)

search images at www.flickr.com/photos/morville/collections/
72157603789246885).

Unlike thesauri and hierarchical taxonomies, faceted taxonomies are often relatively small. Thus, it is often possible to display all the terms within a facet in a single view. If there are not
many terms under the facets and they are not arranged in a hierarchy, then a pulldown menu or popup list may be implemented to
display the terms within each facet. A small taxonomy also allows
for more flexibility with the sort order of terms. The nature of
facets, which tend to describe attributes, also makes them suitable
for logical orderings rather than alphabetic. For example, facets for
date, price, size, age, or other numeric ranges are common, and

you should order these numerically from lowest to highest. For geographic places, with a short list of continents/regions, it might be more logical to start with the user's home continent, such as North America, rather than with the alphabetical leader of Africa.

Just because facets exist within a taxonomy, there is no guarantee that the user interface will implement them for faceted searching. A simple user interface might offer the user the option of searching from one type of metadata value or another but does not support a search on multiple facets in combination. In Boolean search terms, faceted search is based on the AND combination, rather than OR. Figure 9.13 is an example from the Florida Memory site of the State Library & Archives of Florida, where the user can search on only a single term type at once for museum collection items, so while metadata facets exist on the indexing side, facets do not function in this end-user display. (The option to combine facets exists only in advanced search.)

Thus, if you develop a faceted taxonomy, you will want to make sure that it is properly supported in the search user interface.

Fielded Search for Multiple Vocabularies or Other Criteria

Not all cases of fielded search involve facets. As discussed in Chapter 8, a taxonomy project may comprise multiple controlled vocabularies or taxonomics, and users could search each of these vocabularies individually through its own field in a fielded search interface. For example, in a set of controlled vocabularies for indexing a database of articles, personal names and company names (as appearing in article text content) are often maintained in separate vocabularies, and they may appear to the user as separate fields to search as well. This helps avoid ambiguity among term names. These fields are not facets, though, because they are not attributes or dimensions of a periodical article.

In addition to controlled vocabulary fields, fielded search may include fields for nonvocabulary data, such as accession number,

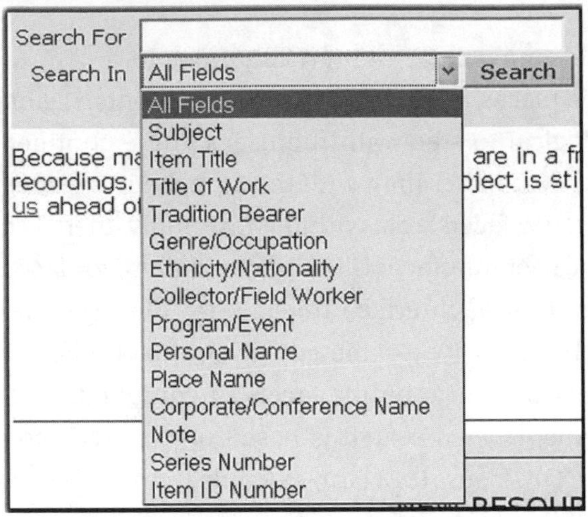

Figure 9.13 Allowing only a single selection among
multiple term types—not a faceted search (Source:
www.floridamemory.com/Collections/folklife/database.cfm)

title, abstract/description, date, etc. While such fields represent useful metadata, they, likewise, are not facets. Figure 9.14 shows an example of a fielded search user interface (from advanced search) for museum objects of the Colorado Springs Pioneer Museum (www.cspm.org), where most of the fields would *not* be considered facets.

A user interface that presents fielded search is often called advanced search. In a graphical display, this is somewhat of a misnomer, since it is very simple to use, and one does not need to be an "advanced" searcher. Often each field type has its own search box. In many cases the listed fields are all predefined, as in the museum example in Figure 9.14, but in other cases there is more flexibility, the user chooses the designation of the field from a dropdown list, and multiple definable search boxes are provided to combine in Boolean searching. This way, multiple terms from the same field can be selected for a search, something that is not usually permitted in faceted search. Boolean operations may also be

Accession Number:	
Collection:	
Title:	
	(the title field pertains mainly to publications)
Author/Maker:	
Description:	
Subjects/Remarks:	
Library of Congress Subject Terms:	
Provenance:	
Publisher:	
Year:	Exact Year ⌄

Figure 9.14 Fielded search options for searching the collections database of the Colorado Springs Pioneer Museum, where not all the fields are facets (Source: www.cspm.org)

selected from a dropdown list. This is where the process becomes a little more "advanced." Figure 9.15 shows an example of the search service Illumina from CSA (www.csa.com/csaillumina trial access), where the user chooses the designation for each field from a dropdown menu. By also selecting the option "Add Row" from the top, the user can add fields and thus make multiple selections from the same field if desired. The Boolean operators are also available in dropdown lists.

"Advanced" online literature retrieval services, such as Dialog, make full use of multiple vocabulary file fields as provided from each of their database vendors. This may be done through an easy-to-use interface display that presents field boxes to the user or through a more traditional command-line interface, in which the skilled searcher specifies the abbreviation of each field to be searched. To support the latter, since the list of fields for fielded search is quite long and varies by database vendor, Dialog provides

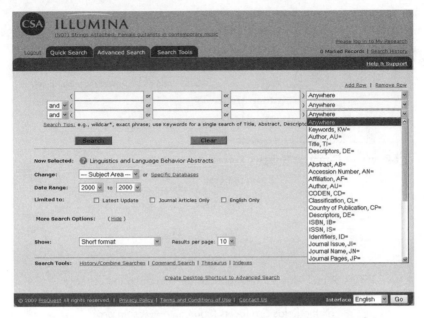

Figure 9.15 Advanced search options of CSA Illumina search
service for literature retrieval, allowing the user to specify
the fields (Source: www.csa.com/csaillumina trial access)

specific guidelines called a "Blue Sheet" for each database. Figure
9.16 is an extract of the Blue Sheet for the Gale Group Trade &
Industry Database (library.dialog.com/bluesheets/html/bl0148.
html#BI), in which the basic fields are defined. The majority of
these are in fact various controlled vocabulary files: Company
Name, Descriptor, Event Name, Geographic Name, Named Person,
Product Name, Statute Name, and Brand Name. (Industry Name
belongs in the Descriptor vocabulary file but is distinguished by a
category designation in the vocabulary management system.[2])
Additional nonvocabulary fields, such as accession number, title,
abstract/description, and date, are available among the extended
fields, which are not shown in Figure 9.16 to save space.

The subject descriptors used for fielded search in a set of taxonomies may be developed and maintained according to thesaurus
standards or just as a simple hierarchy. You should not consider the

BASIC INDEX [top]

SEARCH SUFFIX	DISPLAY CODE	FIELD NAME	INDEXING	SELECT EXAMPLES
None	None	All Basic Index Fields	Word	S AMERICAN(W)BANK?
/AB	AB	Abstract[1]	Word	S CITICORP/AB
/CN	CN	Case Name	Word	S AMERICAN(W)BUSINESS(W)SERVICE?/CN
/CO	CO	Company Name[3]	Word	S CITICORP?/CO
/CP	CP	Caption[2]	Word	S PHOTOGRAPH/CP
/DE	DE	Descriptor[5]	Word & Phrase	S EUROPE/DE S BANKING INDUSTRY/DE
/EN	EN	Event Name[3,4]	Word	S JOINT(W)VENTURES/EN
/GN	GN	Geographic Name[3]	Word	S EUROPE/GN
/IN	IN	Industry Name[3]	Word	S BANKING/IN
/LP	LP	Lead Paragraph[1]	Word	S CHEMICAL(W)BANKING/LP
/NM	NM	Named Person[3,6]	Word	S GATES(1N)PHYLLIS/NM
/PN	PN	Product Name[3]	Word	S BANKING(W)INSTITUTIONS/PN
/ST	ST	Statute Name	Word	S GLASS(W)STEAGALL(W)ACT/ST
/TI	TI	Title	Word	S EUROPE(2W)PROFITS/TI
/TN	TN	Brand Name[3]	Word	S MAESTRO/TN
/TX	TX	Text	Word	S EUROPEAN(W)OPERATION?/TX
/XF	None	All Basic Index Fields Except Full Text	Word	S FOREIGN(W)OPERATIONS/XF

Figure 9.16 Fielded search options listed in the Dialog Blue Sheet for the Gale Group Trade & Industry Database (Source: library.dialog.com/bluesheets/html/bl0148.html#BI)

user interface implementation of fielded search to be in any way a restriction on how you choose to develop the taxonomy.

Endnotes

1. European Centre for the Development of Vocational Training, *European Training Thesaurus* (Luxembourg: Office for Official Publications of the European Communities, 2008), 47, libserver.cedefop. europa.eu/ett/download/ETT_2009_en.pdf
2. Personal experience of the author, who previously worked as an indexer and controlled vocabulary editor of Gale databases.

Chapter 10

Taxonomy Planning, Design, and Creation

Taxonomies: turning data into knowledge
—Nick Berry

Creating, or even revising, a taxonomy is a significant project that eventually becomes a knowledge base that requires continual maintenance. Other books and articles go into the subject of taxonomy planning and project management at greater length than there is space for in this chapter. In one such book, *Organising Knowledge*, the author Patrick Lambe suggests the following six steps for preparing a taxonomy project and discusses each in detail:[1]

1. Meet with the project sponsor (to map key stakeholders and activities, learn the purpose and intent of the project, determine the technology available, and assess the knowledge and information management context).

2. Engage the stakeholders.

3. Refine the project purpose and get the sponsor's agreement.

4. Design the approach.

5. Build a communication plan.

6. Start the process for taxonomy governance.

Another suggested approach to taxonomy projects comes from Darin Stewart in his book *Building Enterprise Taxonomies*. He describes the taxonomy development cycle as comprising five phases:[2]

1. Research (including stakeholder interviews and a content audit)

2. Strategy (developing the taxonomy plan and governance document)

3. Design

4. Implementation (actually building the taxonomy)

5. Administration (maintenance of the taxonomy)

Since accidental taxonomists are not always taxonomy project managers, we will not present detailed project management instructions here. Rather, this chapter looks at key issues pertaining to taxonomies as projects, including their planning, unique issues of enterprise taxonomies, taxonomy creation processes, taxonomy implementation and interoperability, and taxonomy governance.

Planning for a Taxonomy

Because a taxonomy is something created for future long-term use, planning is very important. Planning involves asking questions, conducting research, and preparing a written taxonomy plan, which can also serve as a governance document throughout the taxonomy creation process and for ongoing maintenance of the taxonomy. By now, you should know the details of how to create or edit a taxonomy, but if someone says to you, "We need a taxonomy, and we hear you know how to create taxonomies. What do you need to know to get started?" would you know how to answer and how to proceed? Even people with some taxonomy experience may be unsure how to respond initially to a new and different project. Planning involves asking the right people the right questions, conducting additional research, and developing a taxonomy design and strategy.

Project Questions

The first step in a taxonomy project is to meet with the key person or people connected to the project to get answers to fundamental questions about the intended taxonomy. If a single knowledgeable taxonomy manager is already in place and you come into the project simply to build the taxonomy, then you need only ask the taxonomy project manager the questions listed in this section. If, however, the taxonomy project manager does not yet have all the answers and is hoping that you will help come up with them, or if you *are* the taxonomy project manager, then you need to speak with all of the stakeholders in the project.

A definition of a stakeholder is "anyone who has a vested interest in the project, can be affected by the change initiative that the project represents or has the power to influence the project" (Declan Chellar).[3] Who exactly the stakeholders are will vary depending on the type of organization and purpose of the taxonomy. If, for example, the taxonomy is for a web-based subscription information service, then the stakeholders include the project manager, someone responsible for overseeing content creation or aggregation, any key content vendor(s), someone responsible for indexing, someone responsible for web user interface design (such as an information architect), and someone responsible for marketing and getting user feedback.

Whether you are meeting with the taxonomy owner/manager or are the taxonomy manager meeting with a number of stakeholders, you should be asking the same fundamental questions before beginning work on the taxonomy:

1. Purpose: What will the taxonomy be used for?

2. Users: Who are all the users of the taxonomy, and who are the end users in particular?

3. Content: What content will be covered by the taxonomy?

4. Scope: What are the topic area, scope, and limits?

5. Resources: What are the project's resources and constraints?

If the project owner cannot sufficiently answer all these questions, find out whom else you should ask. Answers may come from more than one person.

Purpose

Although a single taxonomy often serves multiple purposes, typically there is a primary purpose in mind. Recall from Chapter 1 that there are three main applications of taxonomies:

- (Human) indexing support

- Retrieval support (including both search and discovery)

- Organization and navigation support

If a taxonomy's primary purpose is to ensure comprehensive, accurate, and consistent indexing/tagging, then you will probably want more of a thesaurus-type of taxonomy. Nonpreferred terms and relationships should facilitate indexers in finding the preferred terms, and indexing policies must be established. If a taxonomy's primary purpose is to serve retrieval, then a taxonomy structure that best serves end-user needs, such as a hierarchical or faceted structure, is best. Finally, if a taxonomy's objective is to serve website organization and navigation, then it should be hierarchical and relatively small, should have term names that fit well as menu labels, and may not need additional term relationships.

Users

The purpose of a taxonomy will determine to a certain degree who the taxonomy users are (e.g., whether the users include indexers), but there are other variables to consider among users as well. If indexers are involved, it makes a difference whether they are dedicated indexers, content creators/authors, or editors and whether they are experts in the subject matter. Dedicated, trained indexers can deal with a large generalized taxonomy, but expect consistency in depth, breadth, and term style. Authors, on the other hand, seek terms that match the language of their writing and need a simple taxonomy without extensive indexing policies.

End users could be internal organization members, students, subject area specialists, the public, or various subsections of the public. Not only would different audiences look for different preferred terms, but different kinds of users may also have different expectations regarding the display of the term details, including/excluding nonpreferred terms and other relationships. Internal users may expect internal jargon and a structure that reflects the organization. A taxonomy used by students will likely need additional educational features, such as scientifically correct hierarchies and generous use of scope notes. Subject matter experts tend to expect deep taxonomies. A taxonomy for the public ideally is no more than three levels deep if hierarchical, and the display should conform to the same style of popular websites that have displayable taxonomies so that it will look familiar to users.

It can be tricky if the same taxonomy will be used by multiple types of users, which is most often the case with the taxonomies of large information vendors. Margot Diltz, senior manager of editor policy at Cengage Learning, explains:

> It is a challenge to create a single taxonomic system that satisfies the needs of a range of audiences, that is, the expert and the generalist or the child and the adult.

When the taxonomy is meant to meet the needs of all possible users, the results are likely to mean compromises that leave the taxonomist less than satisfied.[4]

Content

The range of content covered by a taxonomy can be a moving target. Once a taxonomy project is proposed, stakeholders may suggest additional content types not originally envisioned in the inclusion. This problem applies to both taxonomies used by information vendors and those used just internally. Thus, when planning a taxonomy, it is important to take a broad view and consider all the types of content likely to be included, even if some will not be incorporated until later.

In addition to the subject area of the content, the type of content affects the taxonomy design. The content could be text only or could consist of other media, such as image files, audio files, or video files, or it could be a combination. Image-only content tends not to make use of broad or abstract taxonomy concepts (such as **diseases**, **mergers & acquisitions**, **human resources**), as text content might. Furthermore, if the type of content is relatively uniform, then a faceted taxonomy might be most suitable. The nature of the content, volume, and rate at which it changes or grows all factor into deciding whether indexing will be manual or automatic, and the type of indexing also affects the taxonomy design.

Scope

While the content to be indexed is the determining factor in the subject scope of the taxonomy, any body of content will include off-topic documents. Thus, a policy is needed from the beginning to determine what types of subjects can be included in the taxonomy. There is also the question of what kinds of named entities should be included for people, organizations, products, places, document titles or names of works, laws, events, etc. If the taxonomy is faceted, you only need to include facets that are relevant to the search process. If not everything is covered, that's still OK. It can be easy to lose sight of a taxonomy's scope, especially if term relationships lead to creating more terms of only marginal relevance to the project.

Resources
Project resources or constraints include the following:

- Skills and expertise: Of project managers, indexers and other taxonomy editors

- Funding: For staff and for software, hardware, and networking services

- Timing: When a completed taxonomy needs to be implemented

- Stakeholder role: Of the project owner, managers, partners, content vendors, and/or key clients, etc., who may have certain expectations for the taxonomy and who may or may not be actively involved

- Technology: Capabilities of the indexing software (human or automated) and the search/retrieval software, the information architecture and user interface design, and how the data is stored (in a database or not)

- Technical support: For software, hardware, and networking/telecommunications requirements and the hosting of the data

Limited resources can obviously affect the size and complexity of the taxonomy.

Additional Considerations

Sometimes the taxonomist reports to a project manager, and sometimes the taxonomist *is* the project manager. In the latter case, such as in the role of a taxonomy manager or taxonomy consultant, there are many other issues to consider. These include typical project management concerns that are covered in other books. Some questions pertaining specifically to taxonomy project management include the following:

- Which people will be involved in the taxonomy creation, management, support, and approval? This typically involves people from different departments.

- Who is required to give approval, and at what level of decision making in creating the taxonomy is approval needed? (Someone other than the taxonomist might decide the taxonomy format, specific top terms, and an approximate number of hierarchical levels.)

- Who will be responsible for setting taxonomy usage policy? Most likely, it will be you, the taxonomist, but the policy will still need approval.

- Who will document taxonomy usage and policies? It might be you, but it might instead be the responsibility of the documentation department.

- How will the taxonomy fit in with other document-level metadata, and who is responsible for this? It's a gray line between taxonomy and other metadata, such as document type, author, and audience, and if a metadata librarian is involved in that area, you need to work together.

- How will ongoing support and maintenance be handled? Who will be responsible, and how much time will be devoted to such tasks?

If you are *not* in a project manager role, and someone else is taking care of all of the preceding issues, you as the taxonomist or taxonomy editor still need to address some key questions before you plunge in and start creating terms and relationships:

- Will the structure of the taxonomy be a relatively flat controlled vocabulary, a hierarchical taxonomy, or a taxonomy organized into facets?

- Will the data be stored in a database with the technology to fully support faceted search?

- If hierarchical, will polyhierarchies be permitted?

- If hierarchical, approximately how many top terms should there be and how many levels deep should the taxonomy go?

- Will associative relationships be included and supported?

- Will the nonpreferred terms be displayed to the end users?

- What kinds of additional information should each term have (such as scope notes or other attributes)?

- Will the taxonomy (or taxonomies) be segmented or classified in such a way that separate files or category designations would be applicable?

In some cases, answers will not be immediately available for these questions. You may need to conduct further research and perhaps even perform some test development of the taxonomy, before the answers become apparent. This is one of the differences between serving as a taxonomy editor versus serving as a taxonomy manager or consultant. If you are a taxonomy editor, someone else should answer these questions for you. As a taxonomy manager or consultant, though, you will need to do research to determine the answers yourself.

Research for a Taxonomy

To a large extent, conducting research for a taxonomy project involves gathering sources for terms (discussed in Chapter 3), but research is also needed to support decisions regarding the taxonomy's size, scope, structure, display, and other features. In some cases, the same research can yield both terms and answers to these other taxonomy design questions.

Possible research tasks include the following:

- More in-depth interviews of primary stakeholders, interviews of additional stakeholders, and perhaps even interviews with some of the potential taxonomy users

- A content audit or content inventory (see Chapter 3 for details and an example)

- Analysis of word or phrase lists generated by simple text analytics tools from sample content

- Analysis of search logs (when a search engine is already in use) and click-trail reports of such reporting tools, if available

- Research into the functions of any existing search/retrieval methods the organization may have and/or methods used for search/retrieval for similar content in similar organizations

Interviewing stakeholders means scheduling individual meetings, either face-to-face or by phone, with the taxonomy project sponsors, leaders, managers, and team members and with key people in other departments who will be involved in or have some stake in the taxonomy. In preparation, you need to identify the stakeholders for interviews and draw up interview questions. Plan for each interview to last perhaps 30 to 60 minutes. The interview questions should seek to understand:

- The goals and objectives of the taxonomy, especially from a business sense

- Weaknesses or failings of the current search/findability

- The basic kinds of content

- The information systems currently used and those that are expected to be added or retired

- The challenges foreseen

- The nature of content creation, by whom, according to what policies, etc.

Questions can deal with both the big picture and with details. You may wish to use a table or spreadsheet to record the results of the interview questions, with a row for each stakeholder and a column for each question. You can then glance at all the results to discern any patterns.

Search query logs record search behavior, and click-trail reports record browse/navigation behavior, and both are useful in different ways. Search query logs provide ideas for preferred and non-preferred terms. They are simple to interpret because they list keywords/search strings that users have entered, presenting them in usage order. Click-trail reports, on the other hand, can provide ideas for what a term's broader term might be. These reports usually show the series of webpage titles that a user clicked through to navigate to the desired information, with a list of trails for each final destination page. Thus, you can discover the most prevalent paths users take to a destination page. These paths provide insight into what most users consider the logical hierarchy or category for the information on the destination page. Query logs are often a standard administrative feature of search software. Click-trail reports might also be included in such software, but if not, there are dedicated web analytics software packages that offer click-trail reports among other features. These packages include ClickTale

(www.clicktale.com), Clicky (www.getclicky.com), iWebTrack (www.
iwebtrack.com), Mint (www.haveamint.com), Unica NetInsight
(www.unica.com), Optimal iQ (www.optimaliq.com), Omniture
SiteCatalyst (www.omniture.com), VisitorVille (www.visitorville.
com), and Webtrends (www.webtrends.com).

Taxonomy Design Plan
The answers to all the aforementioned questions form the basis for
a taxonomy design plan. The extent and details of such a plan will
depend to a certain degree on the organization's documentation
requirements. Formal approval of a plan may or may not be
required prior to starting work on building the taxonomy. The plan
should address at least the following issues:

- Purpose and users of the taxonomy
- Scope of the taxonomy and of the indexed content
- Tools used for creating and managing the taxonomy
- Sources for the taxonomy terms
- Systems used for implementation and end use of the
  taxonomy
- Expected user-interface features
- Indexing method(s)
- Structure/type of taxonomy, relationship types
- Project timetable with milestones and prerequisites

This taxonomy design document—which you may call a project
plan, requirements document, or another name that fits into your
organization's documentation policy—can be considered the first
major "deliverable" of a taxonomy project. The taxonomy design
plan can then be the basis for future documentation of the taxonomy, which you will develop as you create the taxonomy. While the

general taxonomy design issues should be decided in advance, certain details tend to get resolved later, once you actually begin creating the taxonomy. Such details could include term format (such as whether to use parenthetical qualifiers), the use of certain term note/description fields, and procedures for updating the taxonomy. Furthermore, technical requirements can change, especially if the search interface is still under development or the content management/search software is subject to change. (Taxonomy projects are often launched at the same time that new software systems are introduced.) You will update the documentation throughout the taxonomy creation process, and it will be complete only when the taxonomy is complete. Then it is no longer a "plan" but becomes the "governance" document, a policy document to "govern" the taxonomy.

Taxonomy Structural Design
It is at this stage that you will make all structural decisions about the taxonomy, if they have not already been made for you. Structural issues include deciding whether the taxonomy will:

- Have any portions licensed from external sources (see Chapter 1)

- Be predominantly hierarchical, faceted, or organized as a thesaurus

- Have associative relationships

- Be maintained as a single file/thesaurus or as multiple taxonomies/vocabularies/files

- Include additional term types or categories that might be applied to organize the taxonomy

As mentioned in Chapter 5 with respect to taxonomy management software features, assigning categories to terms enables support for certain end-use search interface characteristics and other administrative capabilities. You could also use categories to distinguish:

- Generic terms from named entities
- Terms that the you decide may be permitted to have certain semantic relationships
- Terms that belong within a facet for a faceted taxonomy

There could be a master taxonomy, for example, and subsections categorized for certain audiences or services.

Number of Taxonomists
In planning the timetable for completing the taxonomy, you need to consider how many people will be directly working on it. Whether a single taxonomist will suffice or whether there should be a team of people working on the taxonomy depends, obviously, on the taxonomy size and the project deadline. One taxonomist can create an entire taxonomy for a project if there is sufficient time, perhaps a period of several months. Even if one taxonomist working full time could undertake the entire project, it may be desirable to have multiple taxonomy editors, who would be working only part-time on the project (whether they are on staff or contracted freelancers). As we have seen, there are many subjective decisions that the taxonomist must make, so it is good to have other taxonomists to consult for opinions. If there are multiple taxonomists, the work could be divided among them in different ways:

- By taxonomy hierarchy, facet, authority file, or subject area
- By task/function: interviewing stakeholders, performing a content audit, constructing the initial taxonomy structure, researching terms and relationships, conducting card sorting or other user testing, editing, etc. (some of these tasks must be performed sequentially)

In contrast with the work of indexers, there are no reliable average rates for estimating how many terms a taxonomist can create per hour. There are too many variables, and individual terms may or may not require research. Fortunately, a considerable amount of taxonomy work can be done off-site. Therefore, employing remote freelance taxonomists, which is more appropriate for part-time short-term work anyway, may work quite well for a taxonomy project.

Enterprise Taxonomies

Enterprise taxonomies have recently been receiving a great deal of attention. *Enterprise* is not limited to a company or business but could refer to any large organization, including nonprofits and government agencies. It sometimes seems as if all taxonomies these days are enterprise taxonomies, because 1) it is true that most *new* taxonomies are indeed enterprise taxonomies, and 2) taxonomies that are not created for an enterprise are less likely to be called taxonomies but rather *thesauri* or *controlled vocabularies*. A greater number of new and planned taxonomy projects are for enterprises, simply because that is where the greatest market is. Most information vendors who use taxonomies to provide content for customers or the public, rather than for an internal enterprise, already have taxonomies in place. The number of new information vendors is relatively small, whereas the number of enterprises of various kinds that can benefit from a taxonomy to make their documents and other content easier to manage and find is vast.

Enterprise Taxonomy Characteristics

The significant features of an enterprise taxonomy are the following:

1. Its primary users are members of the enterprise (employees and perhaps also contractors).

2. The content to be indexed with the taxonomy is largely created/authored by members of the enterprise.

3. The taxonomy unifies concepts/vocabularies from various departments to universally serve the entire enterprise (but does not necessarily include all content in an enterprise).

An enterprise taxonomy is often implemented within an enterprise content management system, a document management system, and/or an intranet or extranet (like an intranet, but with additional access to partners, vendors, clients, etc., but not the general public). Access through a public website is also possible but would likely be of secondary importance and may include only parts of the taxonomy.

An enterprise taxonomy is most often a hierarchical taxonomy. Part of the appeal of a taxonomy to an enterprise involves having the taxonomy displayed to the users so that they are aware of it and thus make use of it. A hierarchical taxonomy has the added benefits of educating employees and reinforcing corporate information/knowledge management structures. Vocabulary facets (in contrast to other document-type metadata facets) do not work so well across the divergent content types found throughout an enterprise, although they could serve a subset of enterprise content. A thesaurus may not be suitable for an entire enterprise if it is not displayed or is displayed only as an alphabetical list, which is not the best way to browse for disparate information within an organization.

Developing an enterprise taxonomy has its own particular requirements. Because it involves various departments and people within an organization, a significant number of people have to be consulted in the taxonomy development process, including stakeholders and representative users. Enterprise taxonomy stakeholders include:

- The project sponsor/owner

- The manager (upper management)

- Members of a taxonomy project team

- Managers of departments whose existing vocabulary (which may or may not currently be controlled) will be utilized

- Technical writers or other content creators, who want the documents they write to be found through the taxonomy

- Information technology engineers who will be responsible for implementation and technical support

- The intranet/extranet webmaster(s)

- Key "power" users

Users of an enterprise taxonomy include potentially all employees of an organization. Thus, unlike externally facing taxonomies, test users are easily accessible, although they may be at various remote locations.

The subject matter scope of an enterprise taxonomy can be quite varied and needs to be carefully considered, as there are different options for how inclusive it may be. The scope could include any or all of the following:

- Products and services (names, descriptions, features, user issues)

- Technology and technical terminology (science, research and development oriented)

- People and their areas of expertise

- Human resources and management subjects

- All the information in an enterprise

In addition, you need to recognize the existence of proprietary/nonpublic terminology that would never be known to anyone outside of the enterprise. All enterprises have, to some degree, their own jargon, acronyms, project code names, and so on, that are totally unique and not defined anywhere outside that domain. You need to look for that language and be sure to include it.

Enterprise Taxonomy Project Tasks

The steps for creating an enterprise taxonomy are not too different from those involved in creating any taxonomy, but greater attention is required in certain areas. In addition to interviewing stakeholders, it is both possible and beneficial to interview select users, since the users are people within the enterprise rather than external customers. Web search logs are typically available to analyze for search terms that have been entered, and these should not be overlooked. A content audit is usually relatively involved and complicated in an enterprise, due to the diversity of content. For a hierarchical or faceted taxonomy, you need to look harder to identify organizing principals, problems, and tasks. This is not as simple as a retail product taxonomy. The documented design plan of an enterprise taxonomy also carries more weight, because actually developing the taxonomy may be contingent on acceptance of the plan, which is not necessarily assured. Some managers may be skeptical of the cost-benefits of a taxonomy.

Interviewing Stakeholders and Users

The stakeholders in an enterprise taxonomy project tend to be a larger and more diverse group than stakeholders in a taxonomy for customer-only information services. In addition to the taxonomy project leader, manager, and/or sponsor, you should include a manager from each department whose content will be included and from each department that will use the taxonomy, which essentially includes all departments of an enterprise.

   User interviews, which should come after the stakeholder interviews, ought to include at least two representatives from different functional areas, such as human resources, marketing, sales, customer service, finance, research, and product development. User interviews are typically not as long as the stakeholder interviews. Interview questions should center on what kinds of information are needed within a given function area, how the current system falls short, how a desired search system should work, and any other "wish list" items. At this stage, these are still planning questions. Later, when there is a draft or test taxonomy to review, you will consult with the users and stakeholders again.

Search/Query Log Data

If the enterprise is currently using any kind of search software, its administrative features typically will include search logs, which keep track of the search strings that users have been entering. If available, such logs are an excellent source of both concepts and terms, whether preferred or nonpreferred.

Enterprise Content Audits

As discussed in Chapter 3, a content audit or content inventory is an important step in gathering sources for terms for any taxonomy. In an enterprise, there is an even greater variety of content that the taxonomy may cover, all of which should be included in a content audit. The taxonomy may cover the following types of content:

- Employee handbooks
- Patents
- Manuals and guidelines
- Transaction records
- Policies
- Reports and white papers

- Standards

- Marketing literature

- Product data

- Internal employee newsletters

- R&D development documents

- Training materials

- Lab notebooks

- External publications

- Schematics and drawings

- Customer support documents

- Project documents

- Knowledgebases

Furthermore, there may be a variety of different document types or file formats to consider, including:

- Webpage files (HTML)

- PDF documents

- Word processed documents

- Documents in other publishing formats

- Presentations

- Spreadsheets

- Online help files

- Image files

- Videos

- Database records

- XML files

- Paper (such as from archives or external sources)

Electronic documents could be web/intranet pages or shared files on servers or could be located in document management systems or on individual hard drives.

Although an enterprise taxonomy will be used across the entire enterprise and should include vocabulary for the entire enterprise, this does not necessarily mean that every single piece of content must be included. You might exclude emails, confidential employee records, receipts attached to expense reports, forms, vendor- or partner-produced literature, etc. You might also determine that some content will stay in separate repositories; for example, logs of customer calls will stay in the customer contact system, and forms filled out by individual employees will be kept only in the human resources files.

The content audit needs to be more detailed for an enterprise taxonomy than for other kinds of taxonomies. In addition to writing down the term/concept and its source, other information to record for each concept includes audience, document type, and possibly the content management system in which the document is stored. In *Building Enterprise Taxonomies*, Darin Stewart suggests that data from an audit include:[5]

- Content (or document)
- Category (or document type)
- Source (application, database, or external provider)
- Location (URL, file system path, or hard copy location)
- Stakeholder (author, producer, consumer, or executive)
- Organization (stakeholder affiliation)
- Term

Content determined to be redundant, obsolete, or trivial (ROT) may also be tagged as such.

Guidelines by Jeffrey Veen of the consultancy Adaptive Path suggest a website content inventory include the following inventory items:[6]

- ID# (you provide)

- Name (page title or other)

- Link (URL)

- Document type

- Topics, keywords

- Owner, maintainer

- ROT (redundant, obsolete, or trivial)

- Notes

A similar list of content audit items is included in the web content audit tool (Excel template) on the Information Architecture Institute's "Tools" page provided by John Howe.[7]

A complete content inventory is usually not possible for an enterprise taxonomy. Locating and recording all content in an enterprise would be nearly impossible due to its sheer volume, and much of it may be of little relevance anyway. Rather, you need to identify the most critical content for the audit. Stewart refers to "critical core content" in identifying what should be surveyed during an enterprise taxonomy content audit.[8]

Taxonomy Creation Process

Actually creating a taxonomy involves entering the concepts and terms identified in the planning and research stage into some taxonomy management tool, adding the appropriate term relationships and possible additional information, getting intermittent feedback from stakeholders and test-users, and making further revisions as needed. This is the core of the work of taxonomists and what defines their work. And for most taxonomists, especially those who are not also involved in project management, this is the bulk of their job.

Steps for Building a Taxonomy

Planning for a taxonomy, as described in the first section of this chapter, involves answering basic questions regardless of the kind of taxonomy. But when it comes to actually building the taxonomy, there are different methods. Broadly speaking, the approach to building the taxonomy can be either top-down, bottom-up, or some of each, depending on the type of taxonomy. Hierarchical and faceted taxonomies tend to involve more of a top-down approach. The approach will also depend on the primary source for terms. If a significant number of terms are suggested by the taxonomists, subject matter experts, information architects, or a product manager, then more of a top-down design would result. If most of the terms originate in sample content, a bottom-up approach makes more sense.

Steps for Building a Hierarchical Taxonomy

The basic steps for creating hierarchical taxonomies are the following:

1. Gather term concepts from a content audit, stakeholder interviews, and other sources.

2. Identify the top categories or facets based on analysis of patterns and scope of concepts, and list these (ideally in a spreadsheet).

3. Come up with example second-level terms for each category (but not necessarily all second-level terms), and possibly even a few third-level terms.

4. Present this top-level "straw-man" taxonomy to the taxonomy owner(s) or stakeholders for initial review and feedback and make revisions as requested. ("Straw-man" means that, like straw, it can easily be torn down and rebuilt.)

5. Making full use of all the concepts gathered, fully build the taxonomy out to lower levels, possibly still in spreadsheet software if it is a small taxonomy, or else in a taxonomy/thesaurus management tool.

6. Implement, conduct user testing, and revise as needed.

Since a hierarchical taxonomy is simpler than a thesaurus, at least once the basic hierarchies have been defined, the taxonomist's role could diminish after Step 4. At that point, internal subject matter experts, more intimately familiar with the content, could build out the taxonomy to further depths, as long as the taxonomist provides the guidelines and some review.

Although the top terms are defined first, with sample second-level terms next, often the procedure involves identifying the narrowest terms next, after the top terms, and then grouping the narrowest terms to come up with possible intermediate-level terms. Thus, even for a supposedly top-down hierarchy, you may actually perform some bottom-up taxonomy building, while still presenting a straw-man taxonomy consisting of only the top two levels. It is not unusual to start out creating the taxonomy from both the top and the bottom and to leave the middle for last.

Steps in Building a Thesaurus

The steps for creating literature/digital asset retrieval thesauri are similar to those for creating hierarchical taxonomies but not identical. Top categories may or may not need identifying, and unlike a hierarchical taxonomy, there is no point at which the taxonomist can "pass off" the taxonomy building to subject matter experts.

The taxonomist must do all the development of a thesaurus, except perhaps for named entities:

1   Gather term concepts from samples of the content being indexed.

2. Analyze the collected terms and organize them into lists within the same subject area at the same level "offline," whether in a spreadsheet (preferable) or in a text document.

3. Obtain feedback on some of the more significant term lists as deemed necessary, and then import them into thesaurus management software.

4. Making full use of all the gathered concepts, fully build out the thesaurus of terms and relationships in a thesaurus management tool, consulting reference sources (dictionaries, glossaries, other thesauri) and subject matter experts as needed.

5. Implement the thesaurus, test it with sample indexing, and revise it, filling in apparently "missing" terms and relationships.

When it comes to the most involved phase, actually building out the thesaurus of terms and relationships (Step 4 in the preceding list), there are basically three different possible approaches:

1. Complete each term's set of nonpreferred terms, full relationships, notes, and all attributes, then slowly add more terms. This approach works best for named entities, where interterm relationships are minimal or at least rather simple, but term details might be quite extensive.

2. Add a number of terms quickly and then go back later to add the terms' details and relationships. Adding multiple terms could be done offline and then imported, as mentioned previously, but if the thesaurus software does not

have an easy importing feature, it may be quicker to add terms of less than a dozen or so manually. This approach is more appropriate when there are a significant number of terms at the same level or when you have a list of technical terms that require research and you want to do all of the research later.

3. Adopt a hybrid approach, in which you add terms, create their nonpreferred terms and any scope notes or other term details, then go back and create relationships later; or create hierarchical relationships at the time of term creation, and add only the associative relationships later. This approach can work for various kinds of terms, and the specific procedure is more a matter of how the taxonomist may think: fully defined terms first, relationships second.

If you do postpone any relationship creation after creating a number of terms, obviously you should keep good records of which terms still require relationships.

In either case, whether you are building a hierarchical taxonomy or a thesaurus, you will likely develop a considerable number of terms offline, in a spreadsheet, word processor, or text editor. You can then import or load the terms in batches into a thesaurus management tool, where you can create relationships and add other data. When you add terms later, though, during the taxonomy maintenance phase, you will need to create each one individually. Therefore, you will likely do all maintenance taxonomy work in the thesaurus management software.

Card-Sorting Exercises

The taxonomy-creation process involves periodic input from stakeholders and/or test-users. This input is not limited to approving lists of terms, but could also involve input into the structure in the case of a hierarchical taxonomy. You can gather this input through a procedure called card sorting. As the name implies, card sorting involves having test-users sort into categories small cards or pieces of paper on which you have written the names of candidate taxonomy terms. From the sorting results, you can get an idea how users believe hierarchies should be arranged. Card sorting is usually used for only two levels of a hierarchy at a time, typically the top level and a second level. Card sorting reveals the way searchers think about the concepts and has been a technique utilized by information architects for web navigational taxonomies for some time. While often associated with navigational taxonomies, this method can be used for the top two levels of any hierarchical taxonomy.

The number of cards/terms should be limited so that the card-sorting participants can easily scan the groups and work with them. Ideally, there should be about four to eight top-level categories, and within each of these categories a similar or slightly higher number of terms. Thus, the total number of second-level terms involved might range from 20 to 60. With more than that, the technique becomes unwieldy.

There are two kinds of card-sorting exercises: open card sort and closed card sort. An open card sort does not predefine the broader categories. The participants themselves must categorize the cards as they deem appropriate, determining both the names of the categories and how many categories there should be. A closed card sort is simpler for the participants. You provide them with the top-level categories, and they merely sort the second-level concepts into those predefined categories. You can choose either method or use both in sequence. An open card sort would be useful earlier on in the taxonomy development process, when you have not yet determined the top-level terms, and a closed card sort would come later.

Card sorting no longer requires having participants sort index cards on a conference room table in your presence, although there are benefits to doing it live if you can. Card-sorting software allows you to conduct card-sorting exercises with remote participants.

Web-based software-as-a-service card-sorting tools that offer subscription uses include WebSort (websort.net), OptimalSort (www.optimalsort.com), and MindCanvas (www.themindcanvas. com). These tools, which allow the users to move "cards" by a drag-and-drop feature, offer both open and closed card-sorting exercises. Figure 10.1 is a screenshot of an open card sort via OptimalSort.

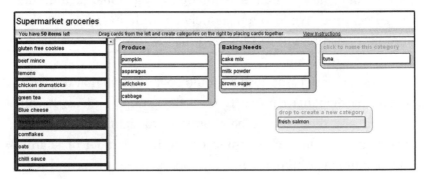

Figure 10.1   OptimalSort card-sorting software for an open card sort

Although conducting a card-sorting exercise is relatively simple, you should design it carefully to get the most out of it. If you have no prior experience with running a card-sorting exercise or merely want to learn more, Donna Spencer's book *Card Sorting: Designing Usable Categories* (Rosenfeld Media, 2009) covers the field in great detail.

Taxonomy Governance

Even after a taxonomy is created and implemented, it is never entirely finished. All taxonomies require some updating over time, some more often than others. Keeping a taxonomy up to date requires having policies, methods, and procedures for maintenance and requires a documented understanding of who is responsible for the taxonomy over time. These documented policies constitute what is called taxonomy governance.

Governance, a term that in the past decade has begun to be used in project management and especially in the information technology sector, refers to all the processes for managing a project, with particular emphasis on accountability. Governance deals with policies and procedures, including roles and accountabilities, standards, process methodologies, and communication methods. For taxonomies, governance is important not only for the design and building phases but also for the continued maintenance of the taxonomy. As mentioned previously, the initial taxonomy design plan document should become the basis of the governance document. This document is both followed and enhanced as the taxonomy is built, implemented, and maintained.

In considering the scope of taxonomy governance, you need to determine the following:

- The kinds of rules that should be followed for adding, changing, moving, or deleting terms or relationships

- The group that should maintain the taxonomy

- The various kinds of changes that may be expected to occur and possibly even their costs

- The kinds of information needed to determine appropriate changes (such as statistics for terms' indexing usage)

- The processes for changes

- Specific methods for handling comments, appeals, issue logs, announcements, update schedules, etc.

Possible methods for communicating with indexers have already been discussed in Chapter 6, but other individuals and groups will also want to propose changes to the taxonomy, so they, too, need to be covered in the governance document. Governance methods vary significantly among organizations and can involve primarily a single person, a couple of people, or a large cross-functional team.

The taxonomist or taxonomists who initially created the taxonomy are not necessarily the persons responsible for carrying out needed updates over time. Creating the taxonomy may involve an outside consultant or contractor or someone temporarily assigned to the project for the time-consuming design and building phase, while the less intensive work of maintenance later becomes someone else's task. The taxonomy could live on for decades after the employee(s) who created it left the organization. Alternatively, the taxonomy may have been inherited through an acquisition or partnership or adopted from another department. No matter what the circumstances, whether you are an employee or contractor, whenever you create a taxonomy, you should expect that the taxonomy will need to be maintained at some time or in some place without your own continued direct involvement. Therefore, documented policies are very important. On the other hand, if you come in to manage or update an existing taxonomy, be sure to ask for all documentation pertaining to the taxonomy.

There might not be a single taxonomy governance document but rather several relevant documents. Taxonomy governance deals with the taxonomy and all associated materials/documents, including:

- An editorial style guide (which may be written for the taxonomy specifically or included within a larger guide for content creation in general)

- An end-user (searcher) manual

- Indexing guidelines for indexers or for people using automated indexing systems

- Any metadata standard of which controlled vocabularies are a part

- A broader product requirements document of which the taxonomy is a part

- Team rules and procedures

An editorial style guide addresses issues involved in creating taxonomy terms and relationships, including capitalization, abbreviations, use of special characters, plurals, length limits, foreign words, inverted forms, punctuation within terms, formats for certain kinds of named entities, etc. Issues concerning term relationships include the number of relationships per term, polyhierarchies, use of associative relationships or additional customized relationships, etc. There may be some overlap between the taxonomy editorial style guide and an indexing guide, especially regarding permission for indexers to create unapproved terms.

Because governance is so closely tied to maintenance, one might assume that taxonomy governance is the same as maintenance, but it is not. As we have seen, governance issues start with the taxonomy design plan. It is important to keep governance issues in mind from the start of a taxonomy project. Chapter 11 discusses taxonomy maintenance.

Endnotes

1. Patrick Lambe, "Preparing for a Taxonomy Project," Chapter 7 in *Organising Knowledge: Taxonomies, Knowledge, and Organisational Effectiveness*, 153–183 (Oxford: Chandos Publishing, 2007).
2. Darin L. Stewart, *Building Enterprise Taxonomies* (Portland, OR: Mokita Press, 2008), 70.
3. Declan Chellar, "Who Are Your Stakeholders?," *The Project Management Hut* (June 25, 2009), www.pmhut.com/who-are-your-stakeholders
4. Margot Diltz, "Taxonomy Work Impressions Survey" survey response, September 22, 2009.
5. Stewart, *Building Enterprise Taxonomies*, 78.

6. Veen, Jeffrey, "Doing a Content Inventory (Or, A Mind-Numbingly Detailed Odyssey Through Your Website)," June 18, 2002, www.adaptive path.com/ideas/essays/archives/000040.php

7. John Howe, Content Development Spreadsheet, iainstitute.org/tools/ content_development_spreadsheets.php

8. Stewart, *Building Enterprise Taxonomies*, 77.

Chapter 11

Taxonomy Implementation and Evolution

*Taxonomies: adding a little to your data so that
you can get a lot more out of it.*
—Bob DuCharme

Taxonomy work involves more than just building new taxonomies. After all, full-time employed taxonomists tend to keep their jobs after they finish building a taxonomy. Chapter 2 lists a number of related duties that taxonomists perform, including documentation, test-searching, and indexing support. In addition, and more significantly, a taxonomy needs to be implemented in different systems, maintained, revised, adapted to new indexing or search implementations, merged or mapped with another taxonomy, and possibly translated into another language. You might maintain, revise, or adapt the taxonomy that you created, but you could also be required to manage and adapt a taxonomy created by someone else. As noted earlier, a taxonomy is never done. Because taxonomies are used to support the indexing of ever-growing and ever-changing content repositories, their terms must be updated and modified in keeping with evolving topics. Over time, you may also be able to collect data on what keywords end users are using, and thus you can modify terms to more closely match.

Taxonomy Interoperability

A taxonomy is not fully functional if left in a taxonomy management system. Although some taxonomy management systems include modules for indexing (manual or automated) and/or search, most likely your content resides somewhere else, and at least some of your end users also use different systems for searching or browsing. Therefore, the completed taxonomy needs to be implemented or deployed into other systems to be used. This process involves exporting the taxonomy from your taxonomy management system and then having it imported into other systems. An existing taxonomy already in use may also need to be implemented into other systems, such as those of third-party partners or vendors. The ability to use data, in this case a taxonomy, in different applications, implementations, or software systems, whether proprietary, commercial, or open source, such as on the web, is known as interoperability.

A taxonomy contains complex information, so a standard interoperable format is needed for exporting and re-importing or for importing an external licensed taxonomy. A CSV (comma separated values) file format works, but it lacks any standard definitions, so CSV format is appropriate only for simple taxonomies and not complex thesauri. A more robust interoperable format, suitable for even complex thesauri, is XML or a format based on XML, such as Zthes, RDF, OWL, or SKOS.

XML

XML (www.w3.org/XML), which stands for extensible markup language, uses nested tags, like HTML, but the creator can define the tags. Definitions for the tags are stored in a related document called a schema. All commercial taxonomy management software supports XML exporting of the taxonomies, so you do not need to create your own XML tags. Figure 11.1 is an example of XML output generated by the thesaurus software MultiTes for a single term,

```
<CONCEPT>
  <DESCRIPTOR>Firewalls</DESCRIPTOR>
  <BT>Intrusion prevention systems</BT>
  <NT>Application firewalls</NT>
  <NT>Network firewalls</NT>
  <N-TYPE>Subject Subject</N-TYPE>
  <TAXONOMY> Risk Management</TAXONOMY>
  <UF>Firewall</UF>
  <UF>packet filtering</UF>
  <UF>packet filters</UF>
  <UF>packet inspection</UF>
  <SN>A device or software configured to permit, deny,
    encrypt, or proxy all computer traffic between different
    security domains based upon a set of rules and other
    criteria</SN>
</CONCEPT>
```

Figure 11.1 An example of XML output for a single term
from the thesaurus software MultiTes

firewalls. In addition to the obvious tags, <BT>, <NT>, and <UF>, this example includes tags for user-defined categories, such as <N-Type> and <Taxonomy>.

As XML tags are user-defined and not standard, in contrast to HTML or various metadata standards (e.g., MARC or Dublin Core), the tags used with an XML taxonomy export file will vary. Each thesaurus software product uses a different format for XML tags. Figure 11.2 is an example of XML output generated from the thesaurus software Smartlogic Semaphore for a single term, *child protection.* This XML utilizes a very different format from that of MultiTes, in that the base tags are more generic, and specific information is contained within the tag attributes. Therefore, instead of a simple pair of tags for each relationship type, there is a tag for "relationship" and the type is described within it.

This kind of XML format makes it more complicated for defining in a schema for importing into another system. Thesaurus software usually does not include a schema document, and even if it did, it would not cover any user-defined relationships, categories, or notes. Therefore, if you want to import the XML file into your content management/search system, you need to write the schema yourself. Most large organizations, though, have technical

```
<term name="Child protection" status="Approved" id="57" type="preferred">
  <relationships>
    <relationship type="hierarchical" name="Broader Term" termId="163">Care</relationship>
    <relationship type="hierarchical" name="Narrower Term" termId="1554">Children at risk</relationship>
    <relationship type="hierarchical" name="Narrower Term" termId="1555">Children in need</relationship>
    <relationship type="equivalence" name="Use For" termId="5534">protecting children</relationship>
    <relationship type="associative" name="Related To" termId="650">Child abuse</relationship>
    <relationship type="associative" name="Related To" termId="2805">Child safety</relationship>
    <relationship type="associative" name="Related To" termId="382">Domestic violence</relationship>
    <relationship type="associative" name="Related To" termId="2478">Sales to children</relationship>
    <relationship type="associative" name="Related To" termId="387">Sex offences</relationship>
    <relationship type="associative" name="Related To" termId="51">Child care</relationship>
  </relationships>
  <notes>
    <note name="Scope Note">Safeguarding children from neglect or physical, emotional or sexual abuse</note>
    <note name="Added In Version">1.00</note>
    <note name="Last Updated In Version">2.00</note>
  </notes>
  <attributes>
    <attribute name="Use for classifying content" />
    <attribute name="Use for concept mapping" />
    <attribute name="A-Z Entry" />
  </attributes>
</term>
```

Figure 11.2 An example of XML output for a single term from the thesaurus software Smartlogic Semaphore (from the Integrated Public Sector Vocabulary)

staff sufficiently proficient with XML, so the task of writing the schema will not necessarily fall to you, the taxonomist. It may also be possible to contract your thesaurus software vendor to write the schema for you. If you are licensing an externally published taxonomy, then you could pay the thesaurus vendor to provide such additional implementation services.

Zthes

In an attempt to provide a standard for the various possible XML tag specifications for thesauri, beginning in 1999 the British software engineer Mike Taylor developed an XML schema specific for the "semantic hierarchies" of terms as described in ISO 2788 and ANSI/NISO Z39.19, which is called Zthes (zthes.z3950.org). Zthes has since gained a reputation as the industry standard, and some commercial software now supports Zthes exporting (and possibly also importing), including Cognatrix, Data Harmony, Synaptica, and Smartlogic Semaphore.

The Zthes schema specifies the following elements: termId, termUpdate, termName, termQualifier, termType, termLanguage, termVocabulary, termCategory, termStatus, termApproval, term Sortkey, termNote, termCreatedDate, termCreatedBy, termModified Date, termModifiedBy, postings, and relation. Subrecords specify the relation (relationship) type. Figure 11.3 is an example of Zthes XML output generated from the thesaurus software Synaptica for a single term from its preloaded Training Thesaurus.

```
< ZThes>
  <term>
    <termId>11572</termId>
    <termUpdate>add</termUpdate>
    <termName>Applied zoology</termName>
    <termVocabulary>Training_Thes</termVocabulary>
    <relation weight="100">
      <relationType>BT</relationType>
      <termId>11573</termId>
      <termName>Zoology</termName>
      <termVocabulary>Training_Thes</termVocabulary>
    </relation>
    <relation weight="100">
      <relationType>NT</relationType>
      <termId>11574</termId>
      <termName>Livestock farming</termName>
      <termVocabulary>Training_Thes</termVocabulary>
    </relation>
  </term>
```

Figure 11.3 An example of Zthes XML output
for a single term from Synaptica

RDF, OWL, and SKOS

The RDF (Resource Description Framework) language, or varia-tions of it, is also used as an interoperable format for taxonomies. RDF (www.w3.org/RDF), which is supported by the World Wide Web Consortium (W3C), is a framework rather than a strict stan-dard. The RDF, which is expressable in XML syntax, was designed for describing resources and giving each resource and the resource's attributes persistent identifiers. An extension of RDF deals specifi-cally with a vocabulary description language but does not get into such specifics as term relationship types. Rather it provides a

326 The Accidental Taxonomist

mechanism for the user to define them. Although RDF uses XML syntax, it is more complex than a tagging language, since it uses what are called *classes, properties, resources,* and *collections.* A better analogy for RDF syntax would be the coding used in object-oriented programming languages.

What may be more interesting for taxonomies are two other standards built on RDF: the Web Ontology Language (OWL) and the Simple Knowledge Organization System (SKOS). OWL (www.w3.org/2007/OWL) is a semantic markup language for publishing and sharing ontologies on the web and supports semantic web applications. OWL features a larger vocabulary, a stronger syntax, and greater machine interpretability than does RDF.[1] As OWL is intended for ontologies rather than simpler taxonomies, it may actually be more than you need. Commercial thesaurus software that supports OWL exporting includes Data Harmony, Synaptica, and Mondeca.

SKOS (www.w3.org/2004/02/skos) is a proposed standard that is an application of RDF specifically for knowledge organization systems such as thesauri and taxonomies. At the time of this writing, SKOS is still a work in progress, with its specifications published as W3C working drafts. In SKOS, the fundamental element is a concept, and SKOS also defines preferred and alternate (nonpreferred) labels for concepts, as well as broader, narrower, and related relationships between concepts. Commercial thesaurus software that supports SKOS exporting includes Data Harmony, Synaptica, and Mondeca.

Taxonomy Updating

A taxonomy is never finished. As soon as it is implemented, it undergoes testing and revision, and continued use will dictate further enhancements. All taxonomies require ongoing maintenance, and many taxonomies also undergo more significant revisions or restructuring over time.

Taxonomy Maintenance

A taxonomy requires continual maintenance. Various kinds of changes can necessitate updates to a taxonomy:

- Ongoing user feedback suggests improvements.

- Quality control indicates preventable indexing inaccuracies.

- Additional content brings up new concepts.

- Certain previously included content is excluded or discontinued.

- New trends, buzzwords, and terminology arise in existing content.

- New audiences, users, markets, or implementations are added.

Taxonomy updating can be done continually or as periodic revision projects. If you have continued responsibility for the taxonomy, then you need to keep abreast of all the possible areas that may affect the taxonomy. This involves reviewing the following:

- Newly added content sources, or the latest issues of periodicals if used with a periodical index

- Parts of the taxonomy or vocabularies covering rapidly changing topics (e.g., current events, politics, technology)

- Direct feedback from users (both indexers and end users)

- End-user search logs for additional search strings entered

- Records of the terms being used in indexing/tagging (human or automated) to determine:

- High-use terms needing further differentiation through addition of more specific terms

- Low/no-use terms that should be removed or merged

- Identifiable indexing errors that point to the need for clarifying terms

When merging one term with another, not only do you convert a preferred term (the obsolete term) into a nonpreferred term for another preferred term, but ideally you want all of the obsolete term's nonpreferred terms to become nonpreferred terms for the newly merged preferred term. If there is a scope note for the obsolete term, that too should be moved over to the designated preferred term, but the taxonomist should review and edit the transferred or combined note. Some, but not all, taxonomy management software has a merge feature that, in a single step, allows a designated preferred term automatically to inherit the nonpreferred terms, notes, and other attributes of an obsolete term that is merged into it.

If the taxonomy set is segmented into subtaxonomies, vocabularies, facets, or authority files, some of these vocabularies will require more frequent updating than others, depending on their coverage. As a rule, named entities require more frequent updates than topical terms. Concepts should have some staying power, whereas relevant people, products, organizations, and so on may come and go. For example, new terms for types of products occur less frequently than new named product models. Simply keeping abreast of the latest news within a field is also a good idea for the taxonomist in charge of taxonomy maintenance.

When it comes to reviewing the indexing, you need to define what the thresholds are for "high-use" terms and "low-use" terms, and determine what counts as an error. High-use may be defined relative to other terms, but you should also consider how search results display. Depending on the user's ability to narrow results, one, two, or three screenfuls of search results per term (10, 20, or 30 records) could be considered enough. Low-use terms could be anything with fewer than three matches, but you also have to consider the time span. In the case of errors, it is necessary to have a clearly defined policy as to what constitutes an error, as well as a procedure to identify and track errors. Indexing is sometimes subjective, so you need to draw the line between "good enough" and "not good enough."

Ideally, you should use the same thesaurus software used in creating the taxonomy (as described in Chapter 5) to make updates to the taxonomy. Updating a taxonomy may include any of the following:

- Creating new terms

- Splitting existing terms (creating two new terms and removing an old one)

- Deleting terms

- Merging terms (including deleting a term and making it nonpreferred for an existing term)

- Changing the wording of a term (including keeping an old name as a nonpreferred term)

- Adding relationships (hierarchical or associative) between existing terms

- Deleting relationships between existing terms

- Changing relationships between existing terms (deleting and replacing with a different relationship)

- Adding nonpreferred terms to existing terms

- Adding scope notes to existing terms

- Adding other new information, attributes, categories, and so on, to existing terms

- Moving a branch/subhierarchy within a hierarchical taxonomy to a new location

If the taxonomy/thesaurus software and the indexing system are integrated, there should be no complications when it comes to updating the taxonomy. But if, as is often the case, the taxonomy is maintained in one software system and indexing and/or search is conducted in a different system, the taxonomy updates need to be ported to it. If possible, set up some kind of schedule for regular updates, whether daily, weekly, or monthly. Taxonomy updates might need to be scheduled during a time when indexing is not taking place, perhaps outside regular working hours.

Then there is the matter of applying new or changed taxonomy terms to previously indexed content. Nonpreferred terms should take care of this automatically in the case of simple term changes. But if you create new terms or split an existing term into two terms, then retroactive indexing can be an issue, and this task may fall to the taxonomist and not the indexers. There may be the resources to retroactively index only selected documents that are considered important rather than all possible documents pertaining to the new term. One option is to have scripting software written to make global changes to indexing when terms change in the taxonomy, or you can make use of interfaces that display term splits along with associated records so that you can assign more precise terminology to older documents.

Taxonomy Revisions

A taxonomy could require significant revisions for various reasons. Its maintenance may have been neglected over several years due to lack of a taxonomist, and evolutionary changes in content and audience/market over time eventually necessitate a more thorough review and overhaul. A conversion from human indexing to automated indexing would require a reexamination of the taxonomy to eliminate ambiguous terms and to increase the number of nonpreferred terms. If accumulated content has increased beyond initial expectations, it might be deemed necessary to expand a relatively small taxonomy in order to support indexing in detail (granularity), for more refined search results. A hierarchical taxonomy that previously excluded polyhierarchies may now permit them. More complex taxonomy revisions involve implementing a decision to convert a controlled vocabulary into a thesaurus or a hierarchical taxonomy, or to convert a thesaurus or hierarchical taxonomy into a faceted taxonomy.

For example, a number of literature retrieval vendors in the U.S. chose initially to base their taxonomies on Library of Congress Subject Headings (LCSH) because it was the largest general-purpose controlled vocabulary available. However, for many decades it lacked hierarchical relationships between terms (with no distinction between hierarchical and associative relationships). Organizations that used controlled vocabularies based on LCSH and later decided it would be better to have a true thesaurus then had to undertake a major taxonomy revision project to convert generic *See also* relationships into proper broader term (BT), narrower term (NT), or related term relationships. For a controlled vocabulary of tens of thousands of terms, this kind of project can take years.

Taxonomy revision projects follow some of the same steps as new taxonomy projects, depending on the type of revision. If there has been a significant change in content, then a content review or audit is required. If a taxonomy is to be totally restructured, then stakeholder interviews would be a good idea. More specifically, if a controlled vocabulary will be converted to a hierarchical taxonomy, then a card-sorting exercise would also be a good idea.

Combining Taxonomies

In addition to revising a single taxonomy, a common taxonomy management project involves combining two or more taxonomies. Different ways to combine taxonomies include the following:

- Integrating: Combining separate taxonomies on different subjects into a single master taxonomy for combined use

- Merging: Combining two redundant taxonomies in the same subject area into one (not retaining them as distinct)

- Mapping: Enabling one taxonomy to be used for another in the same subject area, while retaining them both as continued distinct taxonomies

Integrating focuses more on structure, whereas merging and mapping tend to ignore the structure and the relationships between concepts and focus on the terms. In all cases, the combined taxonomies may have previously been used separately. Integrating or mapping can also be used to combine an existing taxonomy with a newly created one.

Integrating Taxonomies

Integrating taxonomies involves combining previously separate vocabularies, hierarchies, authority files, or subtaxonomies that have different concepts into a single master taxonomy. Integrating allows for combined use in the same search/browse user interface and for a shared content repository. ("Combined use" does not, however, mean that terms from the different taxonomies must be combined in search execution, as in a faceted search.) The subject area scope of the different taxonomies may be related, but for the most part, they should not be overlapping or redundant, as the objective is to have them supplement each other. If the taxonomies were redundant, then the strategy would be to merge, rather than integrate, them. Reasons to integrate taxonomies include, but are not limited to, the following:

- A larger organizational taxonomy is built by combining existing departmental taxonomies.

- An additional facet is added to an existing faceted taxonomy, based on user feedback.

- A manufacturer or distributor adds a new product line, requiring that a new product/topic hierarchy be added to its website.

- An online database provider adds a new database product that requires a new authority file.

- An internally created taxonomy is supplemented by a purchased/licensed taxonomy in a complementary subject area in order to expand its scope.

- A company expands into a new geographic market and needs to add geographic and named organizational terms to cover that area.

- An organization acquires or merges with another organization, and their taxonomies in various operational areas need to be integrated.

Integrating taxonomies works well for hierarchical or faceted taxonomies, in which it is not difficult to add a hierarchy or facet. It is also quite simple to add a new named entity authority file to a collection of controlled vocabularies. Supplementing an existing topical thesaurus with an additional subject area, however, is more complicated. This is because at some point you will need to create relationships between the existing terms and the newly added terms, even if only associative relationships, and you will need to individually identify the relevant terms.

The previously separate taxonomies may have been created within the same organization, but most likely they originate from different sources. In some cases, the taxonomy to be integrated is sufficiently complete and fully structured, while in other cases, it requires significant editing and restructuring to conform to the format and standards of the rest of your taxonomy. While it may even be necessary to build a new subtaxonomy from scratch, this is not likely to occur at this stage, when resources are focused on taxonomy enhancement rather than construction. In other words, the person responsible for managing a taxonomy may not have the additional time needed to build a new subtaxonomy.

The main work for a taxonomist in an integration project is to study the potential issues and make recommendations for the integration, especially with respect to the overall taxonomy structure and any relationships between new terms and those already in the taxonomy. You will also need to come up with indexing and editorial policies for the new taxonomy and incorporate them into the existing governance procedure and documentation.

Assuming that the taxonomy to be integrated comes from an external source, the most crucial issue to deal with is interoperability. As previously mentioned, any taxonomy that is imported in an XML format will need a schema. However, as we have seen, there are different kinds of XML formats, so you will likely need to write a mapping table with instructions on how each XML tag in one taxonomy corresponds with a tag in the other so that the different labels translate from one to the other. Aside from the problem of variations in XML formats and schemas, a taxonomy from another source will inevitably lack some of the values associated with terms in your existing taxonomy. These could include sequential numbers, categories or classes, additional attributes, additional relationship types, and history notes. Some of this information can perhaps be added in batches to the terms in the new taxonomy, while other information may have to be added to terms individually, and some information may simply be omitted because there is no support for it.

Merging Taxonomies

Another type of project involving pre-existing taxonomies is the complete merging of two or more taxonomies. Pre-existing taxonomies in the same or similar subject areas may need to be combined under various circumstances, including but not limited to the following:

- A new enterprise taxonomy replaces the separate taxonomies of multiple administrative departments.

- An information vendor merges different search taxonomies that had previously been used for different search products (used for different markets, media, content, etc.).

- A folksonomy is incorporated into the taxonomy.

- An organization acquires or merges with another organization, and their redundant vocabularies (whether they are enterprise taxonomies or consumer search taxonomies) are merged.

- An internally created taxonomy is combined with a purchased/licensed taxonomy in the same subject area to enhance it.

In merging two or more taxonomies, the process will be simpler if you can designate one taxonomy as the primary or dominant taxonomy into which you will merge the other(s). The decision as to which taxonomy is primary might be made for you, such as when one organization acquires another (typically the acquirer's taxonomy is primary). In other cases, it may not be obvious or even matter which taxonomy should be dominant. You will need to scan both or all taxonomies involved to compare and choose the dominant taxonomy. The dominant taxonomy may be the one that is significantly larger, has greater breadth, has greater depth, has the best skeleton or top structure, is more highly structured if that is important, or is generally a "better" taxonomy in accordance with standards and best practices.

The first step in merging involves automated matching to compare the two taxonomies to identify and classify matches, whether exact or close. Some commercial taxonomy applications, such as Synaptica and Wordmap, include an automatic vocabulary-matching feature, which is especially useful if both taxonomies are already managed in that software. Often one taxonomy is from an external source, so having someone write a custom program or script (e.g, Perl scripting language) to compare the vocabularies might be easier if resources permit. You should compare only two taxonomies at a time. If there are more than two taxonomies to be merged, compare each merging taxonomy with the primary taxonomy separately. Merging focuses on terms only; hierarchical and associative relationships are ignored during merging. Equivalence relationships, on the other hand, are important in merging.

In any case, an output for human review would typically be in a table or a spreadsheet with one column for one taxonomy, a second column for the other taxonomy, and corresponding matched terms in the same row. In a third column to the side or in between, you as the reviewer may enter *y* or *n* for *yes* or *no* to accept or reject the match, or perhaps some other notation to provide a more specific judgment about the relationship between the pairs of terms.

Automated matching should identify and list the following types of matches, along with the match type (the basis of the match). If you are using your own scripting language, then the following should be sequential comparison passes:

1. Exact matches of a preferred term in the merging taxonomy with a preferred term in the primary taxonomy.

2. Exact matches of a preferred term in the merging taxonomy with a nonpreferred term in the primary taxonomy.

For example, the primary taxonomy has the term **cars**, and the merging taxonomy has **automobiles USE cars**.

3. Exact matches of a preferred term in the primary taxonomy with a nonpreferred term in the merging taxonomy (whereby the corresponding preferred term in the merging taxonomy does not match any term in the primary taxonomy). For example, the primary taxonomy has the term cars, and the merging taxonomy has **cars USE automobiles**, but the primary taxonomy does not have automobiles, even as a nonpreferred term. (In these circumstances, automobiles will become a new nonpreferred term in the final merged taxonomy.)

4. Matches of a nonpreferred term in the merging taxonomy with a nonpreferred term in the primary taxonomy (for which the corresponding preferred terms do not exist in either taxonomy), although this would be rare. For example, the primary taxonomy has **cars USE autos**, and the merging taxonomy has **cars USE automobiles**, but the primary taxonomy does not have **automobiles**, and the merging taxonomy does not have **autos**. The corresponding preferred term (**automobiles**) of the nonpreferred term (**cars**) within the merging taxonomy should be considered as an additional nonpreferred term for the corresponding preferred term (**autos**) in the primary taxonomy.

5. Close, but not exact, matches between a preferred term in the merging taxonomy with a preferred term or nonpreferred term in the primary taxonomy, (also called *fuzzy matches*) based on ignoring the following differences between pairs of terms:

   a. Hyphens, parentheses, punctuation, and spaces (such as **healthcare/health care**)

b. Plural/singular (such as **teaching method/teaching methods**)

c. Common abbreviations and acronyms (such as **and/&**, **dept./department**), based on a provided list

d. Words of a term appearing in a different order (such as **photography, digital** and **digital photography**)

e. The addition of certain listed words such as *industry* or *services* (as in **healthcare** and **healthcare services**)

f. Different grammatical endings on the same root word (such as **production/producing**)

For matches to preferred terms in the primary taxonomy (the first and second types of matches in the preceding list), nothing needs to be done, and no human (taxonomist) review is necessary. For all subsequent types, a taxonomist should review the automatically generated matches. Table 11.1 summarizes the kinds of automated term matches and indicates which types require review by a taxonomist.

Additional types of matches will generate candidates for non-preferred terms from the merging taxonomy, and the taxonomist should approve them for addition to the primary taxonomy. Depending on the reason for designating one taxonomy as primary, you might also make use of the match results to consider whether to change the name of a preferred term of the primary taxonomy to that of an equivalent term used in the merging taxonomy, if it seems like a better wording for the concept.

After the automated matches have been generated, you need to analyze the remaining unmatched terms from each taxonomy more closely. You can temporarily sort and interfile them alphabetically, with terms from each taxonomy distinguished from each other in some way, such as font style. Then you can scan the list for additional potential matches based on the start of the terms. It is

Table 11.1 Automated term matches that require review by a taxonomist

Merging Taxonomy	Primary Taxonomy	Review?
Exact matches of:		
Preferred term	*Preferred term*	
Preferred term	*Nonpreferred term*	
Nonpreferred term	*Preferred term*	yes
Nonpreferred term	*Nonpreferred term*	yes
Inexact matches of:		
Preferred term	*Preferred term*	yes

here that your skills in identifying valid equivalence relationships come into play.

Finally, in cases where there are completely different terms in the two taxonomies, there is no need to change terms in the primary taxonomy, and you should evaluate unmatched terms from the merging taxonomy individually for possible inclusion in the taxonomy. You need to pay special attention to where these terms might belong hierarchically when added to the primary taxonomy. If the new terms from the merging taxonomy comprise entirely new hierarchies or subhierarchies, it might make more sense to import the terms along with their relationships, rather than having to recreate the hierarchical relationships between them.

Mapping Taxonomies

In certain circumstances, two pre-existing taxonomies covering the same subject area may be integrated to serve unified retrieval yet remain intact for continued separate use as well. This combination enables one taxonomy to be used at the front end (in the searcher's user interface) while the other taxonomy is used at the back end (indexed to the content) for a specific content set. Thus, the taxonomy that the user sees at the front end continues to retrieve its content as before, along with additional content indexed with the other taxonomy. The taxonomies are matched, or more specifically "mapped," term-by-term where matches are sufficiently equivalent. Hierarchical and associative relationships are largely ignored for mapping.

The notion of mapping is probably most familiar to information professionals who work with metadata, since mapping projects are frequently used to support interoperability among metadata stored in different standards, such as MARC and variations of Dublin Core. As there are standards of metadata, so are there somewhat standardized mapping tables, known as *crosswalks*. Vocabulary or taxonomy mapping is quite different, however. Instead of mapping metadata (instructions for data), you are mapping the actual data, which is every term in a taxonomy.

Situations in which one taxonomy is mapped to another include, but are not limited, to the following:

- Selected internal content from an enterprise taxonomy is made available on a public website that has a different, public-facing taxonomy.

- A content provider with a taxonomy partners with a third-party information vendor with its own taxonomy to expand the market of its content.

- A provider of scientific/technical/medical content, which already has a detailed taxonomy, develops a new information product aimed at laypeople or students and creates a simpler taxonomy for it.

- A large collection of search log query terms needs to be integrated into the taxonomy as additional nonpreferred terms.

- Federated search, involving multiple data repositories, each with its own search engine and taxonomy, is implemented.

- Content will be made available in a different language region, and a comparable taxonomy already exists in the other language.

In a mapping project, it is important to know which taxonomy will appear in the user interface and which taxonomy will be linked to content. You need to be aware of the direction of information flow, which is from content to user, and thus map in this same direction, from the terms in what we will call the *indexing taxonomy* to terms in the *retrieval taxonomy*. Since mapping involves making equivalence relationships between the terms in one taxonomy and the terms in the other taxonomy, one taxonomy is being collectively "used for" the other taxonomy. Therefore one taxonomy needs to be preferred, like a preferred term, and the other taxonomy is nonpreferred. The preferred taxonomy is the retrieval taxonomy, and the nonpreferred taxonomy is the indexing taxonomy.

As with merging projects, mapping involves automatic matching first, followed by a human review. You can use the same series of matching types listed for merging taxonomies for mapping taxonomies, and you can use the same tools to do it. There are two main differences, however, between merging and mapping. First, in projects involving merging, any remaining unmatched terms are simply added to enhance the merged taxonomy, but in mapping, you are not creating a new taxonomy or adding new terms, so any unmatched terms unfortunately cannot be utilized. Second, creating matches for mapping is not limited to equivalence relationships. A narrower term can be mapped to a broader term, as long as it is going from the indexing taxonomy (NT) to the retrieval taxonomy (BT). This is an application of *upward posting*, whereby a broader term can be used for a narrower term. Consequently, it may happen that more than one narrower term in the indexing taxonomy is mapped to a single term that is broader in the retrieval taxonomy. Many-to-one mapping is acceptable but should not be too extensive.

With narrower-to-broader mapping permitted, automated matching could also include phrase matches of terms in the retrieval taxonomy that are phrases within terms in the indexing taxonomy. This is because a noun-phrase found within a longer noun-phrase has a good chance of being more generic (broader) than the longer and thus more specific noun-phrase. For example:

Indexing taxonomy: *Retrieval taxonomy:*
HDTV television sets   **television sets**

Television sets is a noun-phrase within **HDTV television sets**, whereby the shorter phrase of **television sets** is indeed the broader concept. So the narrower term **HDTV television sets** would be automatically mapped "upward" to **television sets**. Not all term-within-a-term phrases are hierarchically related, however, so you should review such automated matches carefully.

As with merging taxonomies, it is easiest for you to quickly review numerous automated matches if they are in a spreadsheet format, where one column is used for the indexing taxonomy and another column for the retrieval taxonomy with matched terms in the same row. Figure 11.4 is an excerpt of a mapping table in which column A contains the indexing taxonomy, column C is for the retrieval taxonomy, and column B is where the taxonomist has marked the acceptability of the mapping as OK, not OK (n), and broader (b, which is acceptable for upward posting). For example **promoters (entertainment)** has **promoters** as a broader term, but **prolactin** is neither equivalent to nor narrower than **prolactin test**, so this is not a match.

In mapping projects, it is all right if you cannot map a term in the retrieval taxonomy to a term in the indexing taxonomy

	A	B	C
	File Edit View Insert Format Tools Data Window Help Adobe PDF		
	F29 ▾ fx		
1	Programmable logic controllers	ok	Programmable controllers
2	Programmable logic devices	ok	PLDs (Programmable logic devices)
3	Programming (Computers)	ok	Computer programming
4	Progressivism (United States politics)	b	Progressive movement
5	Prohibited books	ok	Banned books
6	Project method in teaching	ok	Project method (Education)
7	Projectile points	ok	Projectile points (Archaeology)
8	Projection	n	Projection (Drawing)
9	Projection televisions	ok	Projection television sets
10	Prolactin	n	Prolactin test
11	Proletariat	ok	Working class
12	Prolog (Computer program language)	ok	Prolog (Programming language)
13	Promethazine hydrochloride	b	Promethazine
14	Promoters (Entertainment)	b	Promoters
15	Promotion (School)	ok	Student promotion
16	Pronghorn antelope	ok	Pronghorns
17	Propaganda, American	ok	American propaganda

Figure 11.4 A mapping table representing an indexing
taxonomy in column A, a retrieval taxonomy in column C, and
taxonomist notes in column B: *ok* is equivalent, *b* is broader
(so also ok for upward posting), and *n* is not acceptable

because the retrieval taxonomy terms still have other uses. If, however, you cannot map a term in the indexing taxonomy to a term in the retrieval taxonomy, then any content indexed with that term will not be retrievable with the mapped taxonomy. Whether you should add any preferred terms to the retrieval taxonomy is another question, beyond the scope of the mapping project. This should be decided early on, though, so that you can identify these terms while reviewing the matches.

Multilingual Taxonomies

With the global expansion of business and information these days, adding a second-language version to a taxonomy is not uncommon. A taxonomy in more than one language enables:

1. Users to search content that includes text and/or meta-data in multiple languages, by using a single taxonomy in their own language, which is mapped to the foreign language taxonomies

2. Different users who speak different languages to search the same body of content (which may be in one language or more), using a taxonomy in the user interface in their native language

(In either case, after retrieving a document in a foreign language, the user could have it translated.)

An example of a publicly accessible multilingual online thesaurus linked to multilingual content is the European Thesaurus on International Relations and Area Studies Online (www.ireon-portal.eu), in which a search term in any language will retrieve the same multilingual set of records. A variation on a multilingual taxonomy is one intended to serve multiple audiences in the same language (e.g., departments within the same organization that use different terminology and do not want their term mapped to something that will seem foreign to their end users). In such cases, the displayed preferred terms are different for the separate groups.

A second-language version of a taxonomy should be treated as another way of combining two taxonomies, essentially by mapping, rather than as a simple translation of a taxonomy into another language. Merely adding translations to terms would not support navigation between terms with hierarchical or associative relationships within a second language, and the translation is then no more helpful than a scope note. Furthermore, not every term in one language has an exact translation in another language, especially in the case of nonpreferred terms. In the mapping analogy, the retrieval taxonomy is in the language of the searcher, and the indexing taxonomy is in the language of the content. However, the role of the different language taxonomies is typically dynamic, depending on the language of the user and the accessed content at any given time. The taxonomy in either language could be the retrieval taxonomy or the indexing taxonomy. Therefore, mapping has to go in both directions, which means that matches between terms in both language taxonomies need to be more exact. Narrower-to-broader mappings will not work in both directions. Most commercial thesaurus software supports inclusion of foreign language equivalents for terms, with these equivalents given a distinct designation and handled differently from nonpreferred equivalents. The user-interface display of the taxonomy in each language typically will include the translations. Figure 11.5 shows the displays for two language equivalent terms, in English and French, from the bilingual European Training Thesaurus.[2]

While some taxonomies are designed to be bilingual or multilingual from the start, it is a more typical scenario that an organization adds a second language after a taxonomy has been in use. Either a taxonomy is translated term-by-term, or if an equivalent taxonomy already exists in the desired second language in the same subject area(s), it may be preferable to map the second-language taxonomy to the original (English-language) taxonomy.

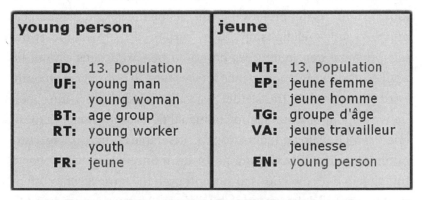

young person	jeune
FD: 13. Population	**MT:** 13. Population
UF: young man	**EP:** jeune femme
young woman	jeune homme
BT: age group	**TG:** groupe d'âge
RT: young worker	**VA:** jeune travailleur
youth	jeunesse
FR: jeune	**EN:** young person

Figure 11.5 Taxonomy term details for two language equivalent terms, in English and French, from the bilingual European Training Thesaurus (Source: libserver.cedefop.europa.eu/ett)

This is not a typical mapping, because, as mentioned previously, equivalence must operate in both directions rather than one-way. A translator, rather than a taxonomist, should handle this mapping, since awareness of broader/narrower distinctions is not even needed, but translation experience is important. It will also likely be necessary to add terms to the second-language taxonomy when it lacks equivalent terms.

Whether translating a taxonomy or mapping to a second-language equivalent taxonomy already in existence, it is important to remember that the matches need to be for concepts, not term names. In addition, even if you are focusing on concepts, not terms, not all relationships between terms will match exactly in another language. When concepts in two languages are not perfect matches, the relationships between them most likely vary slightly as well. There are also cultural influences on what constitutes a relationship.

If a taxonomy is to be translated, it is more complicated than a typical translation project. Professional translators translate text in sentences, and they discern the meaning of potentially ambiguous words from the context. A taxonomy is a list of terms out of context. Instead of reading sentences, the translator of a taxonomy needs to look up a term's nonpreferred terms, scope notes, and hierarchical and associative relationships to be certain of the meaning of the term. Typical translation fees based on per-word rates cannot be applied in such situations, since it takes time to translate each term. Furthermore, while translators typically translate only into their native languages, a sufficiently bilingual translator who has experience translating in both directions is preferable for translating a taxonomy because all translations of taxonomy terms will need to function in both directions to support both the retrieval of multilingual content and the browsing by different language users. In addition, since you are unlikely to find a translator who is also a taxonomist, you should arrange for a native speaker of the second language who is an information specialist/librarian to review the translated taxonomy.

Other matters to take into consideration when developing multilingual taxonomies are support for characters in the writing systems of other languages, translation of the user interface, and adaptations for cultural differences. Remember to have everything in the user interface translated, including menus, instructions, pop-ups, help files, etc. Other language-specific issues to consider include the editorial style for displayed terms (such as the use of plural forms and capitalization) and the "logical" sort orders of terms. Taken collectively, translation plus other language and region-specific adaptations (currencies, measurements, date/time formats, etc.), particularly for software and online user interfaces, is referred to as *localization*. There are companies and consultants that specialize in providing software and interface localization services. Finally, there are cultural differences in user search behavior that you may need to take into consideration. For example, it is possible that in another country, a different facet might be used for the same content because in that culture different criteria are important.

Finally, attention must be paid to governance and maintenance of taxonomies in multiple languages. Often a contract translator translates a taxonomy but is no longer available to help maintain it. When new terms are added or existing terms are changed in the English-language taxonomy, someone needs to take care of adding or changing the second-language equivalents. Too often organizations fail to keep taxonomies in second languages as up-to-date as the taxonomy in the original language. It is also important to have a native speaker of the second language periodically check the function of the taxonomy for quality control purposes.

Endnotes

1. "Introduction to OWL," Web3Schools, www.w3schools.com/RDF/rdf_owl.asp

2. European Centre for the Development of Vocational Training. *European Training Thesaurus*. libserver.cedefop.europa.eu/ett. The 2009 version of the thesaurus is also available for sale in print.

Chapter 12

Taxonomy Work and the Profession

If you find what you're looking for,
thank a taxonomist.

—J. D. Henry

An accidental taxonomist could be asked to create, revise, or map a taxonomy, and after the project is finished, resume his or her previous job responsibilities. Often, however, an accidental taxonomist remains a taxonomist, in both job responsibilities and professional life. This chapter describes the characteristics of taxonomy jobs, whether full-time or freelance, and also suggests sources where taxonomists might look for continuing education and professional networking opportunities.

The Nature of Taxonomy Work

The heart of being a taxonomist is dealing with concepts, figuring out what words are best to describe them, and determining how best to relate and arrange the concepts so that people can find the information they are seeking. The task requires a degree of logic as one must scrupulously analyze relationships between terms. It is neither entirely technical/mathematical nor entirely linguistic but a little of each. You always need to keep in mind how others might look for information when considering how to word a term, create nonpreferred terms, structure relationships, and contribute to the design of the user interface display. Helping people find information is indeed rewarding, but unlike a traditional librarian, you may never meet the people whom you are helping. If, however, you work within a large organization to develop and maintain its internal taxonomies, then you do have the added benefit of constantly being able to check with users to find out how the taxonomy is serving them and how it can be improved.

On the other hand, as a corporate taxonomist, you don't deal with the diversity of subject areas that a taxonomist working for an information provider or a contract taxonomist encounters. Asked what she liked about taxonomy work, Margot Diltz, senior manager of editorial policy at the information provider Cengage Learning, responded:

> The variety of subject areas I get to deal with. My controlled vocabulary is multidisciplinary, with emphasis on business, medical, and science and technology. My job entails making sure we have the terms to cover the literature in all those areas, which means I have to understand the meaning of a term in order to present it correctly in the thesaurus.[1]

A survey of taxonomists of the Taxonomies and Controlled Vocabularies special interest group (SIG) Yahoo! group in September 2009 revealed that taxonomists enjoy their work for two main reasons: They get to organize, and they get to learn. Specific responses included:

- "Verbal play, logic, learning about new subject areas."
- "Taxonomy provides a way of bringing order to the world of information on the internet by relating concepts to each other and narrowing and focusing the user's choices in the sea of synonyms and associated terms in our language. Order out of chaos."

- "I love to research things in the short term, and taxonomy totally allows me to find out a little bit about a lot of things. I also like using research to put things in order."

- "One project involved a review board of 12 experts. The education I got through the work on that project, especially the expert feedback, was like years of university compressed into three months."

The drawbacks and occasional frustrations associated with taxonomy are more varied. The same survey respondents replied:

- "Trying to explain it to outsiders."

- "When I am forced to make a term that is technically incorrect or in the wrong place for the sake of the business or because of the technical limitations."

- "Metrics and spreadsheets. Numbers aren't my strong suit, so using something like analytics to help me choose terms is always a chore."

- "Businesses and publishers are not fully committed to taxonomy projects. Taxonomy creation and maintenance is not seen as comprising a language skill set that is separate from—and as important as—the technology used to implement it."

In Patrick Lambe's survey of 184 taxonomists, the leading frustration reported was lack of understanding/buy-in. His survey also asked taxonomists to list challenges, and the responses included "showing benefits," "becoming technological proficient," and "being taken seriously."[2]

While the skills and qualifications taxonomists need (listed in Chapter 2) are similar for any kind of taxonomy work, the actual working environment, conditions, responsibilities, and related duties can vary greatly. These depend on whether the taxonomist is a full-time employee, a temporary contract employee, a consultant, or a freelancer, and in the case of a full-time employee, whether taxonomy work is the primary job responsibility.

Employment Opportunities

Taxonomists work for varied employers: governments, international agencies, publishers, information providers, online retailers, consultancies, software vendors, and large corporations in any industry. The fact of the matter is that taxonomists often move around from one industry to another, between products and services, between profit-making and nonprofit enterprises, which certainly contributes to interesting careers. Only some fields, such as medical, pharmaceutical, and scientific/technical publishers, require subject matter expertise.

Dedicated full-time permanent taxonomist positions exist, but they are still not very common. Any large corporation or government agency that cares to structure and organize its terminology has enough ongoing information management needs to keep at least one full-time taxonomist busy all the time and at times needs even more assistance. However, one or two taxonomists out of a staff of thousands does not amount to much of the labor force. Businesses involved in the sale of indexed content also employ taxonomists and may even support a small team of taxonomists, but such businesses are rare. The job-seeking taxonomist who does not wish to relocate may have to wait a while before a position opens up.

If you are searching for a *taxonomist* job, you will find relatively few openings. It's not merely a matter of the diversity of job titles used (see Chapter 2), though that does complicate the search. The fact is that the number of positions in which taxonomy is the primary role is rather limited, and the number of open positions is much smaller still. What is more common, however, are positions in which taxonomy is one of several responsibilities. A search on *taxonomy* or *taxonomies* within the job descriptions of open positions yields many more results than a search for *taxonomy* or *taxonomist* limited to the job title. For example, on September 30, 2009, the aggregate job search board Indeed.com listed only six jobs with *taxonomist* or *taxonomy* in the title, but nearly 1,000 with *taxonomy* in the job description (after excluding jobs with the words *biology, biologist, plant,* and *zoology*), and those numbers will surely increase when the economy improves. What this means is that you need not be a *taxonomist* to find yourself using taxonomy skills in your job. A resource for locating jobs that comprise primarily taxonomy work is the Yahoo! mailing list group called Taxonomy Jobs (finance.groups.yahoo.com/group/taxonomy-jobs). Job postings are from employers and recruiters, who proactively submit such job announcements, but many other taxonomy job openings are not included on this list.

Taxonomists as Contractors

A taxonomy project can take a considerable amount of work for only a temporary period of time. This usually applies to the design and creation stage, but revision and integration projects can also demand periods of intensive work. Thus, to supplement internal resources, a great deal of taxonomy work is done by contractors, whether consultants or freelancers. For small operations, these outsiders can take the place of a full-time taxonomist employee, but for larger taxonomy needs, they merely supplement the work of in-house experts.

Some differences in working conditions between employees and contractors are common across industries, but there are also certain specific differences with regard to taxonomy work. For contractors, the biggest benefit is that a lot of taxonomy work can be done at home, and thus they can work for clients in other parts of the country or even in other countries. A number of thesaurus software systems permit remote access, but many contract projects require only Excel. Contractors also encounter a variety of subject areas to work on, and when working on terms, this diversity is important to many. (As a contractor, I have worked on taxonomies for consumer products, industry categories, insurance, news, business management, names of writers, and travel, among other areas.)

On the negative side, contractors usually lack access to the latest software and other technical support services. Tasks such as comparing or merging lists of terms could often benefit from scripts that perhaps only more technical colleagues at an office can provide. It is difficult for a contractor to design a taxonomy for a content management system without the benefit of ever having been the user of such a system. Finally, the self-employed taxonomist does not have the support of workplace colleagues who can provide input and answers to questions for subjective taxonomy-building tasks. (Of course, not all taxonomist employees have as much co-worker support as they would like either, particularly if they are the only person in an organization who is knowledgeable about taxonomies.)

For a self-employed person seeking taxonomy work, there are plenty of opportunities, but there is a distinct difference between working as a *consultant*, directly for a client, and working as a *freelancer*, a step removed from the taxonomy's users. The nature of the work and the working conditions for each role are quite different.

Working as a Consultant

One of the main distinctions between consultants and freelancers is that consultants tell their clients what to do, whereas clients tell their freelancers what to do. To be fair, consultants usually (but not always) undertake work on actually constructing the taxonomy as well, but consultants are expected to do at least some consulting, which means giving formal advice to the client. Thus, consultants need to take more initiative, do more research on the taxonomy's

intended use, and make more decisions, and they may have to per-
suade the client that the taxonomy should be done a certain way.
In compensation for this, of course, consultants get paid more
than freelancers do. It is also more fulfilling to design an entire taxonomy and make the decisions about its structure. However, even
consultants do not always get to design *new* taxonomies.
Increasingly, consulting projects involve reviewing existing taxonomies and making recommendations for improvements.

Following is a summary of what is expected of taxonomy consultants in contrast with taxonomy freelancers:

- Write up a proposal of what you intend to deliver (and
  then deliver it).

- Estimate how much time you need (and then meet these
  deadlines).

- Meet with the client face-to-face at the client's site and
  possibly make several visits to conduct research for the
  taxonomy based on stakeholder interviews, card-sorting
  exercises, and test searching a system within a firewall.

- Write up recommendations that will contribute to the
  taxonomy governance.

- Negotiate any differences of opinion on taxonomy
  design.

- Have your own thesaurus management software (with
  compatible export format options).

- Set a pay rate as high as you dare without risking losing a
  bid to a competing consultant.

Consultants can work for distant clients, too, if they are willing
to travel. Recognizing the fact that there are relatively few qualified
taxonomy consultants, a client does not necessarily expect to find

a local consultant and will look nationally. Thus, the consultants with more business are those who are willing to travel

Working directly with a client on a taxonomy project, especially an enterprise taxonomy project, can be challenging, though. The client might have difficulty communicating the scope and requirements of the project or might not even know, which makes it difficult for the consultant to know what is expected and what to deliver. Indeed some of the complaints taxonomists have about their work pertain specifically to consultant-client relationships. The following is a typical response to the survey question, "Describe a taxonomy project (or part of a project) found especially difficult or frustrating":

> Any project where the perspectives and goals of the client and taxonomist seem consistent at the start but creep and diverge over time—"this isn't what I had in mind"—despite frequent meetings and reviews along the way.

A successful taxonomy project, though, can be very rewarding for the taxonomist.

Finally, consultants need to aggressively market themselves. This includes speaking at conferences and trade shows (commercial and industry shows, more so than librarian/indexer association events), publishing articles in trade journals, participating in professional networking organizations, and actively contributing to discussion lists and social networking sites. The consultant should have both printed brochures and a professional website, and the website should include all relevant informational resources (articles, presentations, etc.) and be optimized for search engines.

Working as a Freelancer

The work of a freelancer, on the other hand, may be less challenging than that of a consultant, but the diversity of projects usually keeps it stimulating. A freelancer usually works on only part of a taxonomy and does not get to see the bigger picture. The freelance taxonomist is usually immersed in terms, not in structure.

Following is a summary of what is expected of taxonomy freelancers in contrast with taxonomy consultants:

- Follow instructions, guidelines, and editorial policy provided by the client.

- Agree to work a set number of hours per week and/or complete a project by the client's deadline.

- Work with little or no contact with the taxonomy users.

- Accept any decisions that have already been made regarding the taxonomy design.

- Expect the client to provide any software that is not part of the standard Microsoft Office suite.

- Expect to do all work from home (other than perhaps an initial meeting/training/orientation, if the client is local). (Note that this applies to a freelancer, not a temporary employee.)

- Accept the hourly rate proposed by the client (with perhaps a little negotiation at the start).

In comparison with in-house taxonomist employees, freelance taxonomists do not usually get involved with full taxonomy and thesaurus development. A large thesaurus may be too complex and interrelated to be broken up into sections for freelancers, even if web-based thesaurus software permits remote access. Also, a project manager might feel that all taxonomists need to have broader overall knowledge of the thesaurus, so only former employees might be deemed sufficiently qualified to work as free-lancers. An exception is work on named entities, whose relation-ships with other terms are generally not as complex (or as interesting). A freelance taxonomist might not even be called a tax-onomist but rather a *taxonomy editor*, with the implication that taxonomists design taxonomies. Freelance projects could include the following:

- Building term hierarchies for website taxonomies
- Building a top-level straw-man taxonomy
- Mapping nonpreferred search terms to taxonomy terms
- Researching, adding, and/or editing named entity terms
- Adding and editing additional attributes to terms (partic-ularly named entities), involving research and data entry
- Providing training documents or writing term rules in support of auto-categorization

Freelance taxonomy work is paid on an hourly basis, and this could be frustrating for the freelancer who comes from an editing or indexing background and is accustomed to being paid per page or per database record. It is impossible to estimate how many terms one can create or edit per hour, because there are too many variables.

Freelance Opportunities
Freelance work is available for taxonomists, but unless you have a steady client, the work is quite sporadic, more so than book indexing or editorial freelance work. Thus, freelance taxonomists usually combine this work with something else, such as consult-ing, teaching, indexing, or a part-time library job. Steady clients might be found among the few taxonomy vendors, information vendors, or software vendors mentioned in Chapter 2, but these opportunities are somewhat rare. Most of the freelance work

offered by information vendors and publishers consists of index-ing/tagging rather than taxonomy work. Sources of intermittent freelance taxonomy work include web/online advertisers and directories, search engines, ecommerce sites, portals, etc. Taxonomy consultancies are also a good source of work for free-lance taxonomists, but their work is never steady or predictable, as it depends on when the consultants win a contract with a client. Then on very short notice, there will be a substantial amount of work to take on. Thus freelancing requires flexibility.

Freelancers must also market and promote themselves, but not necessarily as publicly as consultants do. The best way for free-lancers to get work is through networking, especially among tax-onomy consultants and fellow freelancers. As taxonomy projects vary in size, often one project needs multiple part-time taxonomy editors. Thus, when one freelancer joins a project, the client may ask that freelancer to refer more taxonomy editors to help. In a more concerted effort to support freelance taxonomists in finding projects, the Taxonomies and Controlled Vocabularies SIG of the American Society for Indexing (ASI) has set up a directory of avail-able freelance taxonomists on its website (www.asindexing. org/site/sigs.shtml#taxon).

Education and Training

Taxonomy is still an accidental profession. Dedicated academic programs in the field are lacking. There are no majors, concen-trations, or certificate programs and only a few courses on the subject. Thus, an aspiring professional cannot plan to become a taxonomist and take the necessary university courses for it. Educational opportunities for learning how to create tax-onomies, thesauri, controlled vocabularies, and so on consist of individual courses in library schools, continuing education workshops, organizational and corporate distance learning programs, conference workshops and sessions, and online tutorials.

Information and Library Science Degree Classes

A review of 2008–2009 online course catalogs for the 55 academic institutions with a master's of library science and/or master's of information science or studies program accredited by the American Libraries Association (ALA) in the United States and Canada, with instruction in English, revealed a total of only a dozen courses (typically electives) that could be considered devoted to the topic of taxonomies as we have broadly defined it to include taxonomies, thesauri, controlled vocabularies, and other methods of knowledge organization. Examples of course titles include the following (each with their respective library/information science graduate schools):

- Knowledge Taxonomies at McGill University
- Ontologies at Indiana University Bloomington
- Classification for Information Display and Discovery at Rutgers University
- Knowledge Organization Structures at Syracuse University
- Controlled Vocabularies at the University of Arizona
- Vocabulary Design at San Jose State University
- Thesaurus Construction at the University of Illinois at Urbana-Champaign
- Construction of Indexing Languages and Ontology Design and Interoperability at the University of Washington

Courses that include taxonomies or thesauri, while not dedicated exclusively to these topics, are greater in number. There are

another dozen courses at various ALA-accredited institutions that
mention taxonomy/taxonomies in their descriptions, as one of several topics covered. Course titles include Knowledge Representation,
Subject Analysis, Organization of Information and Knowledge
Resources, and Topics in Subject Access. There are of course many
other courses that may include a single class session on taxonomies but do not mention it in the brief one- to three-sentence
course description.

In addition, the majority of library/information science programs include some instruction on thesaurus construction as part
of a course on information management or indexing. Such literature retrieval thesauri, however, are only one kind of taxonomy. A
class session or project in creating an indexing thesaurus does not
constitute sufficient training to start creating website or enterprise
taxonomies. Nevertheless, even this instruction in the creation of
traditional literature retrieval thesauri is not widespread in library
school, compared with instruction in the cataloging of books.

Although library and information science courses tend to be
limited to students enrolled in the master's degree program, some
graduate schools permit nondegree students to take one or two
regular courses for continuing education (noncredit) purposes.
Distance learning courses are becoming more common, so they
are also an option to consider if no suitable course is offered
locally.

There are a handful of information architecture or information
management degree programs outside ALA-accredited schools of
information science. None of these were found to have *taxonomy*
mentioned in their course descriptions, however.

Information and Library Science Continuing Education Classes

Continuing education or professional development classes are
an especially suitable source of instruction in new or hot fields as
they can be created and added on short notice and may be taught

by practicing professionals rather than academic faculty. These sessions, shorter than a regular college course, do not go into as much depth as this book, but they offer an interactive learning experience. Not all graduate schools of library and information science offer continuing education classes, and those that do sometimes limit them to professionals who already hold an MLIS degree. Dedicated continuing education courses available to the public specifically in the field of taxonomies are still very limited. Examples of such courses offered in online formats are the following:

- Simmons College Graduate School of Library and Information Science—Continuing Education: Taxonomies and Controlled Vocabularies, taught by Heather Hedden, is a five-week session, usually offered quarterly. A full-day onsite version is offered in Boston twice a year (www.simmons.edu/gslis/careers/continuing-education).

- University of Wisconsin Milwaukee, School of Information Studies—Professional Development Institute: Controlled Vocabularies and Thesaurus Design, taught by Steven J. Miller, is a six-week session, offered at least twice a year (www4.uwm.edu/sois/CE).

- University of Toronto Faculty of Information—Professional Learning Centre: Taxonomy Guide: Online Resource and Learning Tool, developed by Linda Farmer, is a self-study course that does not involve an instructor. Registration allows a 12-month subscription (starting any time) to a web-based tutorial consisting of content and exercises (plc.ischool.utoronto.ca/courses_webbased.asp).

There are other library schools with continuing education programs that had no courses on taxonomies at the time of this writing, but this is certainly subject to change on short notice. In addition, regional library networks are a source of continuing education

courses, both on-site and online. These courses are aimed at public librarians and technical staff, however, so taxonomies are typically not within the scope of topics.

Organization Programs

Several professional associations offer online taxonomy workshops and seminars. Others will likely join the list in the near
future. For example, ASI is considering adding thesaurus development to its online indexing course program and also providing
shorter webinars on various topics, similar to those offered by
other professional associations. Examples of such programs are
the following:

- ALA Distance Learning webinars: Webinars, usually 1.5
  hours, tend to be offered through individual divisions
  (www.ala.org/ala/conferencesevents/upcoming/distance
  or www.ala.org/ala/mgrps/divs/acrl/events/elearning).
  For example, Introduction to Taxonomy Development
  has been offered by the Association of College and
  Research Libraries.

- Special Libraries Association (SLA) CLICK University
  webinars: CLICK stands for Continuous Learning to
  Improve Career Knowledge (www.sla.org/content/learn),
  and its webinars, usually 1.5 hours, have included
  sessions on taxonomies in the past and likely will again.

- Association for Information and Image Management
  International (AIIM) Information Organization and
  Access Practitioner course: This program includes
  content inventorying and analysis, metadata, taxonomy,
  ontologies, topic maps, semantic networks, content
  modeling, search techniques, findability and information
  retrieval, and user experience. The course, which is
  actually part of a larger Information Organization and
  Access (IO&A) certificate program, is offered both in an

online format consisting of 10 modules and as a two-day class (www.aiim.org/Education/Information-Organization-Access-Search-Training-Courses.aspx).

- Aslib Public Courses in Library and Information Management Skills: Aslib is the leading information management professional association in the U.K. Constructing a Thesaurus (www.aslib.com/training/open learning/thesaurus.htm) comprising eight (weekly) sessions is its only distance learning course. Aslib also sponsors a comprehensive offering of London-based seminars.

In addition, the Library of Congress Catalogers Learning Workshop/Cooperative Cataloging Training program provides course materials on various topics (a PowerPoint presentation and handouts) to be taught by qualified instructors as one-day workshops. One of these is Controlled Vocabulary and Thesaurus Design (www.loc.gov/catworkshop/courses/thesaurus), which is part of the Digital Library Environment (Cataloging for the 21st Century) series. This particular workshop was co-developed by the Association for Library Collections and Technical Services, a division of the ALA.

Independent Training Programs

Many taxonomy consultancy firms offer some form of customized onsite training classes. Some are more involved in training than others. Some firms (as well as this author) also offer distance learning programs or webinars. The two described here are well-known in the U.S., but instructional programs can be found in other countries, too, such as TFPL (www.tfpl.com/training), which offers on-site training in London. Software vendors also offer free webinars on occasion.

The Montague Institute's (www.montague.com) primary business is offering practical training and published resources in taxonomy and knowledge management. It offers Roundtable Seminars, usually as webinars but occasionally as on-site courses, and also full-length distance learning courses in business taxonomies and related subjects. Courses by teleconference include Taxonomies, Search, and SharePoint and are offered several times per year in three consecutive three-hour sessions. Self-paced distance learning courses include Creating and Using Business Taxonomies, and Integrating Taxonomies, among others. These courses, which include an online "lab" portion, with the participant remotely connecting to the course server for a project, typically take three to six months to complete. There is also a more structured eight-week Metadata, Search, and Productivity Practicum offered three times per year. Courses and roundtables are aimed especially at corporate participants, and discounts are available for additional participants from the same team.

Earley & Associates, a taxonomy consultancy, offers monthly webinars (www.earley.com/webinars) of 60 to 90 minutes each on taxonomy- related topics as part of its Taxonomy Community of Practice Call series. More educational are the occasional four-part Jumpstart webinar series, which are free. Unlike the ALA and SLA webinars, however, these do not offer any interactive component. The company also offers a number of on-site training sessions and workshops ranging from two hours to two days, including a one-day Taxonomy Development and Implementation session, which are conducted at a client's site. As with many consultancies, customized training is also available.

Conference Workshops

If you don't need a corporate program but still prefer a live workshop with instructor interaction, then conference workshops might be your best option. A number of professional associations and commercial conference organizers in the information management field offer pre- or postconference workshops on taxonomy-related topics. The exact programs and speakers will vary from year to year, and the same presenter may turn up at different organization conferences. In the case of professional organization conference workshops, nonmembers are typically permitted to attend at a slightly higher rate. These workshops involve separate registration and fees from the main conference; there is no obligation to attend the main conference when you attend a workshop. With preconference workshops, the posted date range of a conference may not include the workshop date, so make sure to check the dates carefully. Of course, the conferences themselves may also have presentations of interest to taxonomists.

Professional Organization Conference Workshops

Professional organization conference workshops include:

- The SLA Annual Conference (www.sla.org/content/ events/conference) is usually held in June in different U.S. cities. There are both half-day and full-day conference workshops called continuing education courses, and often there is a taxonomy-related workshop.

- The ASI Annual Meeting (www.asindexing.org/site/ mtgs.shtml) is held every spring, usually in May, in different U.S. cities. ASI typically offers a full-day preconference workshop on creating taxonomies and thesauri. Regional ASI chapters have also held taxonomy-related sessions and workshops.

- The American Society for Information Science and Technology (ASIS&T) Annual Meeting (asist.org/ conferences.html), which is usually held in October or November in different North American cities, has two and half days of preconference workshops, and typically there is at least one full-day seminar on taxonomies, which may be introductory, intermediate, or focused on a specific aspect of taxonomy development and implementation.

Although ASIS&T has the reputation of being more academic in its membership and in its regular conference sessions, its preconference workshops are very practical and are more often taught by practitioners than by academics.

- The Information Architecture (IA) Summit (www.ia summit.org), held in March or April in various North American cities and sponsored by ASIS&T, is a conference dedicated to information architecture. Most participants are not ASIS&T members but rather are practicing information architects. Some, but not all, conferences include a taxonomy session among the numerous preconference workshops; and if not, there is typically also a regular session on taxonomies. Euro IA (www.euroia.org) is an affiliated English-language conference that takes place on the European continent in September or October each year.

- The ALA Midwinter Meeting, lasting four days in January, and Annual Conference, in June or July, are held in different major cities every year (www.ala.org/ala/ conferencesevents). Both of these annual events feature full-day and half-day preconference workshops, called Institutes, typically sponsored by ALA divisions. Considering that any topic related to libraries could be on the program, there often is not enough space to include a session on taxonomies, but occasionally a taxonomy workshop is included. ALA is very large, so its divisions are also large and have their own national multiday conferences. These may also be venues for taxonomy-related workshops, especially the Association for Library Collections and Technical Services and the Library and Information Technology Association. Similarly, state/regional ALA chapters also hold full conferences, but not all of these include conference workshops.

- The AIIM Expo (www.aiimexpo.com) is held annually in March or April in different U.S. cities. Its preconference workshops are the same as its certificate programs, which include the Information Organization and Access Practitioner Course described in the previous section on Organization Programs. In addition, the regular conference sessions typically include a session on a taxonomy topic. AIIM regional chapters also have conferences that may include half-day taxonomy workshops.

Commercial Conference Workshops

Commercial conference workshops include:

- The publisher of *KMWorld* magazine, Information Today, Inc., holds the KMWorld conference (www.kmworld.com) every year in San Jose, California, typically in November. In conjunction with KMWorld are two other conferences, Enterprise Search Summit West and Taxonomy Boot Camp, so the preconference workshops of KMWorld also serve the interests of attendees of the other two conferences, and thus there is always at least one workshop on taxonomies. Taxonomy Boot Camp, mean- while, consists of two days of regular conference sessions, all of which are of interest to taxonomists.

- Information Today, Inc., holds Enterprise Search Summit (www.enterprisesearchsummit.com) each May in New York. Preconference workshops typically include a half-day or full-day workshop on creating taxonomies or on some aspect of taxonomy management, even if the conference sessions don't have this focus.

- Semantic Universe (joint venture of Wilshire Conferences, Semantic Arts, and Cerebra) holds the Semantic Technology conference (www.semantic-conference.com) in May or June in San Jose, California. The conference

includes half-day preconference workshops, called
Tutorials, which in the past have included an introduction to taxonomies with Darin Stewart as presenter. In
addition, there are regular conference sessions devoted to
the topic of taxonomies. Tutorials and sessions on ontologies may also be of interest to taxonomists.

- The Gilbane Group, an analyst and consulting firm
  owned by Frank Gilbane and focused on content
  technologies, holds the Gilbane Conference (gilbane
  boston.com and gilbanesf.com), a two-day multitrack
  conference preceded by half-day workshops that may
  include a session dedicated to taxonomies. The
  conference takes place in San Francisco in June and in
  Boston in late November or early December.

- Information Today, Inc., puts on Computers in Libraries
  (www.infotoday.com/cil.htm) annually in late March or
  April in the Washington, D.C., area. Although an
  introduction to taxonomies is not a regular feature of its
  pre- or post-conference workshops, a taxonomy workshop appears on the agenda every few years.

- Henry Stewart Events hosts the Data Asset Management
  Conference (www.damusers.com) and shorter one-day
  briefings several times a year in Los Angeles, New York,
  Chicago, and Atlanta and in London. Presentations often
  include a taxonomy topic, although the preconference
  workshops, called Tutorials, are usually not dedicated to
  taxonomies.

Online Tutorials

In addition to the subscription-based Taxonomy Guide: Online
Resource and Learning Tool, offered by the University of Toronto
Faculty of Information (described previously under Information
and Library Science Continuing Education Classes), there are a

couple of free online tutorials in controlled vocabulary/thesaurus construction:

- Construction of Controlled Vocabularies: A Primer, written by one of the members of the ANSI/NISO Z39.19 Standard Committee (www.slis.kent.edu/~mzeng/Z3919)

- Thesaurus Construction tutorial by Tim Craven, creator of TheW thesaurus freeware (publish.uwo.ca/~craven/ 677/thesaur/main00.htm)

Organizations, Networking, and Resources

Just like job-seeking and self-employed taxonomists, employed taxonomists feel a need for professional networking, perhaps because they are the only taxonomist in their organization or because new projects and technologies always bring new challenges. In addition, since it is often difficult for taxonomists to explain to others what they do, it is nice to get together, even if only virtually, with others in the same profession to exchange experiences.

Professional Associations

There is no professional association dedicated to taxonomists, but it is questionable whether there even should be one, since most taxonomists already belong to at least one, if not two or more, of the professional associations mentioned in the previous section. There is no shortage of conferences, and if a dedicated discussion forum is needed, a number of those already exist independently.

Two established professional associations have recently added dedicated taxonomy subgroups. In April 2008, ASI approved the Taxonomies and Controlled Vocabularies SIG, and in September 2009, SLA formally established a Taxonomy Division based on a member petition. There is some overlap in membership, but most of ASI's members are indexers, especially freelance back-of-the-book indexers, and most of SLA's Taxonomy Division members are corporate/special librarians.

ASI's Taxonomies and Controlled Vocabularies SIG (www. taxonomies-sig.org) is, according to its website, "for those in the indexing profession who are involved in creating or editing taxonomies, thesauri, or controlled vocabularies used for indexing." Some indexers may need to create controlled vocabularies for larger indexing projects, but others are simply attracted to thesaurus creation work due to its similarities with writing book indexes. Most of ASI's members are freelancers, and so are the members of the Taxonomies and Controlled Vocabularies SIG. The SIG's website thus serves the additional purpose of promoting members' freelance services. Membership in the SIG is open to members of ASI and affiliated indexing societies, such as the Indexing Society of Canada, the Society of Indexers (U.K.), and the Australia New Zealand Society of Indexers.

The Taxonomy Division of SLA is "for information professionals interested in organizing and structuring information and specifically in planning, creating, and maintaining taxonomies, thesauri, authority files, and other controlled vocabularies and information structures," according to the SLA website. Previously, SLA taxonomists had to settle for memberships in either the Knowledge Management or Information Technology division. Still in its early phase, the SLA Taxonomy Division has a wiki (wiki.sla.org/display/SLATAX/Taxonomy+Home) accessible by members only, rather than a public website. In contrast with ASI's group, the Taxonomy Division focuses more on conference program planning, educational webinars, and social networking applications. Although membership in the division is limited to SLA members, SLA is an international organization with chapters and members throughout the world.

Other professional associations of possible interest to taxonomists include the IA Institute (www.iainstitute.org), ASIS&T
(www.asist.org), and Content Management Professionals
(www.cmprofessionals.org).

Networking

Well before these new professional organization subgroups were
formed, taxonomists began actively networking through conference gatherings, discussion lists, and other social networking
groups.

Conferences and Meetings

Taxonomy Boot Camp (www.taxonomybootcamp.com), sponsored by Information Today, Inc., is the only conference completely dedicated to taxonomies. As such, it is the best face-to-face
networking event for taxonomists, whether employees or self-
employed. In addition to those who already consider themselves
taxonomists, many attendees simply want to learn more about
taxonomies because of a project they are involved in. Taxonomy
Boot Camp opened in New York in 2005 but has been held every
year since in San Jose, California, usually in November. It is co-
located with the KMWorld Conference and Enterprise Search
Summit, so all three conferences share the same exhibits and preconference workshops.

Local taxonomy gatherings are more difficult to arrange due to
the relatively small numbers of taxonomists, but in Washington,
D.C., where a significant number of taxonomy-related professionals
work, there is a group called Taxonomy Tuesday (semanticommu-
nity. wik.is/Taxonomy_Tuesday). A two-hour afternoon meeting is
held one Tuesday a month, seven or eight times a year. Usually
there is a featured speaker and presentation but sometimes just a
discussion.

Online Discussion Groups

Taxonomy Community of Practice (TaxoCoP; finance.groups.
yahoo.com/group/TaxoCoP) is the main online discussion group
for taxonomists or anyone working with taxonomies. As the name
implies, most of the discussion centers around taxonomy development and maintenance practices, and recent discussion topics
have included merging taxonomies, how many related terms is too
many, navigation taxonomies, taxonomies and SharePoint, and
orphan terms. Both thesauri and enterprise taxonomies are discussed. It is also a forum for announcing events and resources. For
example, dinner gatherings of taxonomists during upcoming
national conferences are often organized through this forum.
Although the group has more than 1,000 members, each new
member is encouraged to make an introduction and is welcomed,
so it is a good networking forum as well.

The Taxonomies and Controlled Vocabularies SIG of ASI also has
a discussion group (finance.groups.yahoo.com/group/taxonomies),
which is not restricted to SIG members, but it is not as active as
TaxoCoP.

Social Networking Groups

Just as taxonomists like to create relationships between concepts, they may also be interested in social networking groups
to create professional relationships among people. In addition
to groups affiliated with professional associations such as SLA
and ASI, relevant social networking groups include several
LinkedIn groups, such as TaxCoP and Thesaurus Professionals.
The professional association groups are much more active in
terms of discussion, but the social networking groups offer a
way to connect to more people. The TaxCoP LinkedIn group
(www.linkedin.com/groups?home= &gid=1750) has just a third as
many members as the Yahoo! discussion group, and Thesaurus
Professionals (www.linkedin.com/groups?home=&gid=1881339)

is a rather new, small group with only about 40 members, many of whom are in Europe. There is also the Indexer's Network, based on Ning, (indexing.ning.com), which includes a Taxonomy and Thesaurus group. Twine, which also includes a form of social tagging, has a Vocabulary and Metadata Management group (www.twine.com/twine/1yyy8g4r-14v/vocabulary-and-metadata-management).

Web Resources

Finally, there are a number of web resources on taxonomies. The following is only a sampling and does not include the websites of organizations previously mentioned in this chapter:

Wikis:
- Taxonomy Community of Practice Wikispace (taxocop.wikispaces.com)

Blogs:
- Green Chameleon, by Patrick Lambe (www.green chameleon.com)
- Lee Romero On Content, Collaboration and Findability (blog.leeromero.org)
- Earley & Associates Blog, (www.earley.com/blog)
- Synaptica Central (www.synapticacentral.com)
- The Taxonomy Blog, by Marlene Rockmore (thetaxonomy blog.wordpress.com)
- Taxonomy Watch, by Linda Farmer (taxonomy2watch.blogspot.com)

Resource-rich consultancy sites:
- Access Innovations, Inc. (www.accessinn.com/library)

- Earley & Associates (www.earley.com/knowledge)
- Taxonomy Strategies
  (www.taxonomystrategies.com/html/library.htm)
- Willpower Information (www.willpowerinfo.co.uk/thesbibl.htm)

In addition to these web resources is, of course, the website of this book (www.accidental-taxonomist.com). The taxonomy profession is definitely an evolving one. New businesses and information needs of organizations and new technologies will impact the field. Taxonomists, too, can help define and direct the field through their professional organization activities, their writing (including blogging), and their speaking engagements. Individuals who are not afraid to try new things, such as taxonomy work, are also not likely to be afraid of changes and evolution within the field over time.

Endnotes

1. Margot Diltz, "Taxonomy Work Impressions Survey" online survey response, September 22, 2009.
2. Patrick Lambe, "Taxonomists: Evolving or Extinct? The Future of Taxonomy Work," presentation delivered at the Taxonomy Boot Camp conference, San Jose, CA, November 19, 2009.

Appendix A

Survey of Taxonomists

Participants in this survey were self-described taxonomists, who responded to a notice posted on the Taxonomy Community of Practice discussion group (finance.groups.yahoo.com/group/ TaxoCoP). Participants replied between November 21, 2008, and January 1, 2009. A total of 65 people responded, although for some questions only 63 or 64 replied.

1. To what extent do you create and maintain taxonomies?

My primary job responsibility	39.1%	25
One of my job responsibilities, but secondary	35.9%	23
A special assigned project, not in my job description or an originally expected responsibility	7.8%	5
Work done as contract/freelance often	12.5%	8
Work done as contract/freelance only occasionally	4.7%	3

2. What is your (usual) employment situation?

Employee of an organization that uses taxonomies primarily internally, for its website, and/or in ecommerce	44.4%	28
Employee of an organization that incorporates taxonomies into a marketed information product or information service	19.0%	12
Employee of a company or agency that provides taxonomy services or custom taxonomies to clients	11.1%	7
Independent contractor or freelancer (obtaining work primarily through subcontracting, working through agencies or other third parties, or as a temp employee)	7.9%	5
Consultant or business owner/partner (obtaining work primarily by bidding or pitching to direct clients)	17.5%	11

3. How long have you been doing work on taxonomies, controlled vocabularies, metadata for classification or tagging, thesauri, or authority files?

Less than 1 year	9.2%	6
1–2 years	7.7%	5
2–4 years	13.8%	9
4–6 years	10.8%	7
6–8 years	12.3%	8
8–10 years	7.7%	5
10–15 years	12.3%	8
Over 15 years	26.2%	17

4. How long have you been doing work specifically called *taxonomy*?

Less than 1 year	14.1%	9
1–2 years	17.2%	11
2–4 years	20.3%	13
4–6 years	10.9%	7
6–8 years	21.9%	14
8–10 years	4.7%	3
10–15 years	4.7%	3
Over 15 years	6.3%	4

5. What degree(s) do you hold? (May make multiple selections)

Associates degree only (2 year college)	4.7%	3
BA only (4 year college)	23.4%	15
BS only (4 year college)	7.8%	5
MA	14.1%	9
MS/M Eng.	14.1%	9
MLS/MLIS	48.4%	31
MBA	3.1%	2
PhD/doctorate	6.3%	4
Other advanced degree	3.1%	2

6. What is your study or training specifically in the field of taxonomy or classification? (May make multiple selections)

Concentration/specialty within a degree program	13.8%	9
Two or more college/university credit courses	16.9%	11
One college/university credit course	3.1%	2
Continuing education course or workshop	13.8%	9
Conference or professional seminar workshop	38.5%	25
On the job formal training	21.5%	14
On the job informal learning and experience	83.1%	54
Self taught through reading	53.8%	35

7. Prior to your work in taxonomies, which best describes your professional background?

Librarian	27.7%	18
Knowledge management	7.7%	5
Content management/ECM	4.6%	3
Document management/records management	4.6%	3
Project management	3.1%	2
Web user experience/information architecture	4.6%	3
Software/IT	12.3%	8
Database design, development, or administration	6.2%	4
Indexing	7.7%	5
Writing, editing, or publishing	4.6%	3
Administrative or clerical	0.0%	0
None/student	7.7%	5
Other	9.2%	6

8. What software do you use to create taxonomies?

Licensed commercial dedicated thesaurus/taxonomy management software	37.5%	24
Licensed open-source ontology/taxonomy development software	4.6%	3
Licensed commercial software, of which taxonomy management is a feature, module, or component	15.6%	10
An internally developed thesaurus/taxonomy management system	23.4%	15
Other commercial software that is not intended for taxonomy creation (such as a word processor, spreadsheet, or database management software)	18.8%	12

9. Are you familiar with and do you generally try to follow any of the following national or international standards: ANSI/NISO Z39.19 (2005) Guidelines for Construction, Format, and Management of Monolingual Controlled Vocabularies; ISO 2788 (1986) Guidelines for the Establishment and Development of Monolingual Thesauri; ISO 5964 (1985) Guidelines for the Establishment and Development of Multilingual Thesauri?

Don't know the standards and thus don't follow them	12.5%	8
Have read at least some of the standards, but don't follow them	17.2%	11
Generally try to follow what is relevant, but not strictly	45.3%	29
Follow or attempt to follow the standards closely and refer to them as needed	25.0%	16

10. Describe how you first got started doing taxonomy work.

Selections from 56 open-ended comments appear in Chapter 2. For the complete list, contact the author.

Glossary

ANSI. American National Standards Institute. A private nonprofit organization that coordinates and oversees the creation and promoting of standards in various industries.

associative relationship. A relationship between two preferred terms, indicating that the terms are related to each other in some way that is not hierarchical. The generic associative relationship is usually called related term with the label RT and is a bidirectional symmetrical relationship.

asymmetrical relationship. A relationship between a pair of terms that is not the same in both directions. Asymmetrical relationships include hierarchical relationships (which point to a broader term in one direction and a narrower term in the opposite direction), equivalence relationships (which point to a preferred term in one direction and a nonpreferred term in the other direction), and sometimes associative relationships if they are customized/semantic.

authority file. Another name for a controlled vocabulary, especially if used just for named entities and restricted to a certain kind of entity (person names, company names, place names, etc.). As such, an authority file lacks the interterm relationships of a thesaurus but may have multiple nonpreferred terms for each preferred term. Also called an authority list.

authorized term. Another name for a preferred term, if nonpreferred terms are called unauthorized terms.

auto-categorization. A form of automated indexing that associates appropriate taxonomy terms with a document, based on one or more different technologies (such as rules or machine-learning) that automatically analyze the text and compare it with data stored with a given taxonomy term and possibly other data. Seeks to automatically discern what a document is about. Also called auto-classification or auto-tagging,

automated indexing. Any indexing done by software and not humans, which could include the indexing done by search engines, and which may or may not involve taxonomies. It includes but is not limited to auto-categorization.

broader term. A preferred term that, in a hierarchical relationship to another term, is broader in meaning, more generic, or a larger whole with respect to its parts. Also called a parent term.

candidate term. A temporary term in a taxonomy, which cannot be used yet for indexing. Taxonomy or thesaurus software typically supports the creation of candidate terms that require an additional approval step before becoming approved terms. Also called a provisional term.

card sorting. A user-testing method for designing hierarchical taxonomies, whereby participants arrange cards of taxonomy terms into categories of their choice, using either physical cards or software to perform the task. There are two kinds: In a closed card sort, the categories are predefined, but in an open card sort, the participants must come up with and name their own categories.

cataloging. The process of both describing an item in a collection by various kinds of metadata and assigning it to an established classification system. Assigning subject terms is also often part of cataloging. Cataloging typically refers to physical items (books, periodicals, photos, music media, museum objects, etc.) but may apply to digitized collections of libraries and museums.

category. 1) Specifically in thesaurus management, any designated classification of terms that is distinct and that can be independent of the hierarchical relationships of the terms. 2) A relatively broad term used for classification of documents (on the whole, document level), rather than more granular indexing, and in particular for terms used in auto-categorization.

child term. Another name for a narrower term, a designation used more in hierarchical taxonomies, than thesauri. A broader term is then called a parent term.

classification. Assigning a class or a classification system code to an object (such as call numbers to a book) so that the object can be located by those who are familiar with the classification system. Classification is used for physical objects, and each can receive only a single classification.

closed indexing. Creating an index for back-of-the-book or a limited set of documents, for which the index project comes to a close once all the pages have been indexed, and the index is published as part of the work. Closed indexing usually does not use a taxonomy. Contrasts with open indexing.

concept. A thing, idea, or shared understanding of something. It is what is meant by a set of synonymous terms. It is, therefore, the combination of both a preferred term and its various nonpreferred terms or of all the linked synonyms within a synonym ring. A concept is more than just a term.

content audit. A comprehensive survey of all representative content (not necessarily every piece of content) that will be indexed with an intended taxonomy, performed to both define the scope of the taxonomy and gather candidate terms.

content management system. Software used typically by an enterprise to manage the internal workflow of digital content through various phases of collaborative writing, commenting and revising, indexing, publishing (to an intranet or externally), search and retrieval, possibly translating, and archiving.

controlled vocabulary. A restricted list of words or terms for some specialized purpose, usually for indexing, but sometimes also for writing. It may refer to any knowledge organization system (synonym ring, taxonomy, or thesaurus) but usually does not include the most complex systems of ontologies or topic maps.

cross-reference. An indication of the direction of a relationship from one term to another, such as *Use*, *See*, or *See also*. Cross-references exist in both taxonomies and indexes, but the term cross-reference is more often used in indexes.

CSV. Comma separated values. A file format, used for storing structured data, whereby associated items are in the same line and separated by a comma, to correspond with rows and columns in a table. It is a multiplatform format useful for exporting data from one system and importing to another and thus serves interoperability.

descriptor. Another name for a preferred term, especially when nonpreferred terms are called nondescriptors.

enterprise taxonomy. A custom-developed taxonomy used within a large organization (an enterprise) as a common knowledge organization system for the entire organization, often implemented in an intranet or an enterprise content management system.

entity. Another name for a concept, which may have multiple equivalent terms, preferred and nonpreferred, to describe it.

entity extraction. A form of automated indexing that uses information extraction technologies to identify and index named entities (proper nouns) in documents.

entry term. Another name for a nonpreferred term.

equivalence relationship. A relationship between two terms that, for the sake of the taxonomy, have a close enough meaning to be treated as equal, with one being used for the other. The term that is used and displayed is the preferred term, and the term that points to the preferred term is called the nonpreferred term.

facet. A categorical grouping of terms in a taxonomy that cover a single dimension of a complex query for an item being searched. Multiple terms, one from each facet, are searched in combination to retrieve the most specific data records. A facet is typically its own hierarchy, but not all separate hierarchies are facets.

facet indicator. A term within a taxonomy that is not used itself for indexing or retrieval (thus a node label) but is rather used specifically to organize a significant number of narrower terms by type, or facet, of narrower term. Sometimes the word "by" is used preceding the facet indicator.

faceted search. A taxonomy structured and a user interface designed to permit the user to select multiple terms, one from each facet, to be searched in combination in order to retrieve the most specific data records that meet all the criteria. Faceted search works best with relatively uniform content records.

federated search. The simultaneous automated search of multiple online databases or web resources, each of which also has its own structure and search system/method, and whose content would not otherwise be externally searchable. This may involve a metasearch engine, which is a search engine that sends user search requests to several other search engines and/or databases and aggregates the results. Taxonomies may or may not be involved in federated search.

fielded search. A type of end-user display that gives the searcher access to the taxonomy through multiple labeled search box fields, which each might be distinct facets, various vocabulary categories, or other kinds of metadata. The user might be able to browse the taxonomy through dropdown scroll lists for each field, or there may be no browsable view of the taxonomy.

flat format display. A common thesaurus display format, in which each term in the thesaurus is listed alphabetically and next to each term appear its details of immediate relationships to other terms and a scope note if any.

folksonomy. A collection of keyword terms or tags that have been assigned to content by multiple users (the creators of content and/or the readers of content). These terms do not belong to any controlled vocabulary but are rather words of the users' own choosing.

governance. Policies and procedures to successfully manage a project and, for a taxonomy, its continual maintenance. These policies and procedures include roles and accountabilities, standards, process methodologies, and communication methods. Governance in project management also includes tasks of defining outcomes, controlling the project and its scope, monitoring the project, measuring outputs, etc.

granularity. Specificity in indexing and retrieval, both with respect to the specificity of the narrowest terms in a taxonomy and with respect to the unit of content being indexed, which could be as specific as a paragraph or sentence.

hierarchical relationship. A relationship between two preferred terms, in which one is broader, or superordinate, and one is narrower, or subordinate.

hierarchical taxonomy. A kind of controlled vocabulary in which each term has a designated broader term (unless it is the top-level term) and one or more narrower terms (unless it is a bottom-level term), and all the terms are connected together into a single large hierarchical structure.

hierarchy. Any collection of terms that are linked to each other by hierarchical relationships. Most controlled vocabularies of subjects contain multiple hierarchies that may be of various sizes.

homographs. Terms with the same name (same spelling) but different meanings. Homographs are typically distinguished from each other in a taxonomy by parenthetical qualifiers. (Homonyms are homographs, but homonyms must also be pronounced identically, whereas for homographs, identical pronunciation is not a requirement.)

index. The structured compilation of index terms associated with a body of content, whereby each index term points to a specific location in the content (document, page, paragraph, or embedded index notation), based on significant mention of that term's concept at that location. An index helps users find content corresponding to a chosen term. An index may be displayed to the user, typically alphabetically, for browsing, or it may be nondisplayed and merely searchable via a search box. The index terms may be restricted to taxonomy terms, or they could be any keywords. The index could be created by a human indexer, or it could be automatically generated.

indexing. The assignment of index terms (which may or may not come from a taxonomy) to content while simultaneously creating an index of terms, which users may then either browse or search to help locate identifiable content. Indexing can be a closed project for a single book or open and ongoing for accumulating content, and it can be manual or automated.

individual. A concept or object in an ontology.

information extraction. A method of automated indexing that uses natural language processing (based on computational linguistics and pattern recognition) to extract useful information, such as subject terms, from varied "unstructured" content. A common form of information extraction is entity extraction for names. Information extraction is also called data extraction.

instance. 1) Another name for an individual in an ontology. 2) A named entity as it relates to the topical term of which it is a narrower term, in an instance-type of broader/narrower relationship. 3) The most specific concept at the narrowest, bottom level of a taxonomy.

interoperability. The ability to use data, in different applications (implementations, software systems, such as a proprietary indexing system, or various proprietary search systems), in a commercial content management system, and on the web. Interoperability involves storing the data in a standard format.

intranet. A private network within an organization built on internet technology and protocols, with web-based content, organized as a large internal website with restricted access.

keyword. A word or phrase that is deemed significant to describe content for retrieval but is not usually part of a taxonomy. It can be assigned to content by an indexer or someone doing social tagging. Keyword may also refer to a word or phrases that an auto-categorization tool identifies within a text as significant. And keyword may also refer to a word that a searcher chooses to enter in a search.

KWIC. Keyword in Context. 1) A kind of permuted or rotated index display of a thesaurus whereby all the terms are sorted alphabetically not merely by their first word but by each of their constituent words (keywords, not prepositions or articles). The terms are indented to varying degrees so that the keyword of each term lines up with the others vertically, and each term is repeatedly mentioned on the occurrence of each of its keywords. The keywords are "in context" because they appear only within their full term phrases. 2) A search retrieval display in which an excerpted line of text is displayed for each returned record, showing where the keyword search term appears in context.

KWOC. Keyword Out of Context. A kind of permuted or rotated index display of a thesaurus whereby all the terms are sorted alphabetically not merely by their first word but by each of their constituent words (keywords, not prepositions or articles). The keywords from the terms appear as the alphabetized headwords in the display, and the terms appear under each of their constituent keywords. Thus, each term is repeatedly mentioned under the heading of each of its keywords. It is simply an index of words within terms. The keywords are "out of context" because they are listed alphabetically rather than in the context of how they appear in the terms.

localization. Translation into another language of software or online information plus other changes needed to adapt the displayed information to the target audience. This includes translating of content, menus, pop-ups, online help, and so on, and supporting documentation. Additional adaptations include country-specific sorting and alphabetizing schemes, use of commas or decimals in numbers, date and time formats, currency and other symbols, etc.

machine learning. A method of auto-categorization whereby sample pre-indexed documents are submitted to the system, which then uses algorithms and performs statistical analysis to "learn" patterns of text content to determine what kind of text typically gets indexed with which taxonomy terms. This method is also known as catalog by example.

mapping. Combining two taxonomies (or one taxonomy and a set of keywords) on the same subject, so as to enable one taxonomy to be used for another while still retaining them both as continued distinct taxonomies. It involves individually matching terms from each taxonomy for equivalences.

merging. Combining two terms or two taxonomies deemed to be sufficiently equivalent, by using one of them in place for both, and the legacy terms not chosen to be used are then converted to non-preferred terms as appropriate.

metadata. Standardized data for a collection of resources/assets/documents/files; sometimes referred to as "data about data," with defined fields, such as title, creator, date, location, audience, subject, etc. Values for some of the metadata fields, such as subject, can be managed with a controlled vocabulary.

named entities. Indexing terms for specific named people, places, organizations, events, creative works, products, laws, and so on, which generally correspond with proper nouns (with the possible addition of years or dates). Named entities in taxonomies are typically managed in distinct vocabulary files, categories, or facets.

narrower term. A preferred term that, in a hierarchical relationship to another term, is narrower in meaning, more specific, or a part with respect to a systematic whole. Also called a child term.

natural language processing. Technologies to automatically discern the meaning of text based on both linguistics and computer science, typically involving the parsing of text so that the grammar is also taken into consideration. Natural language processing technologies are often used in automated indexing.

NISO. National Information Standards Organization. A nonprofit association accredited by the American National Standards Institute that identifies, develops, maintains, and publishes technical standards pertaining to information management.

node. A concept within a hierarchical taxonomy. If a hierarchy is like a tree, then the nodes are the points where branches or leaves come out. A node may refer to the preferred term alone, especially if there are no nonpreferred terms, or to the preferred term plus its nonpreferred variants. But unlike the word *term*, a node is never used to refer to nonpreferred terms.

node label. A dummy term in a displayed hierarchical taxonomy; it holds the place to organize and label a category of narrower terms but is not used in indexing and retrieval itself. Node labels are often distinguished from indexing terms in a display by use of brackets or a different font style.

node name. Another name for a preferred term when the designation node is used for concepts. This is more often an internal, rather than an end-user, designation.

nondescriptor. Another name for a nonpreferred term, especially when preferred terms are called descriptors.

nonpreferred term. A variant term for a concept, for which a different term is preferred. A nonpreferred term points to a preferred term with a *Use* reference and is linked to a preferred term with an equivalence type of relationship. Nonpreferred terms are also sometimes called nondescriptors, nonpostable terms, alternate terms, or synonyms. A nonpreferred term serves as a synonym in a taxonomy but is not necessarily a linguistic synonym.

object. Another name for a concept, especially in an object-oriented database structure. An object also comprises any nonpreferred terms and their definition, notes, and any other attributes. The information on relationships to other terms/objects may also be considered part of an object.

ontology. A complex knowledge organization system that aims to describe a domain of knowledge. Relationships between concepts (also called individuals) in an ontology have various meanings and thus are called semantic relationships.

open indexing. Indexing of periodical or other accumulating content, whereby the index continually grows as content is added or revised. Open indexing usually relies on a taxonomy to maintain consistent use of index terms. Contrasts with closed or back-of-the-book indexing.

orphan term. A preferred term that has no broader terms and no narrower terms. Orphan terms should not exist in a hierarchical taxonomy, but they could be present in a thesaurus, although they are rare.

OWL. Web Ontology Language. Semantic markup language, built on the Resource Description Framework (RDF) for publishing and sharing ontologies on the web; supports semantic web applications. OWL is a set of guidelines supported by the World Wide Web Consortium.

parent term. Another name for a broader term, a designation used more in hierarchical taxonomies than in thesauri. A narrower term is then called a child term.

permuted index. A kind of alphabetical thesaurus display, more common in printed formats, whereby all the terms are sorted alphabetically, not by their first word, but by each of their constituent words (keywords, not prepositions or articles) and thus repeated in the alphabetical list for each word. It is thus an index of words within terms. There are two variations, keyword in context (KWIC) and keyword out of context (KWOC). It is also called a rotated index.

polyhierarchy. A hierarchical structure in which a term has two or more broader terms; also called multiple broader terms (MBT).

postcoordination. The design or tendency of a taxonomy, its indexing, and its retrieval in which terms are kept simple, and usually a specific combination of terms is needed to describe a complex concept. Faceted search makes use of postcoordination, although postcoordination is not limited to faceted search. In any case, concepts are combined after indexing. The opposite taxonomy design approach is precoordinated terms.

precoordination. The design or tendency of a taxonomy to have complex specific terms, typically a noun phrase with multiple adjectives, which describe something that might otherwise be described by two separate terms. Another type of precoordination involves combining two terms, a main entry and subentry, both in indexing and at retrieval. In either case, concepts are combined prior to indexing and retrieval. The opposite taxonomy design is postcoordination.

preferred term. The displayed word or phrase for a concept, which a taxonomist has chosen as the best wording of the concept. Nonpreferred terms are the various synonyms, variants, or other sufficiently equivalent words or phrases used as cross-references pointing to the preferred term. Other names for a preferred term include descriptor, authorized term, and node name.

RDF. Resource Description Framework. A standard supported by the World Wide Web Consortium based on XML syntax for representing information about resources on the World Wide Web.

reciprocal relationships. All relationships between terms in a taxonomy are reciprocal because they function in both directions between a pair of terms, even if the relationship is not identical in both directions.

recursive retrieval. When a user selects a taxonomy term which has narrower terms, content will be retrieved not only for what was indexed with the selected term but also for what was indexed with each of its narrower terms. As a result, broader terms retrieve a greater number of results than narrower terms do.

regular expressions. Special text strings, in a prescribed syntax and scheme, for describing complex search pattern instructions, called regex for short. Regular expressions may be used to contribute to rules-based auto-categorization, among many other uses.

related term. A preferred term in an associative relationship with another term, which is also called a related term, since the relationship is symmetrical.

rotated index. Another name for a permuted index, a kind of alphabetical thesaurus display.

schema. A description of an XML document or set of documents which defines the tags and elements in the document. A schema is needed because XML tags are user-defined. The schema is a separate document, which can be considered as a model, template, or set of instructions.

scope note. A note attached to a preferred term in a thesaurus to clarify usage, such as by restricting the scope of the term. It is similar to but not the same as a definition of a term. Scope notes are used only as needed, not for all terms.

semantic relationships. Relationships between pairs of terms that have a more specific meaning than the generic relationships of broader term, narrower term, related term, and equivalent term. They are customized relationships defined and created by the taxonomist. Semantic relationships can describe any kind of relationship between a pair of concepts that are common among a number of concepts in the taxonomy, while still being based on either a hierarchical, associative, or equivalent relationship type.

sibling term. One of two or more terms that share the same immediate broader term (or parent).

SKOS. Simple Knowledge Organization System. A proposed standard, specifically for knowledge organization systems such as thesauri and taxonomies, built on the RDF to support interoperability for taxonomies.

social tagging. The assignment of tags or keywords by users to content in an unstructured manner without using a taxonomy, whereby anyone in an online community can both create tags and read others' tags, and the popularity of tags also takes on importance. The collection of such tags is called a folksonomy.

stakeholders. People who have a stake in a project, either an interest in it, a responsibility for it, or an influence over it or who will be affected by it. Typically stakeholders include the taxonomy project manager, indexers, executives who control the taxonomy's funding, and key users or clients.

stemming. The stripping of grammatical endings to a word to obtain the root or stem word. The technique is often used in automated search and retrieval systems so that words that differ only in their grammatical endings (e.g., contractors, contracting, contracts) are treated as equivalent matches.

straw-man taxonomy. A first draft of a hierarchical taxonomy, with terms only in the higher levels but not necessarily all levels yet, which could be changed based on feedback. It is called straw-man because, like something built of straw, it can easily be torn down and reconstructed if feedback is critical.

structured indexing. A form of precoordination whereby an indexer assigns a main heading term and then a subdivision term to further narrow or qualify the heading term. For users' benefit, the results should be either a printed browsable alphabetical index or an online interface that permits the user to narrow main term search results by a choice of subdivisions. Structured indexing is standard in book indexing and sometimes used in open/database indexing.

subdivision. A term used in structured indexing to further qualify, narrow, or restrict the application of a main heading term. It may also be called a subheading. Use of subdivisions is a form of pre-coordination in indexing. Subdivisions may or may not be used in a controlled vocabulary. Subdivisions are similar to but not the same as subentries in book indexes.

subject heading. A preferred term or descriptor, especially in a controlled vocabulary used for human indexing; permits precoor-dinated or structured indexing by combining a subject heading with a subheading type of term.

symmetrical relationship. A relationship between a pair of terms that is the same in both directions. The only symmetrical relation-ships are generic associative relationships (related term) and equivalence relationships within a synonym ring.

synonym ring. A simple controlled vocabulary in which all equiv-alent terms (synonyms) of a concept have equal standing and no single term is designated as preferred. Another name is a synset. A synonym ring is thus not displayed to the end user, and usually there are no other relationships (hierarchical or associative) between concepts.

tagging. The assigning of terms to a content item, such as a file or a document, of either taxonomy terms or any keywords that the person doing the tagging thinks up.

taxonomy. 1) A hierarchically structured system of organizing names of concepts. 2) Any knowledge organization system, whether hierarchical or not, involving controlled names of concepts.

term. A label (word or phrase) for a concept. It is the most common, generic designation, which can be in any controlled vocabulary. It may be used to mean any kind of term, including both preferred terms and nonpreferred terms, but is sometimes used to refer to just the preferred term.

term record. The complete information regarding a term, especially as stored and displayed in taxonomy management or indexing software. It includes all of a term's relationships, notes, categories, and any additional attributes, along with administrative information such as approval status, creation and modification dates, and so on; in other words, the metadata for a single term. Not all these details need to be included, though, for it to be called a term record.

text mining. Automated methods of deriving high-quality or useful information from text. It could be based on various technologies, including, statistics, machine learning, computational linguistics, and/or pattern recognition. Text mining may be used to support automated indexing/auto-categorization, but it is not limited to such applications.

thesaurus. A structured type of controlled vocabulary that provides information about each term and its relationships to other terms within the same thesaurus. Typical relationships are equivalent, hierarchical, and associative, and term notes are a common feature. Published standards provide guidance on creating knowledge organization thesauri.

thesaurus software. Full-featured software for the design, creation, and management of thesauri or hierarchical taxonomies. Terms and their reciprocal relationships are maintained, and different displays or outputs are supported. Ideally such software supports creating terms and their relationships in accordance with standards, such as ANSI/NISO Z39.19.

top term. In a thesaurus or hierarchical taxonomy, a term that has no broader terms, only narrower terms. It is the top/highest term of its own hierarchy. A top term hierarchy is a display option, not only for hierarchical taxonomies, but also for thesauri, in which case all the top terms are arranged alphabetically with their hierarchies of narrower terms displayed under each.

topic. Another name for a preferred term, specifically when it is a subject or common noun, not a named entity (proper noun).

topic map. A standard format for representing complex knowledge organization systems comprising topics (concepts), associations (relationships), and occurrences (either attributes or linked content). A topic map can be considered a kind of ontology or a representation of an ontology. It is a standard of the International Standards Organization: ISO 13250.

tuning. Human intervention adjustments to improve the automatic indexing results of machine-learning-based auto-categorization. It involves making changes to the types and numbers of training documents supplied to the auto-categorization system.

unauthorized term. Another name for a nonpreferred term, if preferred terms are called authorized terms.

upward posting. Treating narrower terms as equivalent, nonpreferred terms. A narrower term may be used as a nonpreferred term if users expect it but there is insufficient content. Upward posting is also done when editing a taxonomy to remove low-use terms or when mapping two taxonomies so that one is used for the other and the other taxonomy has a greater number of narrower terms.

weighting. In indexing, the assignment of degrees of strength of linkage between a document and a given index term. If implemented, there are typically only two or three levels of weight from which the indexer may choose. In automated indexing, weighting is usually called relevancy, and there can be various percentages of relevancies. In taxonomy design, there could also be the option of weights between relationships, but this is a level of complexity that is relatively rare.

World Wide Web Consortium. The international standards organization for the World Wide Web, which has offices in various countries. It ensures compatibility for HTML, XML, RDF, OWL, and other coding schemes and their variations used for the web. It is abbreviated as W3C.

XML. Extensible Markup Language. A general-purpose markup language for structuring, storing, and transporting data, which allows the user to define and label all of the tags, following only standard syntax conventions.

Zthes. A standard schema designed specifically for ANSI/NISO Z39.19-based thesauri, using XML syntax, to support interoperability of such thesauri.

Appendix C

Recommended Reading

Chapter 1

Agee, Vicky. "Controlling Our Own Vocabulary: A Primer for Indexers Working in the World of Taxonomy Development." *Key Words* 16, no.1 (2008).

Garshol, Lars Marius. "Metadata? Thesauri? Taxonomies? Topic Maps! Making sense of it all." October 26, 2004. www.ontopia.net/topicmaps/materials/tm-vs-thesauri.html#N773

Gilchrist, Alan. "Thesauri, Taxonomies and Ontologies: An Etymological Note." *Journal of Documentation* 59, no. 1 (2003): 7–18.

Hodge, Gale. *Systems of Knowledge Organization for Digital Libraries: Beyond Traditional Authority Files*. Washington, DC: The Digital Library Federation Council on Library and Information Resources, 2000. www.clir.org/pubs/reports/pub91/pub91.pdf

Lambe, Patrick. "Defining Our Terms" and "Taxonomies Can Take Many Forms." In *Organising Knowledge: Taxonomies, Knowledge and Organisational Effectiveness*. Oxford, U.K.: Chandos, 2007.

Leise, Fred, Karl Fast, and Mike Steckel. "What Is a Controlled Vocabulary?" *Boxes and Arrows* (2002). Retrieved January 13, 2008 from www.boxesandarrows.com/view/creating_a_controlled_vocabulary

Taxonomies & Controlled Vocabularies Special Interest Group. "About Taxonomies & Controlled Vocabularies." (2007). Retrieved January 13, 2008 from www.taxonomies-sig.org/about.htm

Chapter 2

Lambe, Patrick. "Taxonomists: Evolving or Extinct?" Presentation, Taxonomy Boot Camp conference, San Jose, CA. November 19, 2009.

Chapters 3 and 4

Aitchison, Jean, Alan Gilchrist, and David Bawden. "Vocabulary Control," "Specificity and Compound Terms," and "Structure and Relationships." In *Thesaurus Construction and Use: A Practical Manual.* 4th ed. Chicago, IL: Fitzroy Dearborn, 2000.

Broughton, Vanda. *Essential Thesaurus Construction.* London: Facet, 2006.

National Institute of Standards Organization. *ANSI/NISO Z39.19-2005 Guidelines for Construction, Format, and Management of Monolingual Controlled Vocabularie.* Bethesda, MD: NISO Press, 2005.

Zeng, Marcia Lei. "Construction of Controlled Vocabularies." 2005. www.slis.kent.edu/~mzeng/Z3919

Chapter 5

Hedden, Heather. "Taxonomy Tool Roundup." *EContent* 31, no. 3 (April 2008): 40–44.

Will, Leonard D. "Software for Building and Editing Thesauri." www.willpowerinfo.co.uk/thessoft.htm

Chapter 6

Alexander, Fran. "Folksonomies: Business Use." FUMSI. web.fumsi.com/go/article/manage/3791

Bates, Marcia. "Indexing and Access for Digital Libraries and the Internet: Human, Database, and Domain Factors." Department of Information Studies, University of California, Los Angeles (1996). www.gseis.ucla.edu/faculty/bates/articles/indexdlib.html

Chapter 7

Bedford, Denise A. D. "Ontologies, Taxonomies and Search." Presentation, Special Libraries Association conference, Baltimore, MD. June 15, 2006. sla.dsoc.googlepages.com/Bedford2006Ontologies.pdf

Chester, Bernard. "Auto-Categorization and Records Management." *AIIM E-Doc Magazine* 18, no. 2 (March 2004), www.imerge consult.com/img/88BC.pdf

Patkar, Parag. "Eight Considerations for Selecting an Effective Content Categorization Solution." *Computer Technology Review* 22, no. 5 (May 1, 2002).

Reamy, Tom. "Auto-Categorization: Coming to a Library or Intranet Near You!" *EConent* 25, no. 11 (November 2002): 16–22.

Reamy, Tom. "Cyborg Categorization Part 1—The Salvation of Search?" *Intranets Professional* (Jan/Feb 2002). www.intranets today.com/Articles/Default2.aspx?ArticleID=5052&AuthorID=95

Reamy, Tom. "Cyborg Categorization Part 2—How to Build a Cyborg." *Intranets Professional* (Mar/Apr 2002). www.intranets today.com/Articles/Default2.aspx?ArticleID=5056&AuthorID=95

Reamy, Tom. "Selecting Taxonomy Software: Who, Why, How." Presentation, Taxonomy Boot Camp conference, November 2007. www.kapsgroup.com/presentations/Selecting Taxonomy Software.ppt.

Chapter 8

Quintarelli, E., Resmini, A. and Rosati, L. "FaceTag: Integrating Bottom-up and Top-down Classification in a Social Tagging System." *Bulletin of the American Society for Information Science & Technology* 33 (June/July 2007). www.asis.org/Bulletin/Jun-07/quintarelli_et_al.html

Tunkelang, Daniel. *Faceted Search*. San Rafael, CA: Morgan & Claypool, 2009.

Weinberger, David. *Everything Is Miscellaneous: The Power of the New Digital Disorder*. New York: Times Books, 2007.

Chapter 9

Aitchison, Jean, Alan Gilchrist, and David Bawden. "Thesaurus Displays." In *Thesaurus Construction and Use: A Practical Manual*. 4th ed. Chicago, IL: Fitzroy Dearborn, 2000.

Blocks, Dorothee, Daniel Cunliffe, and Douglas Tudhope. "A Reference Model for User-System Interaction in Thesaurus-Based Searching." *Journal of the American Society for Information Science and Technology* 57, no. 12 ((2006): 1655–1665.

Krug, Steve. *Don't Make Me Think! A Common Sense Approach to Web Usability*. 2nd ed. Berkeley, CA: New Riders, 2006.

Gilchrist, Alan, and Barry Mahon, eds. *Information Architecture: Designing Information Environments for Purpose*. New York: Neal-Schuman, 2004.

Morville, Peter. *Ambient Findability: What We Find Changes Who We Become*. Sebastopol, CA: O'Reilly & Associates, 2006.

Rosenfeld, Louis, and Peter Morville. *Information Architecture for the World Wide Web*. 3rd ed. Sebastopol, CA: O'Reilly & Associates, 2007.

Chapter 10

Daniel, Ron, Jr. "Who Owns It & Taking Care of It: Governance & Maintenance Issues." Presentation, Taxonomy Boot Camp conference, Sept. 27–28, 2005, New York. www.taxonomystrategies. com/presentations/Taxonomy Gov and Maint.ppt

Daniel, Ron, Jr., and Joseph Busch. "Taxonomy Governance." Preconference workshop, Enterprise Search Summit, May 16, 2005, New York. www.taxonomystrategies.com/html/archive. htm

Foulonneau, Muriel, and Jenn Riley. *Metadata for Digital Resources: Implementation, Systems Design, and Interoperability*. Oxford, U.K.: Chandos, 2008.

Jansen, Bernard J. "Search Log Analysis: What It Is, What's Been Done, How to Do It." *Library & Information Science Research* 28, no. 3 (2006): 407–432.

Kelway, James. "Creating User Centred Taxonomies: Part One" FUMSI, August 2008. web.fumsi.com/go/article/manage/3126

Kelway, James. "Creating User Centred Taxonomies: Part Two" FUMSI, September 2008. web.fumsi.com/go/article/manage/ 3198

Lambe, Patrick. "Preparing for a Taxonomy Project," "Designing Your Taxonomy," and "Implementing Your Taxonomy." In *Organising Knowledge: Taxonomies, Knowledge and Organisational Effectiveness*. Oxford, U.K.: Chandos, 2007.

Müller, Ralf. *Project Governance*. Aldershot, U.K.: Gower Publishing, 2009.

Owens, Leslie. *How to Build a High-Octane Taxonomy for ECM and Enterprise Search Systems*. Cambridge, MA: Forrester Research, November 17, 2008.

Resnick, Marc, and Misha Vaughan. "Best Practices and Future Visions for Search User Interfaces." *Journal of the American Society for Information Science and Technology* 57, no. 6 (2006).

Spencer, Donna. *Card Sorting: Designing Usable Categories.* New York: Rosenfeld Media, 2009.

Stewart, Darin L. "Preparations." In *Building Enterprise Taxonomies.* Portland, OR: Mokita Press, 2008.

Turbit, Neville. "IT Governance and Project Governance." Project Perfect White Paper Collection. June 27, 2005. Retrieved September 15, 2009, from www.projectperfect.com.au/down loads/Info/info_governance.pdf

Wyllie, Jan. *Taxonomies: Frameworks for Corporate Knowledge.* 2nd ed. London: Ark Group in association with David Skyrme Associates, 2005.

Chapter 11

Aitchison, Jean, Alan Gilchrist, and David Bawden. "Multilingual Thesauri." In *Thesaurus Construction and Use: A Practical Manual.* 4th ed. Chicago, IL: Fitzroy Dearborn, 2000.

Earley, Seth, Marti Heyman, and Denise Bedford. "Multilingual Taxonomies." Presentation, Taxonomy Community of Practice, San Jose, CA, May 30, 2007. www.earley. com/webinars/multi-lingual-taxonomies

Liang, A. C., and M. Sini. "Mapping AGROVOC and the Chinese Agricultural Thesaurus: Definitions, Tools, Procedures." *New Review of Hypermedia and Multimedia* 12, no. 1 (2006): 51–62.

Mili, H., and R. Rada. "Merging Thesauri: Principles and Evaluation." *Pattern Analysis and Machine Intelligence, IEEE Transactions on Pattern Analysis and Machine Intelligence* 10, no. 2 (1988): 204–220.

Powers, Shelley. *Practical RDF.* Sebastopol, CA: O'Reilly & Associates, 2003.

Stewart, Darin L. "Interoperability." In *Building Enterprise Taxonomies.* Portland, OR: Mokita Press, 2008.

Sweeney, Jim, and Daniela Barbarosa. "Synaptica: Automatch Tool Overview." PowerPoint presentation, May 11, 2009. www.slide share.net/danielabarbosa/synaptica-new-feature-auto-match

Chapter 12

Hedden, Heather. "Conference Report: Taxonomy Boot Camp." *Key Words* 16, no. 1 (January–March 2008).

Appendix D

Websites

Chapter 1

International Organization for Standardization (ISO) Standards,
    www.iso.org/iso/iso_catalogue.htm
National Information Standards Organization (NISO) Standards,
    www.niso.org/kst/reports/standards
British Standards Institution, www.bsigroup.com
International Association for Ontology and Its Applications,
    www.iaoa.org
Library of Congress Subject Headings, authorities.loc.gov
Medical Subject Headings,
    www.nlm.nih.gov/mesh/MBrowser.html
ERIC Thesaurus, eric.ed.gov/ERICWebPortal/resources/html/
    thesaurus/about_thesaurus.html
Getty Research Institute Vocabularies,
    www.getty.edu/research/conducting_research/vocabularies
Verizon SuperPages, www.superpages.com/yellowpages
Amazon.com ecommerce site, www.amazon.com/gp/site-
    directory
Shoebuy.com advanced search, www.shoebuy.com/s.jsp/r_as
Microbial Life Education Resources, serc.carleton.edu/micro
    belife/resources
Information Architecture Institute site map,
    iainstitute.org/en/site-map.php
MyFlorida.com site map, www.myflorida.com/taxonomy
Taxonomy Warehouse, www.taxonomywarehouse.com

Chapter 2

Taxonomy Community of Practice,
    finance.groups.yahoo.com/group/TaxoCoP
Taxonomy Jobs Yahoo! list, finance.groups.yahoo.com/group/
    taxonomy-jobs
LinkedIn, www.linkedin.com
Yahoo! Directory, dir.yahoo.com

Chapter 3

World List Expert from MechanicWords,
    www.mechanicwords.com
Online Thesauri and Authority Files, American Society for
    Indexing, www.asindexing.org/site/thesonet.shtml
Thesaurus Sites, Queensland University of Technology,
    www.imresources.fit.qut.edu.au/vocab/thes_sites.jsp
ANSI/NISO Z39.19-2005, www.niso.org/kst/reports/standards

Chapter 5

Xmind, www.xmind.net
FreeMind from SourceForge, freemind.sourceforge.net/
    wiki/index.php/Main_Page
Cmap from the Florida Institute for Human & Machine
    Cognition, cmap.ihmc.us
TheBrain from TheBrain Technologies LP, www.thebrain.com
MindManager from MindJet, www.mindjet.com
VisiMap from Coco Systems Ltd., www.visimap.com
TopBraid Composer from TopQuadrant, www.topquadrant.com
Willpower Information, www.willpowerinfo.co.uk/thessoft.htm
Taxonomy Community of Practice wiki,
    taxocop.wikispaces.com/TaxoTools

TaxoTips, www.taxotips.com/resources/tools

MultiTes Pro from Multisystems, www.multites.com

Cognatrix from LGOSystems, www.lgosys.com

Data Harmony Thesaurus Master from Access Innovations,
   www.dataharmony.com

Synaptica, www.synaptica.com

Wordmap, www.wordmap.com

SchemaLogic, www.schemalogic.com

Semaphore from Smartlogic, www.smartlogic.com

STAR/Thesaurus from Cuadra Associates, www.cuadra.com

SoutronTHESAURUS from Soutron, www.soutron.com/soutron
   thesaurus.html

ITM T3 from Mondeca, www.mondeca.com

TheMa from TRIGA IT-Systeme + Grafik, www.triga-services.de

Amicus Thesaurus, www.amicuscom.com/thesaurus.htm

TemaTres, www.r020.com.ar/tematres/index.en.html

ThManager, thmanager.sourceforge.net

TheW32 and TheW for Java, publish.uwo.ca/~craven/
   freeware.htm

Protégé, protege.stanford.edu

SKOS Editor Plug-in, code.google.cpm/p/skoseditor

Adlib, www.adlibsoft.com

Open Text Collections Server Webtop Thesaurus Manager,
   www.opentext.com

a.k.a. from Synercon Management Consulting, www.a-k-a.com.au

One-2-One from Active Classification Solutions, www.acs121.com

Chapter 6

Delicious, delicious.com

Connotea, www.connotea.org

Diigo, www.diigo.com

Flickr, www.flickr.com

Chapter 7

NetOwl from SRA International, www.sra.com/netowl

Inxight ThingFinder, www.inxightfedsys.com/products/sdks/tf

Rosette Entity Extractor from BASIS Technology,
    www.basistech.com/entity-extraction

Data Harmony Metadata Extractor, www.dataharmony.com/
    products/metadataextractor.html

Autonomy, www.autonomy.com

iQuest Analytics, www.iquestglobal.com

Inxight SmartDiscovery Analysis Server, www.inxightfedsys.com

Autonomy Collaborative Classifier, www.autonomy.com

Autonomy Interwoven MetaTagger, www.interwoven.com

Lexalytics Classifier, www.lexalytics.com

Data Harmony Machine Aided Indexer, www.dataharmony.com

Smartlogic Semaphore Ontology Manager, www.smartlogic.com

SAS Enterprise Content Categorization and Ontology
    Management, www.sas.com/text-analytics

Wordmap Intelligent Text Classifier, www.wordmap.com

Nstein Text Mining Engine, www.nstein.com

conceptSearching, www.conceptsearching.com

Chapter 8

Yahoo! Directory, dir.yahoo.com

Open Directory Project, www.dmoz.org

Monster job board site, jobsearch.monster.com/Browse.aspx

MyRecipes.com, www.myrecipes.com

Kelley Blue Book Perfect Car Finder,
    www.kbb.com/kbb/PerfectCarFinder

Land's End, www.landsend.com

Chapter 9

National Agriculture Library Thesaurus, agclass.nal.usda.gov

ERIC Thesaurus A-Z Browse display, eric.ed.gov

ThomasNet business directory, www.thomasnet.com

Search Harmony, www.accessinn.com:8081/PerfectSearch/
navtree/index.html

Open Directory Project, www.dmoz.org

Buzzillions, www.buzzillions.com

Search Patterns, www.flickr.com/photos/morville/collections

Florida Memory, State Library & Archives of Florida, www.
floridamemory.com/Collections/folklife/database.cfm

Colorado Springs Pioneer Museum, www.cspm.org

CSA Illumina, www.csa.com/csaillumina/login.php

Blue Sheet for the Gale Group Trade & Industry Database,
library.dialog.com/bluesheets/html/bl0148.html#BI

Chapter 10

ClickTale, www.clicktale.com

Clicky, www.getclicky.com

iWebTrack, www.iwebtrack.com

Mint, www.haveamint.com

Unica NetInsight, www.unica.com

Optimal iQ, www.optimaliq.com

Omniture SiteCatalyst, www.omniture.com

VisitorVille, www.visitorville.com

Webtrends, www.webtrends.com

WebSort, websort.net

OptimalSort, www.optimalsort.com

MindCanvas, www.themindcanvas.com

Chapter 11

XML, www.w3.org/XML

Zthes, zthes.z3950.org

RDF, www.w3.org/RDF

OWL, www.w3.org/2007/OWL

SKOS, www.w3.org/2004/02/skos

International Relations and Area Studies Online, www.ireon-portal.eu

European Training Thesaurus, libserver.cedefop.europa.eu/ett

Chapter 12

Taxonomy Jobs Yahoo! list, finance.groups.yahoo.com/group/taxonomy-jobs

Simmons College Graduate School of Library and Information Science—Continuing Education, www.simmons.edu/gslis/careers/continuing-education

University of Wisconsin Milwaukee, School of Information Studies—Professional Development Institute, www4.uwm.edu/sois/CE

University of Toronto Faculty of Information—Professional Learning Centre, plc.ischool.utoronto.ca/courses_webbased.asp

American Library Association—Distance Learning, www.ala.org/ala/conferencesevents/upcoming/distance

e-Learning from Association of College and Research Libraries, www.ala.org/ala/mgrps/divs/acrl/events/elearning

Special Libraries Association CLICK University, www.sla.org/content/learn

AIIM Information Organization & Access Practitioner Course, www.aiim.org/Education

Aslib Public Courses in Library and Information Management Skills, www.aslib.com/training/section4.html

Library of Congress, Controlled Vocabulary & Thesaurus Design,
    www.loc.gov/catworkshop/courses/thesaurus
TFPL Training, www.tfpl.com/training
Montague Institute, www.montague.com
Earley & Associates Webinars, www.earley.com/webinars
Special Libraries Association Annual Conference,
    www.sla.org/content/Events/conference
American Society for Indexing Annual Meeting,
    www.asindexing.org/site/mtgs.shtml
American Society for Information Science & Technology Annual
    Meeting, asist.org/conferences.html
Information Architecture (IA) Summit, www.iasummit.org
Euro IA, www.euroia.org
Amercian Library Association Upcoming Events,
    www.ala.org/ala/conferencesevents
AIIM Expo, www.aiimexpo.com
Taxonomy Boot Camp, www.taxonomybootcamp.com
KMWorld, www.kmworld.com
Enterprise Search Summit, www.enterprisesearchsummit.com
Semantic Technology Conference, www.semantic-
    conferencc.com
Gilbane Conference, gilbaneboston.com and gilbanesf.com
Computers in Libraries, www.infotoday.com/cil.htm
Henry Stewart Data Asset Management Conference,
    www.damusers.com
Construction of Controlled Vocabularies: A Primer,
    www.slis.kent.edu/~mzeng/Z3919/index.htm
Thesaurus Construction tutorial by Tim Craven,
    publish.uwo.ca/~craven/677/thesaur/main00.htm
Taxonomies & Controlled Vocabularies SIG from ASI, www.
    taxonomies-sig.org
SLA Taxonomy Division wiki, wiki.sla.org/display/SLATAX/
    Taxonomy+Home

Information Architecture Institute, www.iainstitute.org

American Society for Information Science & Technology,
www.asist.org

Content Management Professionals, www.cmprofessionals.org

Taxonomy Tuesday, semanticommunity.wik.is/Taxonomy_
Tuesday

Taxonomy Community of Practice from LinkedIn,
www.linkedin.com/groups?home=&gid=1750

Thesaurus Professionals from LinkedIn,
www.linkedin.com/groups?home=&gid=1881339

Indexer's Network, indexing.ning.com

Vocabulary and Metadata Management from Twine,
www.twine.com/twine/1yyy8g4r-14v/vocabulary-and-
metadata-management

Taxonomy Community of Practice Wikispace,
taxocop.wikispaces.com

Green Chameleon, by Patrick Lambe, www.greenchameleon.com

Lee Romero On Content, Collaboration, and Findability,
blog.leeromero.org

Earley & Associates Blog, www.earley.com/blog

Synaptica Central, www.synapticacentral.com

The Taxonomy Blog, by Marlene Rockmore,
thetaxonomyblog.wordpress.com

Taxonomy Watch, by Linda Farmer,
taxonomy2watch.blogspot.com

Access Innovations, Inc., www.accessinn.com/library

Earley & Associates, www.earley.com/knowledge

Taxonomy Strategies, www.taxonomystrategies.com/html/
library.htm

Willpower Information, www.willpowerinfo.co.uk/thesbibl.htm

About the Author

Heather Hedden is a consultant and freelance taxonomist and owner of Hedden Information Management (www.hedden-information.com). She is also an instructor of taxonomy development through the continuing education program of Simmons College Graduate School of Library and Information Science and through independently offered online training. In addition, she does freelance indexing of both books (closed indexing) and database content (open indexing).

Previously, Heather worked for eight years as a controlled vocabulary editor for Information Access Company/Gale. Her work there included converting the controlled vocabularies into ANSI/NISO standard thesauri, updating and adding new taxonomy terms, communicating new terms and policies to indexers, mapping taxonomies, and creating new user-interface taxonomies. Heather then worked as the information taxonomist at an enterprise search software startup, Viziant Corporation, where she was solely responsible for developing all taxonomies used with machine-learning-based auto-categorization. She has also done contract taxonomy work for Gale, Factiva, Dow Jones, Earley & Associates, Bain & Company, and various yellow pages publishers, among other clients.

Heather is the author of *Indexing Specialties: Web Sites* (2007) and of the chapter "Controlled Vocabularies, Thesauri, and Taxonomies" in *Index It Right! Advice From the Experts* (Vol. 2, 2010), both of which are published by Information Today, Inc., on behalf of the American Society for Indexing (ASI). She has also published numerous articles in journals such as *EContent*,

Intranets, Computers in Libraries, The Indexer, and *Key Words* (bulletin of ASI). Heather has given presentations and workshops nationally and internationally at conferences including Taxonomy Boot Camp, Enterprise Search Summit, Gilbane Conference, Content Management Professionals, ASI, Indexing Society of Canada, Society of Indexers (U.K.), and Netherlands Society of Indexers.

Her professional association memberships include Special Libraries Association and its Taxonomy Division, the Information Architecture Institute, and ASI. Heather has served as president of the New England Chapter of ASI, manager of the Web Indexing special interest group of ASI, and founder/manager of the Taxonomies & Controlled Vocabularies special interest group of ASI.

Heather has a BA from Cornell University and an MA from Princeton University. She lives in Carlisle, Massachusetts, with her husband and two children.

Index

A

abbreviations, 179–180

ABI Inform, 28, 29

Abridged Integrated Public Sector Vocabulary, 7

academic institutions, as taxonomist employers, 57, 62

academic thesauri, displaying connection to preferred terms, 107

academic training, taxonomist, 360–361

Access Innovations management tools, 32, 155, 167, 220

Access Innovations web resources, 374

The Accidental Taxonomist website, 375

acronyms
  in automated indexing, 227
  for human indexing, 179–180
  as nonpreferred terms, 103, 105
  semantic relationships, 132
  in terms, 86

action and property associative relationships, 121

action and target/patient associative relationships, 121

Active Classification Solutions software, 168

adjectives in terms, 84–85

Adlib Information Systems software, 166

administrative attributes, term, 94–95

advertisers, as taxonomist employers, 57, 60

agencies as taxonomist employers, information services, 57, 61

agent associative relationships, process and, 121

AIIM (Association for Information and Image Management International) training, 363–364, 368

a.k.a. software, 168

ALA (American Library Association) Subject Headings, 28

ALA (American Library Association) training, 363, 367

all criterion for indexing/searching, 238–239, 240–241, 278

all/some rule of hierarchical relationships, 111, 112

alphabetical displays
  associative relationships, 120–121
  for end users, 108, 267–268
  for human indexers, 105, 185, 186
  thesauri, 120–121, 259–262

alphabetical sort order in hierarchical displays, 274–275

Amazon.com taxonomy, 20, 279–280

American Chemical Society Chemical Abstract Service controlled vocabulary, 29

American Library Association (ALA) Subject Headings, 28